Peasants, Political Economy, and Law

EMPIRE, IDENTITY, AND INDIA

Peasants, Political Economy, and Law

PETER ROBB

OXFORD
UNIVERSITY PRESS

YMCA Library Building, Jai Singh Road, New Delhi 110 001

Oxford University Press is a department of the University of Oxford. It furthers the
University's objective of excellence in research, scholarship, and education
by publishing worldwide in

Oxford New York

Auckland Cape Town Dar es Salaam Hong Kong Karachi Kuala Lumpur
Madrid Melbourne Mexico City Nairobi New Delhi Shanghai Taipei Toronto

With offices in

Argentina Austria Brazil Chile Czech Republic France Greece Guatemala
Hungary Italy Japan Poland Portugal Singapore South Korea Switzerland
Thailand Turkey Ukraine Vietnam

Oxford is a registered trademark of Oxford University Press
in the UK and in certain other countries

Published in India
by Oxford University Press, New Delhi

© Oxford University Press 2007

The moral rights of the author have been asserted
Database right Oxford University Press (maker)

First published 2007

All rights reserved. No part of this publication may be reproduced,
or transmitted in any form or by any means, electronic or mechanical,
including photocopying, recording or by any information storage and
retrieval system, without permission in writing from Oxford University Press.
Enquiries concerning reproduction outside the scope of the above should be
sent to the Rights Department, Oxford University Press, at the address above

You must not circulate this book in any other binding or cover
and you must impose this same condition on any acquirer

ISBN-13: 978-0-19-568160-4
ISBN-10: 0-19-568160-6

Typeset in Sabon 10/13
by Excellent Laser Typesetters, Pitampura, Delhi 110 034
Printed in India by De-Unique, New Delhi-110018
Published by Oxford University Press
YMCA Library Building, Jai Singh Road, New Delhi 110 001

Contents

Preface vii

Acknowledgements ix

PART I
AGRARIAN POLICY AND POLITICAL CHANGE

CHAPTER 1
Agrarian Policy and Law   3

CHAPTER 2
Political Organization   22

CHAPTER 3
Community and Interests   44

PART II
LAW, ECONOMIC CHANGE, INTEREST GROUPS, AND RIGHTS

CHAPTER 4
Agrarian Structure and Economic Development   69

CHAPTER 5
Law and Agrarian Society in India:
The Case of Bihar and the
Nineteenth-century Tenancy Debate   90

CHAPTER 6
Peasants' Choices?
Indian Agriculture and the Limits of
Commercialization in Nineteenth-century Bihar   124

CHAPTER 7
Hierarchy and Resources:
Peasant Stratification in Late Nineteenth-century Bihar   151

CHAPTER 8
Labour in India, 1860–1920:
Typologies, Change, and Regulation   181

Index   219

Preface

This is the second of two volumes resulting from a suggestion by Oxford University Press that they republish some of my essays with extensive new introductions. Part I comprises the introduction and supporting essays follow in Part II. A fuller statement of the rationale for the collections is provided in the companion volume *Liberalism, Modernity, and the Nation* (henceforth *Liberalism*).

Both volumes reprint essays on diverse subjects that may be read in the context of the part played by empire in the modern constitution of identities in India. Except for the first in this volume, which has been rewritten, the supporting essays have not been significantly changed from the form in which they were first published. Instead, the introductory chapters draw out and elaborate upon a connecting theme that was not necessarily the main focus originally.

The particular argument in this volume is that colonial laws and economy, alongside the forces of government interference and regulation discussed in *Liberalism*, helped frame the political identities that emerged in India over the last 150 years or so. I say 'helped frame' because, as insisted in the above-mentioned volume, I am not claiming that colonialism alone explains anything, or that Europeans rather than Indians were the significant agents of change. Also, it is the form and basis of colonial policy that are at issue, not its success. Indeed, its failures and misrepresentations had an important influence on the interest groups and rhetoric that helped decide which identities would emerge and how they would develop.

In these ways, the two volumes share a common theme and purpose. This book looks mainly at the connection between certain features of agrarian policy, revenue and property law, and commercial production, and the emergence of related political identities. But it builds on *Liberalism*, which connects liberal rhetoric and modern technology and governance to the reinforcement of bounded categories and to a discourse of rights. The argument is that such linkages were a necessary part and an instrument of the building of modern identities, including the nation.

The identities are modern not in a chronological sense so much as in their rationale and organization—in particular, as said in *Liberalism*, in their generalizing character and recourse to the concept of rights. This volume is almost all about rural conditions, and hence the relevant identities are those of landlords, tenants, peasants, labourers, and so on. But the points are intended to be more general. In Chapter 8, for example, the impact of the Factory Acts is considered. That discussion provides a useful paradigm, already mentioned briefly in *Liberalism*. A Factory Act defines work in terms of place, time, task, reward, power, and organization. It defines government and law by identifying their responsibilities, and it identifies employers and employees by defining their rights. It assumes a concept of national society and economy in its purposes and rationale—for example, by setting rules that reduce the comparative advantage of the worst employers by applying to all, and by doing so in the public interest and with an eye to the social and economic health of a country and a jurisdiction as a whole. A Factory Act depends too upon skills and technologies—such as scientific measurement and environmental health—and so is a function of modernity. Finally, it reinforces comparable trends and categorizations—just as it defines men, women, and children, so too do many other processes and regulations: age-of-consent laws, demands for compulsory education, franchises for legislatures, administrative policies and departments, and censuses. Inevitably, these categories spawn organizations: unions, political parties, women's groups, or social reform movements. Such processes, or rather the contributions made to them by empire, are the subject of this book.

This book too is dedicated to Lizzie, Ben and Katy, Tom and Emma.

London, 2006   PETER ROBB

Acknowledgements

As said in *Liberalism*, these collections have been put together in moments borrowed from my current 'day job' as Pro-Director of SOAS, a post not designed to permit a scholarly life. As ever, I am thankful for help. Kelly Scott and others created computer-readable texts from some old originals. My wife Elizabeth put up with yet another intrusion of laptop and papers. Some sections and chapters benefited from specific input that is acknowledged in each case.

The following essays are republished with the consent of the publishers named:

Cambridge University Press for 'Law and Agrarian Society in India: The Case of Bihar and the Nineteenth-century Tenancy Debate', *Modern Asian Studies*, 22(2), 1988; 'Hierarchy and Resources: Peasant Stratification in Late Nineteenth Century Bihar', *Modern Asian Studies*, 13(1), 1979; 'Labour in India, 1860–1920: Typologies, Change and Regulation', *Journal of the Royal Asiatic Society*, 4(1), 1994.

Blackwell Publishing for 'Peasants' Choices? Indian Agriculture and the Limits of Commercialization in Nineteenth-century Bihar', *Economic History Review*, XLV(I), 1992.

Note

Chapter 4 is a rewritten version of 'Agrarian Structure and Economic Development' in Rajat Datta, Peter Robb, and Kaoru Sugihara, *Agriculture, Agrarian Structure and Economic Development: Bengal and Japan*, from *Occasional Papers in Third World Economic History*, no. 4, School of Oriental and African Studies, London, 1992.

I
Agrarian Policy and Political Change

1. Agrarian Policy and Law

Villages

In this volume, we will consider some of the changes in political economy under colonialism, with special reference to the countryside. Perhaps the emphasis needs no justification other than the ratio of rural to urban population and the occupational bias of the colonial period. But there is more to it. India could have had an urban-based political revolution, as in some other countries; but by and large it did not. The agricultural sector always mattered politically, even though land revenue provided smaller and smaller proportions of government income. Of course town-based professionals and trading communities, especially the Parsis, were crucial to political developments; but mobilization of the countryside was also evident. Landowners as well as ratepayers formed the earliest representative organizations. Resistance to land-revenue demands and other rural revolts as well as largely urban anti-salt tax protests, expressed popular Indian resistance to the colonial state. The district boards, which helped forge provincial politics, were often peopled by new men from the cities as well as local notables; but they were rooted by their operations, concerns, and character in small towns and mofussils. Broad or specific coalitions of peasants in 'unpolitical' regions chiefly formed the new constituencies of support for M.K. Gandhi and the reformed Congress party (and later for the radical Sikhs, and later still for the separatist Muslims). Importantly, this debunked the myth of the 'loyal peasant' beloved of the British, ensuring that constitutional concessions would continue to be made. Elections in independent India—including those in 2004, which confounded the urban pollsters—demonstrate the enduring importance and the political liveliness of rural voters.

Another reason for concentrating on agrarian conditions is that there is more to be said about their political importance in the context of government policy. There can always be work for historians, but the role of the Western-educated and professional classes in all aspects of nationalism and social development hardly needs re-emphasis. The trade unions have had their chroniclers too, debating the significance of social attitudes and ideologies and the part played by employers, politicians, and the state. Religious and social groups are being extensively studied, usually while noting the new context of colonialism and the challenges of Western theology and science. Not so much, it is true, with reference to the nature or actions of the colonial state itself, beyond 'divide-and-rule'; but those are matters already addressed in *Liberalism*. Of course, the agrarian scene too has been repeatedly examined for its political importance by such diverse scholars as David Ludden, Sugata Bose, David Washbrook, Christopher Baker, Sumit Guha, and Dilip Menon. But a particular issue in such rural histories, more than in the other fields mentioned, seems to be whether or not—or how—colonialism mattered. In *Liberalism*, I mentioned the *Subaltern Studies* emphasis on autonomous classes. Whatever its other merits heuristically, it does not help clarify the articulation of politics between state, elites, and populace, or indeed among castes and within religions. It is odd that the state's influence on the countryside should be controversial, as agrarian society is surely an aspect of India with which the British were very closely involved and in which notable changes clearly occurred. The controversy and that involvement are other good arguments for my emphasis in this book. Finally, in any case, the agrarian sphere provides good examples of more general changes.

Henry Cotton was wrong when he claimed (as quoted in *Liberalism*) that within a few miles of government headquarters there were villages unchanged since Akbar.[1] The persistence of this myth is not remarkable. It suited colonialism, in its supervisory stance, to think Indians conservative and fatalistic, just as it has suited some historians and politicians to overemphasize the alien character of colonialism in India. Both these positions underestimated India. Indians, not Europeans, did the main work of transforming India's economy. Colonial government was overwhelmingly Indian in personnel. Images of European stuffed shirts and soldiers pontificating in council and of paternalistic district collectors taking charge of childlike subjects were encouraged by the empire's own view of itself, but manifestly they were never accurate or complete and after 1920, it should be remembered, Indians were in the majority even in the executive councils of government. Asiaticus had picked it up at once, in the 1780s: Indians were adaptable.[2] Even Indian domestic servants and road-workers quickly took to the Supreme Court's very English law. This was not just going along with change or succumbing to *force majeur*. Indians proved themselves self-interested and very adept at this 'foreign' legal system and at everything else of use that the British had to offer.

1 See Cotton to Ripon, 10 September and 8 November 1893, Add. Mss. 43618.
2 Discussed in *Liberalism*, quoting from the letters of Asiaticus first published in 1784 (reprint, edited W.K. Firminger; 1909) in P. Thankappan Nair, *Calcutta in the 18th Century*, Calcutta, 1984, pp. 169–73.

What then of those unchanged villages? These were the very villages that transformed the Indian economy and its exports of primary materials, that increasingly stored foreign bullion and consumed foreign goods, and that experienced boons or buffeting from international prices. These were the same villages that by 1900 were invariably close to a fixed or weekly market, and often within a day's travel of a railway. Mostly they had a post office even nearer. (See any large-scale map of the time, and search for the little 'PO's.) These were villages that, therefore, sent out and received back more pilgrims and workers and saw more travelling traders or officials than ever before. Leave aside the later impact of local buses and of distribution trucks on metalled roads, or of press, radio, film, television, and the Internet. Can one imagine what it meant for a poor rural family to be able to receive and be able to cash a postal money order sent by a family member working in the mills of Howrah or Bombay? Or that the family member could have journeyed away by buying or being given a ticket on a train that operated according to a timetable and was more or less safe from brigands and warlords? Certainly India had long had sophisticated means of transferring money over distances, potentially to all, but not as a public good provided and guaranteed by the state. So there were old and continuing traditions of migration too, but nothing with the degree of regulation and organization existing only from the nineteenth century. I am not saying that these are good things or bad. I am suggesting that they must have had an effect on people's views of themselves and the world.

Thus part of the origins of modern identities may be traced to economic change and agrarian policy. The intention of raising these questions in this collection is to highlight the kinds of connection that I have often stressed between economy, society, and politics, and particularly between the impact of law and commercialization and the construction of identities and political constituencies. Parts of this volume continue and generalize the arguments of my study of the nature and impact of British agrarian policy, based around the Bengal Tenancy Act.[3] The articles I have included in 'Part II: Law, Economic Change, Interest Groups, and Rights', do not pay much direct attention to identities or politics, but they offer a basis for understanding how new kinds of interest groups and class interest might have arisen. Chapter 4 outlines the limits of the sway of capitalism under colonial rule, a subject taken up in specific ways in the essays that follow it. Chapter 5 discusses the impact of law. Chapter 6 asks similar questions with regard to the actualities of production. Chapter 7 explores the fluidity and contingency of rural hierarchies,

3 Peter Robb, *Ancient Rights and Future Comfort: Bihar, British Rule in India and the Bengal Tenancy Act of 1885*, Richmond, Surrey, 1996.

except within broad class-like categories. Chapter 8 considers in particular the impact of indigo and tea production, and the fate of labour. All five imply continuities with the past, the mixed impact of colonial administration and trade, and the ability of already advanced or well-resourced groups to prosper at the expense of others. Chapter 8 also widens the discussion beyond agriculture—those aspects have been described in the Preface. Together, the essays define conditions in which new expressions of identity were needed and were possible. The introductory chapters are concerned with antecedents or contexts, and with the ways they were translated into identities.

Government and the Countryside

Agrarian policy comprises all the actions of government towards rural society and agriculture.[4] It includes policies relating to land revenue, surveying, and records; to land ownership, tenancy, and rural labour; to agricultural production and trade; and to the science and development of cultivation. It is complex; its detail may seem dull; but it is very important. It affects politics, among other things—how power is exercised in the countryside; how the state tries to gain support; what interests it represents. It affects government—what it can and cannot do, and what it is for; the state's income and how it is spent. It affects the economy—the terms on which societies organize the production of food and the exchange of goods; the comparative importance of cultivation, processing, industry, and services; a country's or a region's standing among others. It helps determine well-being—the social distribution of food, work, and wealth; levels of health and population. Finally, it is part of culture—attitudes towards property, employment, family, and inheritance; other social and moral values, such as the significance and purpose of cultivation; how people think about socio-economic classes and 'rights'. Later, these elements together will bring us back to identity and politics.

For a foreign government, agrarian policy provided (as said) what is arguably the most important point of influence upon the subject people and territory. In India the British, though so few and distant from the majority of people, could change the nature of landholding, the availability of land, and the capacity of people to move from one place or one job to another. They could influence the kinds of crop that were grown, the manner in which credit was provided to cultivators, and the ways crops were marketed. They could affect the patterns of consumption, the basis of prestige, and the terms on which some Indians gained dominance over others. They could control and reward favoured classes. They could transform India's internal and international economy. Or,

---

[4] The following paragraphs were originally written for a course at the Indira Gandhi Open University, at the request of Abha Singh.

more precisely, as we should not think of any government as being all-powerful and all-knowing, they could introduce policies for a variety of motives and find that they produced a range of intended and unintended effects in these various aspects of life. With hindsight, we can see that agrarian policies led to a transformation in India. Though agrarian legacies and continuities were important and the picture of an India of unchanging villages had never been true, yet the integration of the countryside with broader systems of government, law, and trade became markedly greater than before, during the nineteenth and twentieth centuries.

Let us concern ourselves at first with only one aspect of colonial agrarian policy, the large aspect related to land rights. This is a very well-known story, but there may be benefits from my telling it again as lucidly as I can, with an emphasis on the elements relevant to this book. There are two main contexts, relating to the motives lying behind the policies. First is the motive of *control*. Land policies are partly about ensuring that there is order in the countryside and that revenue is readily relinquished to the state. This does not mean that land policies were merely a form of coercion. Just as important, they offered a means of persuasion. The British wanted to support or create classes which would have an interest in collaborating with them and which would be able to curb those who tried to resist or avoid the state's authority. The British also intended to ensure (though they did not succeed in this) basic levels of well-being in the population as a whole so as to avoid the costs and dislocation of famine, disease, and desertion, and thus protect future state revenues.

Second, there is the question of *trade*. In the eighteenth century, British trade with India centred on exchanging cotton goods manufactured in India for bullion (silver and gold). This was partly because there was little market in India for British produce, but also because silver and gold were not simply money but commodities wanted by India that Europe could supply relatively cheaply. Even cheaper for the British East India Company, however, was to make its purchases in India using revenues from Indian territories and using profits from the sale of products in which the Company established a monopoly, such as salt and opium. Such strategies also implied land policies.

Later, from the mid-nineteenth century, this not very efficient system gave way to one that sought to draw on a much wider range of products and to involve a much bigger proportion of Indian consumers. This meant that land policies became even more important. Overseas land and labour resources were now beginning to support and enrich the population and the capitalists of Britain as its industrialization progressed. At first, slave plantations, North American development, and the newer settlement colonies played a larger part in this process than India. But India soon became a source of raw materials (cotton, jute, indigo) and of some foods and drugs (opium, tea, coffee, wheat), and also a market for British manufactures. The surpluses earned by India's foreign trade (except with Britain) helped Britain to finance its own deficits in trade with some other countries. India was also a vital site for British employment, services, and investment.

Contrary to what is sometimes thought, colonial land policies were not exactly calculated to achieve these effects. They were the outcome of countless individual economic decisions and not of any farsighted state plan. But certainly Indian land policies were expected to help (or at least, not hinder) British economic interests, which were also supported by the economic theories of those days. The success of the policies can be seen in the extent to which India's countryside *did* perform the roles required of it by British industrialists, merchants, and consumers.

The basis of land policy was the revenue settlement, meaning the decision of how much would be paid to the state for land, who would pay it, and on what terms and conditions. The tendency in India was for strong states to reach down as near as possible to the actual cultivators for information about agriculture and landholding as well as to fix responsibility for the payment of land revenue. No pre-colonial states managed to do without local intermediaries—lords, record keepers, headmen, and so on—but many kept careful records relating to landholding and revenue payment. The most celebrated survey was that ordered by Todar Mal, finance minister of the Mughal emperor, Akbar. During much of the seventeenth century, this and further surveys permitted a system of regulated revenue settlement based on assessments of agricultural output.

In the eighteenth century, however, there was an ever-increasing demand for revenue. This was attributable to a number of factors: the growth of stronger regional states, the cost of warfare, investment in production and trade, tributes paid to others (especially the Marathas and the British East India Company), and loss of income to intermediaries or to the powerful, again including the European trading companies which generally avoided local tolls and taxes. This need for money led to agreements between local rulers and either the powerful elites (a few zamindars, then meaning the territorial lords and official revenue collectors) or efficient 'fixers', so-called revenue-farmers or *ijaradar*s chosen by the auction of rights to the highest bidder. In general these arrangements implied short-term increases in revenue in return for a reduction of central control.

In 1765, the British East India Company gained hold of the revenues of Bengal and Bihar. At first the Company worked through deputies who also served the nawab of Bengal; and even when it took control directly at the behest of the Governor, Warren Hastings, in 1772, it still awarded the revenue-collecting right to the highest bidders for terms of one or more years. But the

Company was gaining information through access to the revenue records (moved to Calcutta), the experience of some European collectors, and also a commission of inquiry in the districts. Strong theoretical and practical arguments were advanced, notably by Council member Philip Francis, that short-term revenue-farming was unwise.

In 1789, therefore, a 10-year settlement was declared by the Acting Governor, Sir John Shore. In 1793, under the new Governor General, Lord Cornwallis, this was superseded by a settlement that was declared permanent—that is, the rate of tax was fixed for ever. The settlement was to be made by local arrangements using the existing records, without survey, and with what were thought to be (but in many instances were not) hereditary landed interests, the zamindars.

Many considerations lay behind this system, which was ordered from Britain. It provided a means of running India through general rules set out in a long list of Regulations enforceable by the courts. Such minimal direct government was favoured by the political theories of the time. The system was also thought suited to Indian expectations and to conditions in Bengal, where the self-seeking servants of an imperfectly organized commercial company were now in possession of an empire. Making the settlement with zamindars would secure, or if necessary create, an indigenous rural aristocracy. Permanence would place a clear and fixed limit to the government's share of production and thus encourage investment, higher productivity, and trade, which then would increase the government's income indirectly.

To some extent these goals were achieved, though the Company soon turned against the Bengal system. The cultivated area increased and more crops were grown for local and international markets, adding to an already commercialized agriculture and to established means for the reclamation of land. Zamindars, despite pockets of resistance, gave up their broader military and political roles and became adjuncts to a new political order and so subjects of the Company's government. Gradually, from the early years when land could barely be sold at any price, a valuable land market grew along with the population, giving meaning to the rights created in and after 1793. New landlords, at first often resisted by local communities, were able to call on state force to ensure their possession. A tendency in favour of separate rather than shared landholding led to partitions under official scrutiny, so that the number of zamindars increased markedly, especially in some districts. Land became a reliable security for borrowing and mortgages, but also therefore a means whereby traders and moneylenders could extract agrarian produce at lower cost and somewhat reduced risk to themselves.

The Permanent Settlement attached possession to revenue payment. In the past, non-payers could be punished in their person by imprisonment or torture, for example. Now their property was at risk. Some great zamindars lost out as the revenue demand was often set at rates that were initially very high (a notional 90 per cent of income). But new regulations were introduced to help the remainder over the next few decades by giving them near-absolute powers over their tenants and over their tenants' property, including standing crops.

Some other agrarian classes had their pre-existing rights recognized. This qualified those given to zamindars. In some areas, intermediary landholders (*jotedars*) gained most from the Permanent Settlement through directly managing production. On the whole, however, the legal position of cultivators was weakened. For most of the nineteenth century, until changes in the law and in official attitudes, they did not share in the benefits as incomes from agriculture improved. Even in the eighteenth century, dispossessed and opportunistic people had formed criminal gangs (as dacoits) in the countryside. In the nineteenth century, armed or concerted resistance broke out, expressing various mixtures of religious, social, and economic grievances. Disease, scarcity, and famine worsened in rural communities, partly because of the gradual spread of the effect of these changes in property law.

Very soon after the introduction of the Permanent Settlement in north-east India, it was challenged by Company officials, especially Thomas Munro, who, as remarked in *Liberalism*, held that it was inappropriate to the regions they knew. In Munro's case, this meant parts of the Madras Presidency, where (despite a permanent settlement along the Andhra coast) he claimed that either there were no identifiable landlords or the local chiefs threatened British rule and should be removed, not revived. More generally, he argued that a zamindari settlement was contrary to Indian understandings of landholding and revenue obligations. A little later, around 1812, these conservative arguments were allied with the reformist and anti-aristocratic tendencies of Utilitarian thinkers and political economists, such as James Mill, who now controlled the London administration of the Company. The alliance ensured that no further settlements would be permanent. It was argued that landlords did not generally contribute to prosperity and were not doing so in Bengal, and that production would be best increased by giving property rights to those responsible for tilling the soil. It was claimed in this context that Indians did not understand, or were abusing, the elaborate legal system that had been set up in Bengal and that they would be better served by rulers who combined executive and judicial functions.

In future, therefore, most settlements were *raiyatwari*, that is made with the *raiyat*s (those regarded as actual cultivators) rather than with landlords. Such settlements were introduced in southern and western India. Similar but modified versions were later devised for village communities (*mahalwari* settlements) based around co-sharers (*pattidari* or *bhaiachara*) in parts of north

India, especially the Punjab. Broadly speaking, these temporary settlements relied on close surveys of the countryside and on regularly revised records. Revenue rates for each cultivated plot were set for a limited period, commonly 30 years. Actual payments depended on annual reports on the use of that plot. Temporary settlements therefore implied close and personal, rather than distant and legalistic, government. They nevertheless standardized the categories of landholding and replaced systems based on shares or collective liabilities with ones based on individual title.

The surveys were always elaborate and became more time-consuming and 'scientific' as the nineteenth century went on. Measurement and the drawing of plans were separated from the recording of landholders and from economic, social, and historical assessments of the conditions in every village and in regions (called 'circles') of similar character. Revenue rates were increasingly set at levels related to the supposed capacity of the soil (not current output) in order to discourage idleness. They were calculated in accordance with the definition of rent by the classical economist David Ricardo—namely, that rent was merely the unearned extra produce from better land compared with returns from the least favourable land, and therefore that it was both measurable and safe to tax. When this (in fact very imprecise) calculation led to overly high revenue demands, these were modified by more subjective assessments of what areas could afford to pay.

The Punjab, in particular, in the late nineteenth century advocated a peasant-proprietary model of agrarian policy and turned the survey and settlement report into an expensive intellectual exercise, one of the founts of today's anthropology and development studies. By contrast, the United Provinces saw a resurgence of belief in aristocratic land-control, especially in Awadh following the rebellion of 1857-8. There a settlement was made with superior landlords (*taluqdars*) in replacement of a village-level settlement introduced immediately after the British annexation. It was debated whether this and other settlements should be made permanent. In the end (as already mentioned) they remained temporary, even where superior revenue collectors were again recognized, for example in central India as well as in Awadh.

There were subsequent adjustments, of course. The systems introduced between 1770s and the 1850s did not remain unchanged. New ideas and perceived problems prompted reforms, which continued upto and after the end of British rule. These expansions in government responsibilities were significant. Many measures were taken to preserve property. On larger estates, the British encouraged primogeniture so as to avoid the risk of subdivision upon inheritance. Legislation was passed to ease the burden on 'encumbered estates' whose survival was threatened by bad management or misfortune. The Court of Wards, first introduced in Bengal in 1790 and 1793, provided for the temporary administration of an estate by the Board of Revenue, where necessary or requested, in the stead of an 'incapable zamindar' (a description often held to include women). In the twentieth century too, many (though less effectual) efforts were made to halt the fragmentation of plots of cultivation and to facilitate land swaps that would consolidate scattered holdings.

Especially after riots in the Deccan in 1875, a host of more general measures sought to protect landholders in the temporarily settled areas against moneylenders who, supposedly, were snapping up land rights and disturbing the time-honoured political and social equilibrium of the countryside. Various laws qualified the advantage given to creditors by the increased security of landed property, including tenancies, and by the operation of the laws of contract. The most extreme of these was the Punjab Alienation of Land Act of 1900, which tried to restrict land transfer (and hence mortgages on rural land) to recognized agriculturists, members of the 'tribes and castes' listed in a schedule to the Act.

Whereas in the first half of the nineteenth century the government sought mainly to ensure that revenue was paid promptly, in the second half it became more concerned with agricultural development. This matched the demands of British industry for raw materials and markets, but also responded to worries about rural unrest and about the condition and vulnerability of the poor. Such concerns had become important to policy and to political debate from the late 1830s onwards. One consequence was an attempt once again to use property rights as a means of securing political and economic goals. Gradually the idea of state-enforced rights was applied further and further down the tenurial and social scale. This was an important change, and it will be useful to summarize the story again here, relating it to the colonial management of the countryside.

Various Tenancy Acts set out both to protect superior landowning interests and to provide a measure of security to the cultivators. In the second half of the nineteenth century, these enactments began to give some rights to those who held land from landlords rather than directly or indirectly from the state. In Bengal, the Rent Act of 1859, while purporting to help zamindars collect rents, also recorded as settled or occupancy tenants those who had held land for 12 years. It placed restrictions on the enhancement of rents. It also sought improvements in landlord–tenant relations and the more effective resolution of agrarian disputes.

Defects in this legislation and more radical impulses for reform in the aftermath of further famine and rural unrest led to the Bengal Tenancy Act of 1885, which added two major points. Firstly, there were more elaborate classifications of tenants and gradations of rights, with a presumption of occupancy status in a village for all those holding any land in that village. In many areas, this status now applied to large majorities of first-tier tenants (that is, excluding those who were the tenants of other tenants). Secondly, there was provision for survey and settlement to establish and record rights, holdings, and rents by analogy with the procedures in temporarily settled areas. These had the effect, as operations proceeded, of establishing tenant rights and familiarizing people with them.

Indian legislation was influenced by the ideas of fair and fixed rents and of secure tenure that had been popularized during tenancy debates in Ireland, where they took on a populist and nationalist hue. More important, however, was that the 1885 Act extended the Punjab peasant-proprietary model. The occupancy tenants of Bengal and Bihar (the latter region being the immediate focus of attention in view of the poverty of the region) were being ensured a kind of property in their landholdings in order to encourage them to invest in agriculture: to make them, in short, rich peasants.

The trend after 1885 was for the principles of the Bengal Act to be extended elsewhere, such as to the Central Provinces in 1895. But it was overtaken by measures designed to regulate all aspects of agrarian relations. Other regions had also had tenancy legislation, but the needs were different where numerous cultivators rather than landlords were the ostensible revenue payers. In the twentieth century, too, further measures were taken in Bengal and Bihar (as elsewhere) to afford some legal protection to subtenants, sharecroppers, and labour. None of these strictly related to property. Rather they built on arguments about equity (also heard during the debates over the 1885 Act).

Tenancy reform was thus advocated by leading officials in most provinces. Ideas included placing limits on rents and providing more secure occupancy for tenants. It was claimed, as one minute put it with regard to the Central and the North-Western Provinces in 1883, that the law had developed by merely 'ascertaining and defining prescriptive rights and customary privileges of certain classes' rather than by intervening 'so as to regulate beneficially'.[5] In short, colonial law merely 'recognized', it did not create.[6] Rights had been declared or revived through appealing to principles that sometimes arose in remote antiquity but were still preserved 'within the hearts of the people'.[7] These rights, however, now bore all the exclusivity and protection of English

---

5 J. Woodburn, Secretary to the NWP Government, to the Government of India (henceforth GOI), Proceedings of the GOI, Revenue and Agriculture Department (henceforth R&A), 21 December 1883, Add. Mss. 43584, British Library.

6 T.W. H[olderness], note, 21 July 1884, quoting William Muir, note on Oudh Tenant Right, Tenancy papers, 1867, and A. Colvin, Memorandum of Settlements, 1833–4; Add. Mss. 43584. After Thomason's rule in 1844, repeated in the 1859 Bengal Tenancy Act, land rights were subject to a prescription of 12 years' occupancy, the period derived from English law but also claimed as an ancient custom of India.

7 Woodburn note, 21 July 1883, *loc. cit.*

law, which among other things placed a 'very powerful engine of [rent] enhancement in the hands of the landlords'.[8] Many non-privileged tenure-holders and most actual cultivators had suffered. Hence 'further remedial legislation' was needed, though it required great caution.[9] Within this rather timid argumentation, there was a bold proposal to change the government's role in agrarian society from protection and facilitation to regulation and reform. As I have shown elsewhere, it was a goal shift from preserving 'ancient rights' to promoting 'future comfort' hinted at by famine policy in Lytton's day, but worked out above all under Ripon and in the Bengal Tenancy Act of 1885. That Act (as would be expected of a moment of transition) embodied complex and contradictory attitudes to custom, property rights, economic advance, and social reconstruction.[10]

Increasingly, a 'hands-on' approach was demanded. The 1880s saw the end of a long debate about permanently fixing the land-revenue demand (as in eastern India since 1793, but not elsewhere in India) and the ridiculing of a scheme advanced by Edward Buck for a self-regulating variable demand based on agricultural price statistics.[11] Instead, programmes of agricultural improvement were planned. In 1870, by initiative of a Conservative, Lord Mayo, agricultural departments had been set up, partly to relieve others of administrative burdens, but also to collect information and to promote experiment and good practice, with one model farm planned for every district. This partly followed the scheme of a statistical committee set up in 1866 after the north Indian famine of 1861. Initially agricultural returns were made only in temporarily settled areas; but in the 1870s, after famine in Orissa, George Campbell, a reforming Lieutenant Governor, ensured that Bengal followed suit, though its local agency remained very weak. These separate agricultural departments were soon abandoned; but in the 1880s, with the impetus provided by a major new Famine Commission, they were re-established on a more professional and permanent footing.

Ashley Eden, architect of legal rights for enterprising tenants, was dismayed. He thought the departments a sham, though he was willing to have a roving commissioner who would learn from his travels and advise the local and central governments.[12] Bengal zamindars were also generally opposed to further scrutiny by state officials. But Eden's successor Rivers Thompson disagreed.

8 Holderness note, *loc. cit.*
9 Woodburn note, 21 December 1883, *loc. cit.*
10 Peter Robb, *Ancient Rights and Future Comfort*—this book offers a specially focused exposition of this and several of the other arguments in this introduction.
11 See J.R. Reid, Secretary to the NWP Government to R&A Dept., 17 May 1884, and extensive other papers, Add. Mss. 43584, and, on Buck's scheme, Bayley to Ripon, 22 August [1882], Add. Mss. 43612.
12 Eden to Ripon, 13 November 1882, Add. Mss. 43592.

He wanted a department, a Director of Agriculture, experimental centres, and various training schools, arguing that agrarian issues had 'always been a chief object' of the land-taxing Indian powers, and moreover that every 'civilized country in the world' now recognized that agricultural improvement could no longer be left 'entirely to private enterprise'. There was 'room for neither doubt or discussion', he wrote, '...of the principle' that a 'duty' of development 'attaches to the State'.[13] This was the change already described in *Liberalism*. Between Eden and Thompson, who both admitted that governments had allowed the utter decay of Bengal's old village reporting and accounting system, one moves from a framework of law to the creation of means for improvement. It was symptomatic of a major extension of the government's responsibilities. It occurred generally in India as in Britain and other countries. Experiments in scientific agriculture and later interventions in credit and marketing were also important politically—more so somewhat after Ripon's time—as markers of the widening role for the state.[14]

Land reform was thus a key example of the way that the role of government was being extended. The British were no longer content merely to frame the agrarian structure (that is, establish and define landed property) in the hope of promoting commercial expansion and securing its revenue. They now placed a new emphasis on investigation and statistics, on agricultural experiments and credit provision, and even on direct intervention (committees for particular crops, price fixing, and finally development planning), as part of broader social and economic strategies. It is true that, nonetheless, policy towards land rights, considered in isolation, retained an echo of the minimal government favoured in the eighteenth century and by laissez-faire doctrines in the nineteenth century. But even that policy, in some ways, had been radically different from what had gone before. Colonial policy introduced new ideas about land use and types of land control. These ideas were common to the different kinds of agrarian policy. This is one of the keys to the political impact of the policies, and so I shall explore it more fully.

Property and Tax

Earlier it was believed that British laws created landownership in India, but it is now plain that this depends on what is meant by the term. In some senses,

13 Bayley to Primrose, 16 June [1883] and A.P. MacDonnell to Secretary, GOI R&A Dept., 1 June 1883, Add. Mss. 43612. See also Secretary of State's despatch (Revenue), 16 June 1881, and Resolutions, of the GOI, R&A, 8 December 1881 and 9 January 1882, Add. Mss. 43584.

14 For further discussion, see Peter Robb, 'Bihar, the Colonial State and Agricultural Development in India, 1880–1920', *Indian Economic and Social History Review*, 25(2), 1988.

there was private property in land in India from the earliest historical times. Religious notions of renunciation depended on it, as did payments and grants to kings, temples, elites, co-sharers, workers, and artisans. Over time, different states found sophisticated ways of measuring and defining land rights, including surveys, records, and title deeds. Land rights could be sold and inherited; there were stories and theories about their ultimate origins and about the proper behaviour of landholders. The holders would enjoy one or more of very many specific kinds of tenure. Of course, land rights were not absolute—they never are—and they could be lost to force or usurpation. They would be qualified by obligations to pay land taxes and/or to supply materials and manpower. They were subject to communal and joint-family obligations and generally to the rights of others, both superiors and inferiors. All these things also applied to land rights under the British.

What colonial laws and policies did to land rights was more subtle, in theory and also increasingly in practice. They reduced the number of different types of right to only those which the law specified. They made each type's benefits and obligations more definite—by legal definitions, by more precise measurement through scientific surveys, by more exact records, and by the decisions of a hierarchy of courts. They applied uniform concepts to all land—that is, they tried to deny the existence of land of doubtful or shared ownership. There were no sacred groves or shrines that did not belong to a temple or a *mahant*; no forest or flood plain without owners; no house, well, *ghat*, or bazaar without a proprietor. The owner did not need to be an individual, of course. The owner could be a family, a village, a corporation, or the state. But for all that, only one kind of 'ownership' was to be recognized, the kind established in the state's law.

Many local variants and distinctions, and some pragmatic responses to circumstance were ignored or overridden, for example between kinds of co-sharers, between resident and non-resident landholders, or between high and low castes. Other pre-existing types were reinforced and generalized, at least in the law, as new categories of landlords, intermediary tenure-holders, tenants, and subtenants, and later as settled and occupancy tenants or tenants-at-will.

Now the characteristics or 'incidents' of property were always spelled out. A zamindar in Mughal times had any of a range of possible rights, but in particular he had the duty to collect revenue for the state, retaining a proportion for himself (supposedly 10 per cent). His revenue-collecting (*malguzari*) right derived from Mughal authority; in regulation districts, even the amounts of the collections were theoretically specified by surveys and rules. In addition, the zamindar might have chiefly powers derived from his local socio-political standing—his character, caste, or lineage and his command of retainers. These powers carried some obligations to the community and certainly produced further income, for example through tolls, control over markets, payments for credit, use of forced labour, and further shares of produce. There would have also been others occupying and using *the same land*, who might similarly have had effective rights over it—for example, a right to cultivate, or to reside in a village and exploit village resources. Such rights too fell into particular categories and had specific names, and—just like zamindari rights—they could be derived from licence, or custom, or power. Pre-colonial rights therefore could be of different types and degrees, and could overlap in relation to the same plot of land.

Within British territory (that is, leaving aside the Indian states, though these were influenced by the same processes), all landowning became in one sense identical; as a complete collection of rights to land, unless some legal provision said otherwise. Landlords were given exclusive titles to specified areas, with qualifications made by law reserving certain other rights for the state, for sub-proprietors, or for privileged tenants. All these rights derived from the state and its laws, while any unspecified sub-rights derived only from the landlord. The *khudkasht* raiyat—a cultivator with superior and residence rights in a locality—was turned into a 'tenant', for example. And if he was not provided for in the state's regulations, he could legally gain the right to use land only by *contract*—that is, through an agreement he made with the landlord. He might have privileges or he might have no security of tenure—in theory, this was decided by law, not force.

Several provisions turned land into a commodity that could be readily bought and sold, firstly because it could not be arbitrarily seized by the powerful, not even by the state itself; and secondly because it was largely free from encumbrances (that is, subordinate rights that would reduce its value). One consequence was that 'rents' and hence '*abwabs*' (illegal cesses) also changed their meaning. Payments of various kinds had always been made to social and political superiors on different pretexts, sanctioned partly by the state and partly by custom and according to what was thought fair or affordable, or what could be extorted given the relative power of the parties involved. Now there was merely 'rent', meaning a contractual payment for the use of land. Anything beyond 'rent' became illegal. In the absence of formal leases, and given colonial expressions of respect for Indian 'custom', it took a long time before this legal distinction meant anything much in reality. But ultimately rents became more regulated while 'illegal' cesses and dues became harder to exact. These changes placed pressure upon landlords and forced them to devise new ways of securing their incomes. Some left the land to better-resourced managers (including European planters) or more skilful agriculturists. Others improved their own management, or cultivated more on their own account, or hardened the terms offered to bonded labour and sharecroppers.

This leads on to another important point, that the British related ownership to *use*. Like most other states, they favoured settled agriculture over all other modes of land utilization, though they also created reserved forests (as the Mughals did hunting tracts). They deliberately set land-revenue rates—and designed the systems and chose the revenue payers—in order to maximize commercial production, though oddly they chose to do this while thinking they were conserving an old order and while trying to make land tenure more secure.

Moreover, land that was not in regular use the British defined as 'waste'. Much of such 'waste' they denied to landholders and communities who had had informal shared control over it; they resumed it for the state or allocated it to private owners. They greatly reduced the areas that were revenue-free (*inam* or *lakhiraj*). Earlier regimes had left vast amounts of land and its produce in the hands of others to pay for public services and goods (officials, armies, temples, mosques, schools), and had drawn much government income from their own state lands (*khalsa*). The colonial government was not eager to manage lands directly or to look to state land as a major source of income. It recognized revenue-free lands only where it could not avoid doing so. Because they wanted to ensure the validity of titles to land, the British had to respect specific, unimpeachable, written revenue-free rights, whether from before or after British rule. But for their own part, even when they wanted to show particular marks of favour by making land grants, for example to soldiers in the Punjab, they very seldom awarded them revenue-free. They preferred to encourage market production and to collect cash into the treasuries, and then to govern through employees who were paid in money.

What all this also implies is a particular idea of the purpose of land. Above all, it was to be cultivated to produce crops that could be sold. The land had to pay, to its owner and then to the state. This was not wholly new of course, as all states and for that matter all settled cultivators had always had much the same idea about land. Exploitation of land resources and the human shaping of landscape certainly long preceded colonial rule in India, and one should not imagine that there was some kind of pre-colonial ecological harmony between man and soil. But the commercial use of land did become, in British rhetoric, almost the *only*, the hegemonic idea of what land was for— and this undoubtedly reduced the grip of alternative views: for example, of land as a place of ritual in such activities as ploughing, sowing, and harvesting; of land as sacred and as the basis of the political order; of land as patrimony, or a common good for kin or community; of land as a public store of wealth to be drawn on as necessary; of land as a means of expressing and enforcing social customs and distinctions.

There are some further general points to be made about this from the administrative stand point. There seem to have been five distinct stages in India, as also in Britain, that mark a development towards a 'modern' fiscal structure. First, there was the institution of fixed property, which provided security against the payment of tax—here the example is land in recorded ownership, in place of personal liability, which led to forced sales in place of imprisonment or torture. Secondly, there was a limited but definite demand, whether permanently as in Bengal or on a periodically fixed scale as in so-called temporarily settled areas. The intention was to free the income of both taxpayers and the state from the uncertainties of negotiation or force. Thirdly, there was an attempt at standardizing payments between individuals or regions in comparable conditions. This is different from earlier times both because all payments tended to be less uncertain and because taxes were likely to be highest in areas or from persons over which the ruler exercised closest sway. Broadly, one can call this objectification, a reduction of personal obligations as the basis of taxation and accumulation, as of much else. Indian states had repeatedly tried for some standardization; the British succeeded more fully than their predecessors. Madras land-revenue payers continued to resent the lower rates in Bengal, but could do so because of the existence of public accounts and of notions of parity. Meanwhile, defenders of the system could cite the overall tax burden, taking account of taxes on income and trade. Fourthly—and this really marks a second stage of development—there was growing importance of those alternative sources of revenue: more indirect taxes, more taxes on consumption, taxes on income, user payments for state services, and so on. In India, the land revenue declined markedly in importance compared with such alternatives from the late nineteenth century onwards. It followed that, though formerly taxation may have been extremely high for some payers and these excesses declined over time, yet the *total* income of the state vastly expanded as the system developed. Fifthly, there was a great widening in the range and number of taxpayers, necessarily accompanied by a certain shift towards graduated or progressive taxation. This consolidated standardization by linking tax to the ability to pay. British officials tried to ensure equitable demand in India by calculating, for example, land revenue according to the qualities of different soils and after careful economic assessments. Similarly, as expenditure began to be redistributed from private to public purposes, this prepared the way for demands that the rich should support the poor not only out of charity but via the objective intervention of the state. Such demands were rather imperfectly answered in India, and remain so; but in principle it is still plain that the evolution in taxation was the counterpart of the revolution in the state's purposes and justification. Both income and expenditure matched the changes in the jurisdiction of government within borders, and hence the shift from oligarchy to democracy. It was not just a matter of representation following taxation. The duality of tax and spending, the greater definition *and* the widening ambitions of the state all encouraged and reinforced the nationalist demand for self-determination. It was not admitted by the protagonists, but this meant higher rather than lower taxation, with a view to the state's mobilization of the 'national' resources. The colonial state's inability to do this was one of the strongest economic arguments against it. If the nation's management were the job of the state, it was said, it would be done better by those who (supposedly) represented all the people.

Another consequence of all this, I argue, was the firming up of social classes and the hardening of divisions between them. With regard to landholdings, the evidence is unequivocal. There was a tendency for larger holdings to become relatively more profitable, to preserve their integrity (as seen in statistics of average number and size), and to maintain or even increase their share of total cultivated area. There was also a tendency for the number of smaller holdings to increase and for their size and share to diminish. These related tendencies had different starting points and took different forms in different places. There were differences between permanently and temporarily settled tracts, between irrigated and dry lands. But broadly these same two features can be seen everywhere—among and between holdings with many different kinds of title, in lands dominated by large landowners and in lands under peasant-proprietors.

There had always been many landless in India, and migrant populations of many kinds. Under colonial rule (and since), the pressure increased for people to settle on land and cultivate it, but larger proportions than ever were unable to subsist from the land in their possession. The growing numbers in cities and factories were too small proportionately to compensate for this change, especially as population and average life-expectancy rose. Microholdings and sharecropping, and food from landlords' home farms often became devices to lower cash wages. There was an impoverishment of large sections of India's population. Many factors contributed to this, but an important contribution was made by the very large increase in the numbers of people who could not live by their land alone but had to rely on employment by others.

Behind this differentiation was a major change in agricultural production, which seems somewhat paradoxically to have been related to a significant rise in population. I have often argued that the key factor in impoverishment was not just the subordination of Indian cultivation to world and especially

British consumers. It also mattered that the colonial economy did *not* entirely transform India's countryside and the mode of production, and that the new production and trade were in some large part *created by Indians*. There is indeed the important issue of the economic exploitation of India by Britain, but also the not inconsiderable matter of the exploitation of some Indians by others. The colonial economy seems to have caused, for India, a proportionately major loss of international market share by value. But the terms of trade for Indian agriculture were not uniformly bad, and the trade itself undoubtedly generated extra income. For whom? For British wholesalers, shippers, and insurers certainly; but also for some Indian intermediaries and producers.

2. Political Organization

Land and Status

Did agrarian policy matter politically? To answer, we need first to examine the nature and extent of social change in the colonial period, which means establishing a point of departure with regard to social categories. In pre-colonial times, the predominant forms of socio-political organization seem to have been the household, the local community, the caste, and the kingdom. The household alone is the focus of *Krsi-paràsara*,[1] one of the few early works devoted to agriculture and hence informative of the status and role of cultivators. By its account, society is by no means unstratified, but the kingdom is only just mentioned, caste barely referred to (though purity is required of those performing rites),[2] and the community visible only on a few occasions involving agricultural and seasonal rituals.[3] Cultivating households are implied as being the norm. Within them, the householder's father is to be put in charge of the zenana, his mother is to be placed in the kitchen, the householder is personally to manage the cultivation, and a person 'like himself' is to be set to supervise the cattle. The only people of different kinds directly mentioned are cowherds and kings.

On the other hand, a strong emphasis on supervision (well-supervised agriculture producing gold; poorly supervised, poverty) implies that the household contained or employed other workers. That workers were employed

---

1 *Krsi-paràsara*, edited and translated by Girija Prasanna Majumdar and Sures Chandra Banerji, Bibliotheca Indica, 285(1579), Asiatic Society, Calcutta, 1960. Supposedly this is the only work of its kind, derived from a period before (or certainly not later than) the eleventh century AD. This edition compares different manuscripts and gives texts in Bengali and English. For the discussion following, see especially stanzas 1–11, 30, 79–104, and 145–7. Bhaskar Mukhopadhyay kindly provided me with his own copy of this text.

2 The text mostly appears to enjoin rituals upon the cultivators themselves, and only in the requirements for the ceremony before ploughing (*hala-prasarana*) is there mention of worshipping a twice-born man.

3 Community participation is implied in stanzas 100–3 (a village procession of a bull, cowherds, and cultivators) and 221–37 (*pusyayatra*, a pre-harvest festival), and possibly 178–81 (a festival and feast for the sowing of paddy).

is reinforced by comments relating degrees of comfort to the numbers of ploughs for each household—five to ten implying wealth, two or three a bare sufficiency, and one indebtedness. There are hints too in the observation that the good husbandman cares not only for rituals and cattle, but also for the welfare of other people. Sumit Guha has provided a portrait of a peasant household's labouring dependants, which might well serve as a model for the relations implied here.[4]

An undifferentiated picture amidst hints of stratification implies a lack of self-consciousness about the status of the peasant. On the other hand, *Krsiparàsara* also embodies an image of the cultivator and is a eulogy on his status and importance. In addition to having the attributes already mentioned, the ideal cultivator is energetic, is regular in his attendance on the fields, and is knowledgeable about seasons, rainfall, signs, portents, and seeds. He is the lynchpin of society on whom others, however wealthy, must depend, the one to whom they come as supplicants. Do these attributes and distinctions imply a self-consciousness and a practical solidarity on the part of cultivators *as a class*?

One may take up this question towards the end of the early modern era by interpreting colonial reports, such as those of Buchanan-Hamilton. It is hard to discern any change. We might look, in Marxian terms, for unfree and then landless labour, and primitive and then capitalist accumulation; we might expect, following the work of C.A. Bayly in particular, that the colonial state's successful drive for secure (landlord) property and settled agriculture was a necessary prerequisite for the evolution of a range of agricultural classes, at least beyond the gentry and merchants for whom Bayly ascribes an earlier existence.[5] However, in Purnea for example, Buchanan already reported a fairly clear range of socio-economic categories in the early nineteenth century.[6] First came the dominant and independent rural elite, the zamindars, augmented by area intermediaries: the zamindari *dewan* and other agents, and revenue

---

[4] Sumit Guha, 'Time and Money: The Meaning and Measurement of Labour in Indian Agriculture' in Peter Robb (ed.), *Meanings of Agriculture: Essays in South Asian History and Economics*, Delhi, 1996.

[5] C.A. Bayly, *Rulers, Townsmen and Bazaars: North Indian Society in the Age of British Expansion 1770–1870*, Cambridge, 1983; see p. 30: 'It is easy for us to assume that the state was the only political organization in pre-colonial Indian society, and that the peasant family farm was wholly predominant as an economic form. But in this period the state was only one of the political formations which existed, and a large part of the population subsisted through petty carrying, plunder and pastoralism.' Thus Bayly focuses in the ensuing period on 'the triumph of the state, both Indian and British, over its competitors, and the settlement of the agrarian and commercial economy'—though without taking up the 'class' attributes of pre-colonial peasants.

[6] Francis Buchanan-Hamilton, *An Account of the District of Purnea in 1819–10*, edited by V.H. Jackson, Patna, 1928, pp. 117–19.

farmers (*mostajirs*). Next came village elites, people outside the mostajirs' authority (those occupying unassessed land, paying low rents in perpetuity, or paying directly to the zamindars; and all high castes, Hindu and Muslim, 'exempted from rent for their houses and gardens'). Such elites, and perhaps some other landholders, expressed their dominance by employing and controlling labour, including one specialist ploughman for every six cattle. In another category were village officers, the watchmen, and messengers. Then came other cultivators (*adhiyars*) who held land through mostajirs or other agents. Finally there were the slaves and poor labourers, who at least 'procured room for their houses from those for whom they work'. Within this broad pattern, types of tenure also certainly existed, their names and character briefly recorded by Buchanan: various kinds and degrees of fixed-rent tenants, tenants in perpetuity, short-leaseholders, and so on.[7] Such categories (not being wholly invented by Buchanan) must imply degrees of power and wealth, as well as solidarities perceived by people themselves.

On the other hand, as in *Krsi-paràsara*, the indications are of relatively limited common identities.[8] It does seem that, for every tenurial categorization or social layer, there were many other connections and identities that overlapped, as well as a general fluidity, ambiguity, and contingency of status.[9] First, there were large numbers of servants and hired workers in Purnea, but outsiders found it very difficult to obtain labour, as workers could not escape the vertical control provided by debt bondage. Secondly, broader identities were expressed, but possibly, like caste and community, cut across economic strata. 'More than half the Hindus', reported Buchanan, 'consider themselves as belonging to foreign nations, either from the west of India or Bengal, although many of them have no tradition concerning the time of their emigration and may have no knowledge of the particular part of the country from whence they came.' Thirdly, among such broad categories, caste was plainly fluid. For example, as 'Hindu law' was strongly enforced, the numerous high-caste families found 'great difficulty in procuring proper marriages for their daughters'. Should they fail before the onset of puberty, as often they did, daughter and parents risked disgrace. Some then would convert to Islam, according to Buchanan, and some be 'lowered to an inferior degree' of society.[10]

---

7 Ibid., pp. 438–43.

8 Social consensus was at work when, as Buchanan noted, groups of people concealed information of which they were perfectly aware. (The East India Company was gullible and accepted partial and improbable reports.) Buchanan may have missed social structures either for want of information or because of his presuppositions.

9 Richard M. Eaton's characterization of Muslim 'conversion' is suggestive here (see his *The Rise of Islam and the Bengal Frontier, 1204–1760*, Berkeley, 1993) as are other works on syncretism.

10 Buchanan, *Purnea*, pp. 121–3.

Fourthly, castes were also ambiguous as occupational categories. Buchanan records many that were not confined to their 'proper profession'. Only 10 per cent of Maithila Brahmans 'stud[ied] more or less, and reject[ed] service', some 'carr[ied] arms', and more than two-thirds 'occup[ied] lands...and attend[ed] chiefly to their cultivation'. Lavana Brahmans lived 'entirely by commerce'. Rajputs would not 'condescend to such drudgery' as to hold the plough, except that one in eight did so; while others were traders or went for service in other districts. Mithila Kayasthas still adhered 'to the proper duties of their caste, being writers and accountants, but many rent[ed] land' without cultivating it themselves. Many Telis ('oilmen') worked as traders. Finally, nonetheless, considerations of 'purity' did matter. Buchanan refers to the many castes of 'pure cultivators' and others apparently confined in practice to their ritual occupation. Small sections, such as Malis who worked as garland-makers, were 'admitted to be a very pure order of Sudras', and similar positions of relative prestige seemed to adhere to Potters, Blacksmiths, and Barbers, all of whom 'generally confine[d] their labours to their profession'. Similarly, impure and 'vile' castes identified by Buchanan reflected their actual occupations, though also apparently 'aboriginal origin'.[11] There are echoes of supposed Hindu decline in Buchanan's account; but we may assume that he described conditions that had long been fluid.

All these distinctions affected the rights and perceptions, and hence divided the body of tenants and cultivators. Above all, although stable bands of people can be discerned amidst the diversity, and though some 'types' were becoming richer or poorer, an unambiguous class identity for 'cultivators' was unlikely. This was because of non-'class' distinctions, such as the avoidance of physical labour that was important for the higher castes, who generally paid lower rents and might hold their household plots free. Because social categories were of mixed basis, caste, tenure, and occupation were each important but not decisive. Moreover, they usually derived from hierarchical and dependent relationships more than from horizontal commonalities. Into this setting came the colonial state, bearing with it not only the legal and administrative changes already discussed, but also the priorities of aggressive international trade. There were two known outcomes: a discourse of the 'peasant' and organized 'peasant' protest.

Indigo and Class Awareness

One might therefore suppose that, under colonial rule, commercialization plus commoditization (especially of landed property) produced classes as if by a

---

11 Ibid., pp. 202–57. There are some exaggerated accounts of the 'invention' of caste under colonial rule. What seems to have occurred was a development of the nature of caste, as discussed below.

simple equation. As Marx would have it, a 'definite organization of the labour of society' would be created by 'the separation of the labourers from all property in the means by which they can realise their labour', and in short by a capitalism that 'seizes upon, not only the economical, but every other sphere of society'.[12] To consider whether that was what was happening in India, I shall examine the context of the very celebrated protest movement by indigo-growing raiyats in Bihar as an example of possible economic influences on identity.

Bihari indigo was produced for export; production was dominated by Europeans. Here, if anywhere, commercialization, capitalism, and colonialism should have created peasant solidarity. Yet I shall not quite be saying that it did so. Here was an archetypical instance of exploitation and the emergence of new, consolidated political interests. But did the exploitation produce the classes; if so, how? In particular, was the mode of production so different as to give rise to a different consciousness? I shall propose a complex set of relationships and influences. The indigo example, once one analyses it in detail, shows this complexity well. (Similar issues are considered in Chapter 6.)

The key to the encouragement or enforcement of indigo cultivation was the European or indeed Indian planters' status as intermediary leaseholders (*thikadars*) or more rarely zamindars of suitable villages.[13] The directly

---

12 Karl Marx, *Capital*, revised 4th edn, translated by F. Engels; translated by S. Moore and E. Aveling; New York, 1906, pp. 389, 400, and 785–6.

13 There are extensive sources in official records on indigo cultivation. For some details of indigo acreage and outturn see Government of India Proceedings, Revenue and Agriculture Department (hereafter R&A), Agric. [Branch], C series, Nos 12 and 20, January 1890 and Agric C 8, October 1898, National Archives of India. A convenient summary, unintentionally revealing about changes between the 1870s and 1890s, is used here unless otherwise stated: R&A Agric A 17–18, January 1891. See also Jacques Pouchepadass, *Land, Power and Market: A Bihar District under Colonial Rule, 1860–1947*, New Delhi, 2000 (translated from the French) and *Champaran and Gandhi: Planters, Peasants and Gandhian Politics*, Delhi, 1986, revised edition 1999; and Colin M. Fisher, 'Planters and Peasants: The Ecological Context of Agrarian Unrest on Indigo Plantations of North Bihar, 1820–1920' in Clive Dewey and W.G. Hopkins (eds), *The Imperial Impact: Studies in the Economic History of Africa and India*, London, 1978. The situation in Bihar was different from that in Bengal, on which see Blair B. Kling, *The Blue Mutiny: The Indigo Disturbances in Bengal 1859–1862*, Calcutta, 1977. To Kling, the indigo industry, which 'later had to take refuge' in Bihar, was a mercantilist trade shamefully dependant on forced labour. In the event, he regrets, the peasant exchanged the tyranny of the planter for that of the moneylender. Nonetheless, the disturbances and debates over indigo marked the beginnings of a colonial concern for rural welfare: a new interest in peasant capitalism and the Whiggish assertion of judicial supremacy. Bengal's problems may have convinced Bihar planters that a plantation system would run into labour difficulties. Also in most of north Bihar the extent of large zamindari estates made direct ownership unlikely.

commercial hold of the alternative *khuski* or free system (in which there was no tenurial relationship) was relatively rare during most of the nineteenth century. The usual *thikadari* arrangements occurred in two forms. About half the area under indigo was managed on the *zerat* system: the planters, in the place of the zamindars, took possession of the *sir* or demesne lands of the estate, on which they would arrange for the cultivation of indigo, appointing their own agents and workers. Otherwise production was mainly *asamiwar*, that is, the planter induced raiyats to enter into contractual agreements to devote a proportion of their holdings to the growing of indigo for the factory, in return for which the planter provided seed and at least one advance payment amounting to some 20 per cent of the amount payable for the harvested crop. Sometimes—and this appears to have been the original system, though one beginning to change from the 1880s—a price per *bigha* was stipulated, with a minimum payment even when the crop failed. At other times, and increasingly, a rate per *maund* was fixed. Severe damages against a defaulting raiyat were provided for. All these arrangements depended upon written contracts for a limited term and, with one exception, were restricted to a single harvest. The system as a whole nonetheless enmeshed the raiyats politically and socially as well as economically.

We noted in *Liberalism* when discussing Ripon's policies that nineteenth-century officials were concerned about this system, their attention alerted by the deplorable condition of many in north Bihar as well as by serious rural disorders in Bengal, partly over a different indigo system there. The official impulse was at first to extirpate what they saw as a pre-modern or Asiatic feature: the fact that cultivators were subject to a general social oppression by those who desired their crop. The officials appealed to the European planters to conduct themselves in a 'commercial' and indeed a 'British' fashion. They were concerned secondly, as we know, from a more conservative stance to erect a body of law and administration to regulate 'rights' at different levels of society and production. Thus the indigo question also reflected their less optimistic view of the likely impact of economic change on Indian society. By the 1870s, the officials were sensitive to reports that the raiyats objected to indigo cultivation, that its profits compared unfavourably with those from other crops, and that there was resentment because the planters repeatedly commandeered the best lands. It was in this context that Ashley Eden first took up the indigo question in 1876. He instructed that the leaseholding (thikadari) and contract (asamiwar) systems should be discouraged, and the cultivators' occupancy and other rights supported. The later self-regulation of the Indigo Planters' Association not only increased the contract rate at which the crop was bought, but also introduced a uniform standard for the measurement of lands and professed to abandon various abuses of the thikadari system, including demands on the labour and the non-indigo produce of the raiyats.[14]

At this time, apologists for the Bihar indigo system noted that the indigo planter paid much more to the zamindar than he could hope to receive on the basis of the rent roll, even including the returns from zerat and all the revenue-free land. He did so because as a thikadar he would receive indigo cheaply. On the other hand—so the argument went—the cultivator did not lose out because under the asamiwar or contract system he paid a low rent on his entire holding in return for growing indigo on a small proportion of it.[15] Moreover, the crop, though unprofitable in itself in comparison with say rice or wheat, was not grown as an alternative to other cash crops; it did not dominate the cultivator's production strategies. It required little or no manure, was 'far from exhausting' to the soil, and occupied the ground 'when nothing else could be there'—it was commonly preceded or followed by a rabi (spring) crop.[16]

In contrast to this, critics considered the indigo planters, because of their methods, to be a plague on Bihar (as observed in *Liberalism* in the case of C.J. O'Donnell). They were, in the planter D.N. Reid's colourful phrase, 'like a herd of elephants in a field of sugar-cane'. They not only carried away the produce with annual profits at around 60 per cent of outlay, judging from Reid's own factories in 1890/1, but also caused permanent injury because they 'trampled under foot' any independence of the cultivators.[17] The second of these points was really an indictment of the planters for placing impediments

14 See Chapter 1. The planter, D.N. Reid, later argued that the price increase was compensated for by a new practice of insisting on indigo from the very best fields and that none of Eden's other reforms were carried out; Reid to Under-Secretary of State for India, 25 September 1894, R&A Rev B 18, December 1894. The verdict of Girish Mishra, *Agrarian Problems of Permanent Settlement: A Case Study of Champaran*, New Delhi, 1978, is that indigo helped zamindars, introduced new and improved implements of cultivation (stimulating production of other crops), provided employment to large numbers of labourers (the district's population rose through in-migration), increased the money supply, and helped fix rents. But the cultivation was compulsory, and the price fixed by area (not outturn) and subject to political and not market forces, preventing the peasants from becoming entrepreneurial (p. 310).

15 Patna Commissioner to Board of Revenue, 7 April 1888, Patna Commissioner's Records (hereafter PCR), 350 21/5 (1888/9), Bihar Records Office.

16 Appendix B, Government of India Revenue Despatch (no. 8, 1889), R&A Agric A 30, February 1890.

17 Reid to Charles Bernard, 14 August 1894, R&A Rev B 18, December 1894. The calculation was from a year in which average prices were the 'very lowest on record', and from the indigo factories at Sadowa and Maniora, where Reid considered his expenditure lavish, some 25 or 50 per cent more than his neighbours in the amounts paid to raiyats and labourers. Lower outlays and the failing value of the rupee, which raised the Indian price for indigo, led Reid to suppose that a 65 per cent return was obtainable in the early 1890s.

in the way of so-called 'natural' development. Reid mentioned the planters' opposition to railway construction in north Bihar on the grounds that it might raise the cost of labour. He represented the local officials as partners in a conspiracy of greed and despair (despair at the allegedly hopeless condition of the raiyats and of agriculture in Bihar). This combination conveniently prevented reforms that conflicted with the planters' appetite for profits. W.B. Hudson, the head of the planters' association, had allegedly advised Reid to make friends with his district collectors, because it would 'pay... better than any amount of fair dealing'. Officials could improve the planter's standing with zamindars or the educated classes, and would ignore the condition of the raiyats so long as they were quiet.[18] The industry was an evil, according to this argument, because it was so far from being worked on a commercial basis. Behind Reid's attack lay the commonplaces of a libertarian political economy: objections to restraint of trade as well as preference for the enterprise of peasant proprietors.[19]

But why should indigo have been produced under such a system? Was it not contrary to British expectations? Perhaps so; but it was maintained despite efforts to change it. After the reforms of the 1870s, the indigo industry entered into a period of high profitability. This, in combination with legal developments, led to changes and intensification in the control over the raiyats and their cultivation. With one possible exception (payment by weight of produce rather than area under cultivation), the planters sought to increase supply of the crop by the easiest means: extension of cultivation. Existing concerns, taking advantage of a run of good seasons for indigo, established branch factories to corner the production opportunities of new areas. They even became competitive amongst themselves and with other crops. Some opium lands were given over to indigo in the 1880s, and, as the acreage under indigo increased, there were reports in areas with long-established indigo factories of 'interlopers' entering rival bids for leases from zamindars and even offering improved terms to cultivators.[20]

At this time, however, the planters' enthusiasm was predominantly for an extension of the free (khuski) system, whereby they could encourage the raiyats to take up indigo on holdings too tangled and scattered to be managed directly or through the tenurial structure. Some of the means for this development were provided in the new tenancy law; part of the motive was to be found in the increasing rivalry between the planters and the zamindars, which was

18 Reid's letter of 25 September 1894, R&A Rev A 3, December 1894.
19 Compare Adam Smith, *The Wealth of Nations*, 1776; Harmondsworth, 1976, p. 488: 'If great improvements are seldom to be expected from great proprietors, they are least of all to be expected when they employ slaves for their workmen.'
20 For this and the following paragraphs see note 13 and other sources cited.

sufficiently acute for there to be fears of disorder in several areas. British administration favoured the planter in possession, and to some extent the raiyats. Heavy fines were imposed on one *malik* for example, when, having opened an indigo factory in opposition to an existing company, he claimed the indigo lands as his zerat. Nonetheless, it ceased to be every planter's goal to obtain thikadari leases and bring as much land as possible under zerat management. There was also strong official discouragement of the old practice of planters illegally seizing raiyati land to form factory zerats. A better plan seemed to be to convert or extend indigo agreements with the raiyats independently of the zamindars. The khuski system began to be much discussed. In the event, it considerably reduced the importance of the zerat system but never replaced the asamiwar. Nonetheless, its advocacy was an impulse for change, while its fate is of some significance.

Several factories tried a fully fledged commercial system in the late 1880s. At Bahrauli in Saran, for example, they paid no advances and entered into no agreements, but at harvest offered double the usual price for indigo. The factory thus saved interest charges on the usual outlay for seeds and advance payments, and sidestepped any arguments with zamindars in that tenants remained responsible for their own rent payments. But such schemes were shortlived. A high price margin was needed to attract voluntary supplies, and thus, despite the savings early in the season, the factories were left with too little leeway to cope with varying agricultural conditions at the harvest. The Bahrauli experiment was seen off by a crop of low quality that the factory was forced to buy at a loss. Moreover, until cultivators were generally independent in their property and in agricultural decision making, it was dangerous for any one interest to rely solely on market forces to deliver a particular crop. Pure khuski had no answer to command over produce originating in social or economic power, or even from advance payments. Accordingly, the extension of indigo cultivation depended very largely on the control over the raiyats that the planters were able to gain.

In this they may well have followed a more general pattern. If they relied less upon tenurial relationships, they had to make greater use of debt through mortgages or the enticement of harvest loans at much higher rates than under the asamiwar arrangements. A financial compensation was necessary to provide the same level of control as smaller loans offered in conjunction with tenurial subordination. The factories had first consolidated their relations with the raiyats in times of hardship by offering credit on more favourable terms than professional moneylenders. Quite suddenly, this practice developed into what could be regarded as a version of the thikadari system applied directly to the raiyats. There began a form of *kurtaoli* leases, or subtenancies, once a genuine transfer to the planter (in the capacity of an under-raiyat) of a small proportion of an occupancy holding for zerat cultivation; but increasingly from the 1880s the notional subletting of entire holdings. The raiyat received a loan and, in practice, remained in occupation in return for an obligation to grow indigo on the usual proportion of land and with the usual annual advance payments.

The initial advantage to the raiyat was money borrowed on easy terms. He could settle old debts, replace his bullocks, marry off his daughters, or survive a poor season. (The bad harvests of 1883/4 gave considerable impetus to these agreements.) He gained a possible ally in rent disputes with his zamindar. He had some defence against the planter too at first, in the complexity of raiyati holdings thus brought under indigo cultivation. Without the focus of a tenurial relationship, it was naturally difficult to enforce an oppressive or contested agreement. The advantage to the planter was that he could invade another's sphere of influence, even undermine the usefulness of his thikadari status, without having to come to terms with a zamindar. It was also, and more importantly in the longer term, that for a single outlay—perhaps Rs 20 per bigha—he could capture the raiyat virtually in perpetuity.

At first it was the zamindars rather than the raiyats who opposed these changes. In the Gopalganj area of Saran, for example, where subletting agreements became very common, one of the factories involved was at Maniara, managed by the aforementioned D.N. Reid. His real opponent was the Hathwa management. Reid attempted to deal directly with the raiyats, advancing them money on the security of their holdings. The Hathwa estate (to which the villages belonged) vigorously contested this interference. The raiyats reneged on the agreements with Reid, under inducement from Hathwa or otherwise, and when he tried to foreclose the estate resisted by denying the transferability of the holdings under the 1885 Tenancy Act (section 183 left this issue to local custom). Reid filed 300 suits for breach of contract. As a result, it became necessary to open a *munsif*'s court in Gopalganj. Such quarrels, and a host of others involving less prominent protagonists, were really about the control of production. Reid was not interfering directly with the payment of rent. But his measures had coincided with the assertion by the Maharaja of Hathwa and other zamindars of a more direct and complete management of their estates. The zamindars were seeking more effective means of tapping the profits of agricultural production. The planters' shift from the exploitation of a tenurial relationship to their use of commercial weapons was symbolic of a more general movement in the means of economic and social oppression.[21]

21 I shall detail Reid's experiences and failure more fully on another occasion; see Reid to Under-Secretary of State for India, 25 September 1894, note by A.P. M[acdonnell], 8 December, R&A Rev B 18, December 1894; and Reid to the Maharaja of Hathwa (Krishen Pertabh Sahi), 9 December 1892, R&A Agric B 3, May 1891.

These features tell us about changes in the economic system, but also about limitations in the power of both landlords and planters. For all the European capital and the planters' attempt at hegemony over commercial production, they were unable to choose a system at will. Their even greater weakness in the face of larger forces became obvious at the end of the nineteenth century, when there was a collapse in the market for indigo due to competition from artificial substitutes made in Germany. The decline of indigo was in part a phenomenon of European-influenced production. The trade collapsed throughout India; but in Madras, where Indian smallholders predominated, the area under cultivation and the quantities produced did not experience continual decline. In the Punjab, production actually increased between 1902 and 1907. Apparently European-influenced production was more vulnerable, being directed towards export, and more price-sensitive, being dependent upon capital; but it was also less efficient in terms of land use.[22]

The connection between European capital and export dependence is obvious. But it is less clear why capitalist involvement should have, in effect, reduced productivity. The planters had paid very little attention in the era of easy profits to the maximizing and development of either the crop or the processing methods. They first began to seek expert advice only in 1897, when the dangers were already imminent. Their questions could not be answered without experiments on the yield of dye rather than the weight of the crop. The planters had impressions that more dye was obtained after dry weather than wet, and from raiyats' rather than factory lands; but no certainties. The botanist's view was that the real failure of the planters was ignorance of the plant that they were actually using. None had 'made the slightest effort to follow the time immemorial usages in seed production'; they had merely taken what was on offer in Kanpur, Delhi, or Multan in the hope that if the seed was expensive, it would be good enough.[23]

Yet at a deeper level the unpreparedness of the industry related to the fact that it had been no more 'modern', that is, scientific and maximizing, in its production methods than it had been 'modern', that is, commercial and capitalist, in its production relations. The planters did not have the ability to monitor and improve productivity. Rather, they had assets of two kinds: on the one hand, their marketing and financial connections and their

---

22 See J. Thomas & Co. to C.R. MacDonald, Daulatpur, 13 December 1906, and memorial of the General Committee of the Bihar Planters' Association, R&A Agric B 14, July 1908. I prepared indices from R&A Agric B 14, July 1908. Taking 1902/3 as 100, the area under indigo production in Bengal (mainly Bihar) was only 54 in 1906/7, whereas it was 100 in Madras and 148 in the Punjab.

23 Note by Leather, R&A Agric C 3–5, May 1899, and by Watt, R&A Agric A 6–8, August 1900.

manufacturting capacity; on the other, their social and economic control over cultivators and labour. Defeat on one of these fronts led directly to a reassessment of the other. Planters cast about for other ways of exploiting their local influence. Early in the twentieth century, they tried shifting to cotton and to sugar. This was of course just another example of extension rather than intensification. It was also illustrative of the familiar paradox of a supposed capitalism (that is, growth-oriented, profit-led production) that had to coexist with strong socio-political means of accumulation and distribution (see Chapter 6).

Some aspects of the problem may be summarized as follows (they are relevant for assessing economic development too). The indigo was grown through systems that were never truly commercial. The buyer of the crop was always either a landlord or a moneylender (in effect). But the buyer never monopolized the production of his suppliers—the indigo crop represented only a proportion of their cultivation. The planters therefore found it relatively difficult to intervene in production methods; they set out rules that were impossible to enforce, while the cultivator himself had little or no incentive to improve the quality of his product. This was a low-cost, low-quality system producing high profits for the planter. Some of the reasons for this were undoubtedly 'colonial'—the alliance with government, the uses of law, the management and financial structures of the plantation, and the links with external capital and markets. But some were also indigenous: the conditions of agriculture, the expectations of the people, and the nature of landholding.

What are the lessons here for the understanding of Indian political development? The primary one is surely that these were not circumstances in which one would imagine that a 'modern' kind of class awareness would readily develop; that is, an identity based primarily on a sense of common economic interests. Here, economic controls were intermixed with political ones and it is hardly surprising that the social order was correspondingly complex. Later Mahatma Gandhi intervened in the indigo disputes during the First World War, when planters had tried either to revive production or to take enhanced compensation for relinquishing their leases. This has been presented both as the inclusion of a new class—indigo raiyats—into the world of modern politics, and as a continuation and extension of existing local interests and influences: leading cultivators anxious to take advantage of higher prices for rice, former factory agents dissatisfied with their terms, local school-teachers and other government employees influenced by nationalist ideas, and journalists and local politicians making names for themselves. It was all these things, but what it was not was a unified movement of peasants uniformly trodden down by capitalists.

The terms on which cultivators became involved in the indigo system (and hence their political perspectives) were intricate and changing. Their interests often diverged amongst themselves. For all their oppression—and there is much anecdotal evidence of brutality—even the planters were subject to local conditions rather than able to transform them at will. The message of commercialization and the view of the world that it provided was therefore somewhat fuzzy. The proper targets of resentment were unclear. Even planters might have their uses against local landlords or moneylenders. And was the government an ally of the cultivator or the planters? Gandhi's initial prestige and the part he was able to play in Bihar owed much to his fame, and the impression that he was influential with government at the highest levels, as well as with leading Indian politicians. There was a need for explanation, for ideology, and for organization in order to coalesce 'class' interests and to focus the protest movements. We start from the involvement of Bihar in a world economy. But we end by concluding that it did not bring an unequivocal political transformation or confrontation. The situation did not explain itself. How then did peasant movements arise?

Becoming Peasants

Our earlier assessment of pre-colonial rural society and the evidence of Buchanan-Hamilton implied that notions of 'peasant' characteristics, rights, or solidarities, insofar as they have appeared in India, did require to be constructed—just like all the other modern identities which have been analysed by scholars. Even in late nineteenth century Bihar, Indians were reported typically still to emphasize their caste or ritual status before their occupation when identifying themselves to enumerators. Stevenson-Moore remarked of Champaran district:

> No person will state his chief means of livelihood to be other than the recognized occupation of his caste. Thus a very large number of Brahmins, who live entirely by cultivation, assert their main occupation to be that of a priest. Again, a barber, who lives mainly by cultivating his land, asserts his hereditary profession to be his chief means of livelihood. Conversely a Koiri, who has been mulcted of his land and lives by labouring for others, still claims to be a cultivator....[24]

The echo of Buchanan-Hamilton is not surprising. Stevenson-Moore's evidence was of identities apparently being asserted irrespective of status, and of caste being immutable. But we also know that very many attempts at upward mobility were already being made, including ones which involved a change in 'hereditary occupation' as well as in *varna* standing. For the purposes of the present discussion, the real issue was raised when, according to Stevenson-Moore, the Koiris, the 'backbone of the Bihar peasantry', were determined to assert their status as peasants. Would they do so in common with non-Koiris

[24] C.J. Stevenson-Moore, *Final Report on the Survey and Settlement Operations in the Champaran District, 1892 to 1899*, Calcutta, 1900, p. 16.

even in contradistinction from Koiris who were not cultivators, and thus accept modern definitions of 'peasants' and 'peasant rights'? Or were the misconceptions of definition self-fulfilling—did they prevent the creation of peasants *as a class*, a process different from the regionalization of *jati* that was also occurring?

Stevenson-Moore was writing of a region where agrarian interests were hotly contested because of indigo disputes. As yet, he suggested, the raiyats did not like indigo but their attitude remained one of 'passive acquiescence'. He attributed the apathy to a want of competition where villages were held entirely by one influential zamindar. There also may have been less need of contestation in a district described as having relatively sparse population, low rents, abundant cultivable waste, uncertain measurement, and few petty proprietors, and where survey disclosed 'large excess areas in the holdings of the tenants for which no rents were paid'.[25] But more to the point, the circumstance was that raiyats were 'ignorant of the value of their rights' and that 'Assistant Settlement Officers often had great trouble in inducing them to understand a question sufficiently to give an intelligent answer'.[26] In short, it may be deduced that such 'apathy' as existed was no necessary reflection of lack of intelligence or self-assertion; the problem was that the raiyats did not recognize the (Western, external) frame in which the questions were asked or the rights conceived.

That was to change quickly enough, not least through the settlement operations. These too were not undisputed. Even in the Champaran of the 1890s, there were some tenants thought less ignorant and less 'apathetic' than others. In two places, raiyats already 'united to assert their rights'. On the estates of the Madhubani Babu (*tappa* Duho Suho, *thana* Alapur) the landlord claimed a rent of between 8 and 9 rupees per bigha, and the raiyats denied that it was more than 3 to 6. In tappa Bahas in the same thana, where the raiyats were more independent and better off than elsewhere in the district owing to the great richness of the soil, they were also on bad terms with their effective landlord, the Murla indigo factory. They collectively denied holding excess area when the factory sued for increased rents. The protests were not futile. Most of the Duho Suho raiyats won their case before the settlement officers. The Murla raiyats also won, as no prior measurement could be proved.[27] Was this class action or one orchestrated by local leaders? It is unclear; but such claims, successfully prosecuted, may be assumed to have encouraged an awareness of the possibilities people now enjoyed as 'tenants', say, rather than as Koiris or Rajputs, even in a situation in which high castes might still enjoy favourable rents.

25 Ibid., p. 63.
26 Ibid., p. 58.
27 Ibid., pp. 58 and 72–3.

On an average, about one third of all holdings in the district were subject to fair rent suits during the settlement operations of the 1890s. Mostly the outcomes disadvantaged tenants, but as a process the record was expected to stabilize rents somewhat and to 'retard the advancement of rent-rates enormously, and so secure to the tillers of the soil a larger share of the unearned increment'.[28] The status of land also was contested, as well as rights of possession. For the latter, there were 122 cases between landlords, 1298 by landlords against tenants, 217 by raiyats against landlords, and 572 between raiyats. In all, only about 3 per cent of holdings were subject to dispute, but these totalled 12,432 in number (there were 3,64,659 raiyati holdings). Such statistics indicate a substantial, even a 'modern', involvement of subjects with the state. This has significance in a region where investigations revealed that there had been no general custom of measuring land even at transfer. A new tenant accepted the *jama* irrespective of the actual area of the land.[29] It means that the state was promoting particular views of people's interests: not only introducing ways of resolving disputes, but also before that defining their nature.

Peasant consciousness is notoriously difficult to gauge, but it may be assumed from peasant actions. If so, then J.A. Sweeney's revision report on Champaran, prepared between 1913 and 1919, reveals a change.[30] The munsif's court at Motihari (covering Champaran) entertained considerable civil litigation between 1907 and 1917. Except for 1907 with 4763, the total number of cases instituted ranged between about 3000 and 4000 a year, but rose to 6033 in 1916 and 7690 in 1917, 'swollen' by settlement and indigo disputes.[31] In preparing his revision, Sweeney found disagreements far more numerous than expected, on average 19 per square mile, and suits for the enhancement of rents affected nearly 40 per cent of all tenancies in the district.[32] This was partly because landlords and their agents were using the system even more vigorously than before in order to extend their power. But, Sweeney concluded, it was also attributable to the bad relations between landlords and tenants, especially with regard to indigo, dating from at least 1907/8.

He commented on this at length. The murder of one factory manager arose out of an 'isolated' dispute, but also 'there was a general feeling of uneasiness.... Continual meetings of the Muhammadan raiyats were held in the Sathi area under the guidance of one Shaikh Gulab. Acts of violence were committed on

28 Ibid., p. 76.
29 Ibid., p. 71.
30 J.A. Sweeney, *Final Report on the Survey and Settlement Operations (Revision) in the District of Champaran (1913–1919)*, Patna, 1922.
31 Ibid., p. 12.
32 Ibid., pp. 35 and 82.

factory servants by raiyats who refused to labour for the factory after they had received advances [obliging them to do so].... Arson followed and, most significant of all, the mowing down of the raiyat's own crops in the...fields set aside for indigo...'. The dispute was prosecuted through the courts and with the government. 'A common fund was raised for contesting cases and petitions were put in against the factory.' Arenas for resolving the argument were also provided by an official investigation and report, involving the planters' association. The remedies were equally generalized. They included an agreed increase in the price paid to the raiyats and a local by-law reducing the area to be set aside for indigo cultivation. The terms of the raiyats' complaints themselves anticipated these procedures and bases for a solution. They referred to the failure of due process (damages taken for not growing indigo although no *satta*s, or agreements, had been executed); they alleged illegal cesses; and they claimed that payment was not made for labour and services.[33]

One 'remarkable effect of our operations', observed P.N. Gupta in his revision report for Saran district, was 'the large increase in the number of suits for arrears of rent...in every district in North Bihar'. The average more than doubled in Saran and Champaran, and 'in many villages where serious rent disputes existed, the raiyats combined during the process of the settlement operations and withheld payments of rent altogether'. 'The raiyats', Gupta went on, 'or the more intelligent of them, now understand that the [earlier] enhancements and the methods of realising them, were illegal.' He regarded this as a 'revolution from a system...where the landlord kept no proper rent accounts, and issued no receipts, but collected as much as he could from raiyats who paid as little as they could, to a system where every man's rent is accurately known'.[34] Friction was inevitable during such a change; but so too, surely, was combination based on an appreciation of common experience and collective force.

I do not mean to be chronologically prescriptive. Some features evident in this account had occurred earlier in other agrarian disputes and perhaps had parallels over very long periods. As a package, however, I suggest these conditions were distinctive. They contributed to a context in which there seems to be an inevitability about peasant agitations such as those led by Gandhi or the Bihari *kisan* leader Swami Vidyananda. Given this experience of the new laws at work and the consciousness that they spread new kinds of right, it begins to seem less remarkable that peasant associations emerged despite the ambiguities of economic change. These were not just caste associations by

33 Ibid., pp. 18–25.
34 Phanindra Nath Gupta, *Final Report on the Survey and Settlement Operations (Revision) in the District of Saran (1915–1921)*, Patna, 1923, p. 186.

another name. They came complete with a partly imported anti-landlord rhetoric and an armoury of tenant rights conceived as 'property' both for peasants and defining them.[35] In the past, rural people had tried to resist or avoid oppressors by a variety of means. It is uncertain whether these also constituted a frame for class identity or formal organization as 'peasants' or 'tenants'.

If the first part of this argument concerns experiences under colonial law and government, the second must be the spread of ideas to give the experiences meaning. Another Bihari leader, Swami Sahajanand Saraswati, provides a striking case study of attitudes and arguments that also contributed to the construction of peasant identities. I shall now examine two tracts of the 1940s, recovered, translated, and edited by Walter Hauser.[36] I will suggest not only that Sahajanand was a product of his times in his understandings and his goals, but also that it is possible to observe in him a direct response to the colonial conditions that we have just been considering.

The first text is *Khet Mazdoor*, a treatise on agricultural labour. Its political message is that landless labourers and poor peasants share a common oppression though their roles and status are analytically distinct. The three main elements in the argument are a scientific, evolutionist approach using ancient texts as well as interpretive reasoning; a Marxist, class-based analysis of economic factors and power; and the deployment of statistical data and other empirical evidence. The second text is *Jharkhand ke Kisan*, a tract on the condition of and remedies for the peasants and especially the Santhals of Jharkhand. This uses similar means but elaborates more fully the measures needed to improve conditions, a significant list that equates with many of the demands for rights or reforms set out by protesters.

Khet Mazdoor, or 'Rural Labour', takes a long and pessimistic view of the origins of the problems of twentieth-century Bihar. Sahajanand starts in ancient times, with everyone engaged in agriculture in an age of equality. (The concept of equality itself is his own arguably 'modern' addition to his sources, though they do talk of a lack of social differentiation.) In the second phase, Sahajanand explained, occupational specialization developed through population growth

35 This is one of the arguments more fully developed in Robb, *Ancient Rights*.
36 Walter Hauser (ed.), *Sahajanand on Agricultural Labour and the Rural Poor*, New Delhi, 1994, an annotated Hindi and English edition of *Khet Mazdoor*, written but not published in 1941; and, in the same format, Hauser (ed.), *Swami Sahajanand and the Peasants of Jharkhand: A View from 1941*, New Delhi, 1995. Sahajanand was a Bhumihar Brahman who began his political career as a supporter of Bhumihars. In the 1920s and 1930s, he was involved in political activism with the Kisan Sabha—it included upper-caste tenants and also those of lower status. In the late 1930s, under the Congress ministry, his concern was mostly for those of lower standing, including landless labourers.

and warfare. As a result, though even Brahmans (say) might continue to cultivate, cultivation was not their defining role; instead they sought to use the labour of others, and so a new class emerged. 'Vaishya' ceased to mean the people at large, but instead signified the section that cultivated. 'Sudras' appeared, being those who undertook physical work. The third and current phase in this evolution, according to Sahajanand, was characterized by full land use, and hence by four classes among the cultivators: rich, middle, and poor peasants, and the labourers (*khet mazdoori*), all defined effectively by access to land and consequently means of production. The rich employed labour; middle peasants mostly used family resources; the poor had to sell their labour, having insufficient land; and the landless relied wholly on finding work. Sahajanand produced a predictable pedigree for this analysis: Marx had argued that slaves were themselves sold, but labourers sold some or all of their labour. Serfs did so as a tribute to the landholder; others did so for payment or subsistence. Russian sources and examples were cited.

In India as elsewhere, according to Sahajanand, the rush for private property and the subdivision of holdings over the generations deepened the social differentiation. Finally, more recently the interrelated factors of loss of industries, growing dependency on agriculture, and excess labour-supply led to increasing numbers and proportions of landless agriculturists. Sahajanand argued that daily-wage labour was inherently precarious and that total wages, whether in cash or in kind, could readily fall below the minimum needed for subsistence. Since the First World War, debt bondage had been increasing and real wage levels had dropped sharply, having been more or less stable since the early nineteenth century. Behind this interpretation, even though Sahajanand was writing in prison, was a host of statistics from census and other reports—not all of them accurate. Some were taken indirectly from the writings of the Marxist Palme Dutt, calculations of the agrarian economist Radhakamal Mukerjee, studies by the British official Harold Mann, and the findings of the Commission of Agriculture chaired by Linlithgow.

Workers' interests obviously diverged from those of their 'peasant' employers. Sahajanand called for solidarity among the oppressed groups, noting that it was an oppressor's ploy to divide the oppressed against each other. He considered that only plantation workers could be described as proletarian in Lenin's sense, and that otherwise class formation was interrupted by rivalries and occupational distinctions (such as for ploughmen) as well as by caste and religion. His take on the perennial importance of intermediaries and the minute distinctions within Indian society was that everything was *ek upar ek*, or 'one above the other'. He objected to those who focused on socio-religious disadvantage (as he interpreted the use of terms such as Dalit or Harijan), arguing that they missed the common oppression of which untouchability, say, was only a part. More, they implied that there was a problem in terms of fixed classes, whereas there was an ever-growing body of the dispossessed and impoverished. The main point of Sahajanand's evolutionary explanations was to show that oppression was dynamic.

Where did these kinds of explanation come from, or lead? Sahajanand's analysis was socialist and *à la mode*, spiked with specific calculations, given that he sought political cooperation between labourers and kisans (or at least those who were not effectively landlords). He had access to the ideas of Marx, Lenin, and even Stalin, as well as to now-printed Sanskrit texts and the accounts of some of the officials, experts, and nationalists who had investigated agrarian conditions in India. In short, he had both an ideology and a methodology with which to develop his ideas and inform his politics. For him, oppression was due to competition for land and surplus labour. More land, or the effect of it through greater productivity, would bring social improvements. Sahajanand favoured the confiscation of zamindari land. He held up as an example Lenin's support for the poorest peasants and workers on model farms, though he did not propose collectivization. He decided the capital for economic improvements would have to come from the state, both for practical reasons and to break the cycle of oppression by landlords and capitalists. But change would only be achieved through popular organization and action. Initially it was realistic to expect separate movements for kisans and for labourers, but a merged public movement would be more effective and should be achievable eventually through informed cooperation and enlightened self-interest.

For Jharkhand, Sahajanand's verdict was less historical and more specific, though again dependant in part on colonial statistics, gazetteers, and inquiries, this time the evidence of the recent Santhal Parganas Inquiry Committee set up under a British official by the Congress government of Bihar. Sahajanand thought Adivasis (tribals) were at the mercy of exploiters and let down by the measures designed to protect them. He discussed different kinds of tenure provided in custom and law, and the impact of British legislation. He believed that landlords were looting the country and that Adivasis were 'literally trapped by the law',[37] unable to defend themselves under a system operating in the English language and with English concepts. He considered forest reservation another exploitation by law as well as greed. He noted the problem of debt—this too related to contract law and to the spread of moneylending and commercialism. He did not blame the British alone as he considered doing so a weak excuse. Moreover, his remedies were remarkably similar to theirs, by type if not in every detail.

---

37 Hauser, *Jharkhand*, p. 4.

His principal demands were as follows. Protect kisans from landlords by regulating rents and fixing them for five-year periods; relate rent to the land revenue and provide safeguards for tenants in proceedings for rent arrears; enforce zamindari responsibilities; unify the region's tenancy acts, with special protection for Adivasis and 'backward' tenants; ensure 'traditional' rights to forest and other products; provide pure drinking water and irrigation; furnish kisans with government loans; introduce compulsory education; and improve various aspects of the administration. These sound like the goals of a colonial policy minute or the promises of a modern election manifesto. Sahajanand was demanding reform of the land-tenure system despite the imperfections he had identified in the operation of the law. He was calling for education as a public good, arguing that Hindus should follow the example of Christian missionaries and empower the downtrodden (though he did not quite use those words). His assumption was of a modern state in a world conceived as it had been by colonial power: a world of forests and agrarian land, of landlords and tenants, of tribals and Hindus; a modern state concerned with legality and transgression, with citizen-subjects, and with rights, responsibilities, and the public interest.

Nothing in Sahajanand's diagnoses was particularly original, and very little would have been possible except under the circumstances that colonialism helped create—especially the access to intellectual trends, theories, and methods, some of it through the English language. All of it was politically important at the time and has been influential since, not just because Sahajanand was a significant figure but because some of these ideas influenced policy well after Independence (not least zamindari 'abolition'). More than this, however, the explanations related specifically to the circumstances of British colonial government: its agrarian laws, its belief in development through capital (partly to face a perceived demographic crisis), its use of categories and collection of statistics, and its construction of a specific form of responsible and managerial state. These were not just taken for granted by Sahajanand; they were central to his explanations and prescriptions.

My conclusion is that in the twentieth century a different vocabulary became widely available to Indians agitating for agrarian and other rights. It can be traced to official categorizations and policies as well as to political theorists and leaders. It represented an available identity, though not of course an exclusive one or one invariably chosen. (This is not intended to revive the old debates *between* class, caste, or faction as guiding principles of Indian society and politics.) My argument once again is that capitalist practices and colonial categorizations, and the contested politics of rights which they engendered, helped create politico-economic classes and aided their organization *as interests*—indicated for example in the Landholders'

Association of 1838 or the British Indian Association of Awadh; the peasant protests against indigo, opium, or outside moneylenders of the nineteenth century; or the kisan sabhas and peasant parties of the twentieth century.

Let us return briefly to the indigo raiyats. In the end, they showed considerable solidarity. As is well known, peasants in general were repeatedly involved in movements claiming tenurial and, latterly, political rights. Among more general explanations of these developments, we may place the property laws and agrarian policies of the colonial state. They provided concepts to describe felt economic and social disabilities. They were related to a number of different ideas of political economy: landownership, property in and from work, and village community. Indigo cultivators, for example, had rights and were entitled to state protection. It was in large part these rights and entitlements that defined the actual category of the 'indigo raiyat'. Such ideas were influential partly because exemplified in real measures of government and law.

Many groups identified themselves through class interests that also drew on policy debates and the broader European discourse to which they had been indebted. As said, the zamindars came first, with societies defending their political interests and seeking to reduce their liabilities. In Bengal in the 1870s and 1880s, both additional local taxation and tenancy laws were resisted as a 'confiscation of property'. On the other hand, as a deliberate official defence of property, land revenue was repeatedly reduced as a proportion of incomes and of total tax during the colonial period, and rural taxation has remained comparatively low since Independence.

Later, each formation of a kisan sabha, for example, also reflected a complex indigenous and colonial inheritance. Where a society was active, there were usually more successful agriculturists operating within a market economy, and new rivalries as a result of that upward mobility. And there were always claims about fair tenancy and enjoyment of property, concepts that had been imbedded in colonial laws and transmitted through administration, courts, surveys, and settlements. Colonial rule's generalizing features helped to direct or limit indigenous processes, and thus to influence how India changed. The spread of commercial production and the widening of international trade helped define goals and interests for the state and (some) people despite a limited penetration of capitalist modes of production. New forms of social association were created in India by colonial law, policies, and assumptions in advance of thorough social transformation.

In short, influences from agrarian policies can be seen in assumptions that nowadays are scarcely questioned. More than that, they may be traced in the very fabric of society. Take the case of Calcutta (Kolkata). It has long been dominated by the upper-caste literate service and professional elite, the *bhadralok*. These were not the direct descendants of the mixed bag of landed magnates, merchants, bankers, and office-bearers who ran the eighteenth-century city. They were the product of a society made in large part by the permanent zamindari settlement. After an upheaval in which some great families were dispossessed, the settlement permitted the emergence of secure and increasingly wealthy landed classes. It allowed them to live away from the land in the city; to build houses, temples, schools, and hospitals; and to sponsor societies, printing, and other civic goods. True, it created many smaller and subordinate landed interests that were less secure, indeed insufficient; but on the other hand it also demanded a range of lesser employees—the agents, managers, and clerks who worked the system in practice, plus a host of professionals, especially lawyers. The Permanent Settlement was based on regulation and then on statute, implying top-heavy and centralized private and public bureaucracies regulated by the law courts, rather than on dispersed, day-to-day, hands-on administration by landholder and state. Calcutta's concentration of writers and literate workers was the result, and they in turn required and manned Calcutta's offices, schools, newspapers, and associations.

Other kinds of revenue settlement encouraged other kinds of government and society—too many to be detailed here. Colonial Calcutta and Bengal might be contrasted with Bombay (Mumbai) and Madras (Chennai), the administrative, commercial, and industrial centres of regions with temporary raiyatwari settlements. They might also be compared with colonial Lahore and Punjab. The priorities of military recruitment as reflected in revenue and land policy, the emphasis on peasant proprietorship of the so-called agricultural castes, the preservation of some great landed families, and in general a paternalist government defending its personalized rule and customary law—these agrarian policies help explain much of the Punjab's twentieth-century political history before and after Partition, and once again remind us of the formative influence of agrarian policies.

Mahatma Gandhi had a different vision of an India of self-regulating, self-sufficient communities. But this too was in some respects indistinguishable from the ideal advanced by European anti-materialists and moralists, and also claimed by many as the indigenous Indian way. They tried to recreate it not only in the Punjab but also elsewhere as a basis for tenancy and commercial cultivation (such as Bengal in 1885) and even for local policing (such as the dream of a village watch supported by a local community). Independent India sought zamindari abolition and land ceilings partly because of these colonial debates about the best means of securing economic progress and social equity. This was another victory for the peasant-proprietary school, but also (in the event) for the subterfuge, pragmatism, and compromise that had nonetheless preserved the wealth and power of landed families.

3. Community and Interests

Culture and Category

More indigenous, alternative senses of peasant community also existed, for example as identified by William Pinch. In apparent contrast with the story just told, he has claimed that peasant assertiveness arose out of religious and social attitudes and change.[1] It is not my purpose to deny these bases of identity, nor to imply that there were no distinctive, even general features of 'Indian' peasants. I am suggesting that the forms and vocabulary of the alliances and struggles that occurred in modern India were strongly influenced by the legacy of colonial rule—not so much by the legal–political relations that the state purported to shape (for it was never able to achieve what it proposed), but by the working of its categorizations upon existing and continuing relations, both in practice and in terms of ideology and understanding.

Pinch describes peasants thinking of themselves as Kshatriya rather than Shudra, and of sadhus articulating Vaishnava and hence relatively egalitarian ambitions to underpin agrarian radicalism. It is certainly true that where there were active agrarian movements, there was often also evidence of social mobility—among the Vellalas, Ezhavas, and Mapillas in the south, Patidars in the west, Jats in the north, and so on. In Bihar, there were religious and social movements drawing on older texts and traditions, making claims to status within an increasingly generalized varna hierarchy. Pinch does not deny that there were external influences in promoting changes, noting for example Ashis Nandy's and others' insistence that an emphasis on 'masculinity' was an anti-colonial *response* or, as Pinch puts it, 'a coming to terms' with colonially reconstructed hierarchy and terminology. His emphasis, however, is on 'indigenous' forces. On the other hand, he does not support extreme versions of indigenism or even the concept of 'subaltern' autonomy. Rather, he sets himself against the colonial stereotyping that criticized sadhus as 'men in disguise' (W.H. Sleeman's phrase) *because* they could be drawn from any caste or community, or as dangerous frauds because they were 'political' rather

1 William R. Pinch, *Peasants and Monks in British India*, Berkeley, 1996.

than 'religious' in their aims.² When Pinch seeks to reassert the religious element of peasant sensibility and politics, it is on a broad definition of what is religious. My conclusion is that the ambitions he identifies swam in a sea of other influences, including the ones I have stressed, and that upward mobility for an agrarian caste within a Hindu hierarchy, say, could be *of a type* with demands for rights as a tenant, honour as a cultivator, and profit as a producer.

One objection I expressed at the outset of these volumes was to the privileging of a supposed Indian essence. Implicit in Pinch's account is the recognition that debates about the degrees of colonial or 'external' influence on 'indigenous' processes of change are less interesting than examinations of the logic of the processes themselves. Because social forms evolve continually in conjunction with historical and rhetorical forces, the distinction between internal and external features continually dissolves. The key questions concern how the actors in each drama fashion events and identities out of the variety of components available to them. This makes it unsatisfactory to privilege the 'external', as in versions of modernization theory. By the same argument, one also should not privilege the 'internal' as if it were immutable, essential, and wholly autochthonous. In less cautious hands than those of Pinch and in some current Indian debates, this principle has been overturned. It is certainly violated in current notions about distinct and antagonistic religious 'civilizations', notions that are essentialist or primordialist but ahistorical.³

Therefore we are entitled to ask once again what were the roles in peasant mobilization of the old stalwarts—the evolution of the state and its standardizations; the emergence of new institutions, professions, and expectations; the growth, increased speed, and reduced cost of communications, through transport, language, and print; the increasingly shared economic and political experiences; the awareness of Western ideas and examples with regard to the nation, to class, and to individual or equitable 'rights'. As argued throughout this introduction, it cannot be that such influences played no part in peasant mobilization or consciousness, for example. Nor did indigenous or religious forces operate in some kind of pristine arena. As others have noticed, to assume that they did is merely to produce a new Orientalism.⁴ How

2 W.H. Sleeman, *A Report on the System of Meg punnaism* or, *The Murder of Indigent Parents for their Young Children (Who are sold as Slaves) as it Prevails in the Delhi Territories, and the Native States of Rajpootana, Ulwar, and Bhurtpore*, Calcutta, 1839, p. 11, cited by Pinch, *Peasants and Monks*, p. 8.
3 This would apply to Samuel Huntington's 'clash of civilizations'.
4 Walter Hauser has made a parallel point about assumptions that the 'subaltern' school alone have recovered the extent of dissent and resistance among Indian subordinate classes. He has questioned the privileging of colonial discourse, but also

then did the religious and inherited elements emphasized by Pinch combine and react with selective borrowings from other traditions and reactions to new circumstances?

In principle, that is the question that I have tried to examine. I have not said that 'the domain of legal-political relations constituted by the state' *had* to be the 'exclusive...site of peasant struggle'. But nor have I succumbed to the view—paralleled by colonialism's own faith in Indian primordialism—that 'popular culture' in India was a 'storehouse' that 'preserved an enormously rich collection...of forms of popular protest'.[5] I have suggested that Indians did not just preserve and draw on their own essence, but engaged in a *process* and a *negotiation*. I have suggested that the allegiances and vocabulary of India were strongly influenced by colonial rule, even though the state alone never wholly 'constituted' the legal-political domain. Communal or class labels did not serve all purposes. Identity had to be constantly reiterated; borders and unity were contested and needed to be reinforced. Texts and norms were not wholly followed in practice—especially where the categories were contradictory. Caste, for example, defines Hindus and is complementary to or constituent of the idea of a single Hinduism, but it also divides Hindus, contradicting their unity. Hence, many Hindu movements tried to do away with caste, raising the question of whether and in what senses they remained Hindu. So too a Bihari might be a Kurmi, an indigo raiyat, or an occupancy tenant. The choice was not unlimited, however, and it was not only self-defined. Nor was it the same at different periods of history. In these contexts, Indians were subjected to a 'modern' view of their society. They were not objects but actors. European categorizations worked upon continuing relations; pre-colonial inheritances channelled Western influence. Colonial rhetoric emphasized given identities of language, tribe, caste, or community, but British policies also helped create class interests.

Acts of state, in defining the quality and borders of classes and types, gave definite rights to, and encouraged the political representation of, sections of society that the law itself had defined. In Europe, unlike in India, there was a significant element of *recognition* in these definitions. Some large elements did exist from which these categories were constructed. In some respects, the

---

the existence of 'official history'. For this and other relevant comments, see *American Historical Review*, vol. 96, February 1991, pp. 241–3 and vol. 97, October 1992, pp. 1269–70, and the *Journal of Asian Studies*, 50(4), November 1991, pp. 968–9. For a good brief discussion of Orientalism and religion in politics see David Ludden (ed.), *Contesting the Nation: Religion, Community and the Politics of Democracy in India*, Philadelphia, 1996, introduction, pp. 1–23.

5 The quotations are from Partha Chatterjee, *The Nation and its Fragments*, Delhi, 1994, pp. 170–1.

changes marked an internalized standardization, an existing consciousness of operative classes and communities. For India, what I have been describing is the creation of institutions of civil society. It is not helpful to use this term either with a narrow definition (that is, meaning intermediary institutions pitted against the state) or with a broad one (meaning effectively any social institution whatever). But we may use it to cover those institutions that, distinct from the state and from the household, are relatively open and representative in their membership and impersonal in their organization and purpose. This supposes a restricted delineation of the state and a relatively fluid model of society. In colonial India, this civil society extended first to the equivalents of 'aristocracy' and 'bourgeoisie' because legal rights were less effective at lower levels of society. This result looked a little like Habermas' public sphere (given that the German *bürgerliche* means civil, public, *and* middle-class). On the other hand, as I have argued, in India as in Europe (though much more tentatively), there were growing pastoral, welfare, and developmental functions for the state and a need to respond in some way to the democratic imperative. As a result, lower-class people also made appeals through a discourse of rights and through organizations that were very close in form to those of the elites. This civil society was not about equality, but about groups organizing to make claims in terms of individual, legal, or economic entitlements. The state and the elites equated their interests with the general good; but thus encouraged a more general assertion of civil rights, as opposed to duties to god, king, or kin.

In feudal Europe or in pre-colonial southern India, for example, it is hard to identify civil society because it is not easy to distinguish the state from various forms of social and ritual authority, and the prevailing mindset relates to shares and obligations within social categories (as in *kaniyatchi*) rather than to individual rights. Habermas' explanation was that 'publicness was not constituted as a social realm... rather, it was something like a status attribute'.[6] The Mughals—and to some extent the Marathas, Tipu Sultan, and so on— definitely were trying to separate out the state and state functionaries, but they did not really succeed. The British tried to do the same and, though they did not wholly succeed either, they got a good deal further than their predecessors. By the present day, we do have distinguishable spheres that may overlap in practice but are recognizably state, or public (but non-state), or private.

The British imposed their Eurocentric designs upon peoples and institutions then following a different logic. Habermas describes a process in western

---

6 Jürgen Habermas, *The Structural Transformation of the Public Sphere: An Inquiry into a Category of Bourgeois Society*, tr. Thomas Burger with the assistance of Frederick Lawrence, Cambridge, 1992.

Europe whereby the extension of the state (the construction of the bourgeois public sphere) helped and was helped by parallel developments in society, economy, law, and culture.[7] Though used, for example by Partha Chatterjee, the public/private dichotomy (like other binaries) does not self-evidently work for India. In the West, the Greek, Roman, and Christian notions of the household and individual may be seen in contradistinction to the development of the state—in law, politics, economic management (slavery, feudalism, capitalism), humanism or romanticism, and so on. In India, the divides have been notably blurred, perhaps from ideas of *advaita*, as for caste, pre-eminently concerned not only with supposedly 'public' matters of work, education, or socio-political role, but also with 'private' issues of family, household, marriage, birth, death, dining, and menstruation—many of these matters being themselves further divided as *kachcha/pakka*, heating/cooling, left/right, and so on. The spread of the state, in both the East and the West, did involve intrusions or even extension from courtly to social regulation; but starting points and means were strikingly different.

What makes the public sphere into a civil society is its discourse of individual rights and the representative and objective nature of its institutions and methods. But Indian civil society is not the same as European. Even institutions that seem most 'Western'—scientific societies or the Indian Constitution—are not wholly so in their practices. Trade unions and voluntary groups in India could also be 'Hindu' or caste-based. Different ideas of science fitted with different ideas of the nation and its needs. Despite their undoubted theoretical sophistication, Indians' constitutional debates also accommodated to the priorities and experiences of Indian actors. Tragically, religion and politics mixed. However, these incongruities also reinforce the argument that economic, social, and technological change and the active role of the state and Western ideology are necessary to any account of where we are now. True, the colonial state produced or reproduced some institutions that were out of kilter with Indian conditions. We see this, for example, in the gaps between class-defined urban citizenship or the village community myth and the actualities of Indian life or even indigenous representations of it. We see it in the difference between, say, 'landlord' and 'malik', or between 'middle-class' and 'bhadralok'. Nonetheless, the social constructions that the British recognized did form so-called 'communities' or classes. Whatever their many components and origins, such communities could be found whenever authority was deployed to affect everyday conduct. Texts and norms were given authority over negotiation and contingency. The 'Other' was identified, bounded, and often demonized. These processes provided trajectories of change.

---

7 Ibid., p. 7. Habermas was referring to lordship in the high middle ages in Europe.

Colonial laws in India were devised according to theories of social category in which nuances and contradictions had no part. In their search for identities, the rulers drew on devices that their own history had led them to expect, though India helped cast the European examples into sharper relief as it was seen as a test of universal principles. First came the need to fix places and then people in space, and later to determine their relations one with another. Aspects of the colonial project in India took this form, insisting on settlement (the units being the village, estate, district, and region) and then on social category (linguistic family, caste, and religion). Management and improvement came together in comprehensive surveys. In eastern India, they were instituted systematically from about the turn of the nineteenth century. They measured place astronomically and by triangulation, but also sought to identify, describe, and explain it. This was one of the subjects of *Liberalism*.

The Politics of Famine

The creation of boundaries of all kinds was accompanied by their politicization. Hitherto, these books have tended to assume there was a more or less 'natural' movement from colonial categorization to political representation and organization. Since the discussion of Sahajanand above, not much emphasis has been placed on the fact that, intellectually, there was also a process of *interpretation*. I want to return therefore to the relationship between categories and rights, the identification of which both defines and activates groups. In turn, that leads us to the politicization of issues.

This kind of argument is familiar from other accounts of the creation or production of identities. It is not a denial of what is 'given', nor of non-human, non-subjective influences. For example, classes and status must owe something to ecology. Without succumbing to a crude determinism, we can relate social forms to land and water management as many scholars have done in the past. If dry lands require shifting and adaptable cultivation in regions that are also strategically vulnerable, then we are not surprised to find relatively egalitarian 'brotherhoods' with chieftains or warlords and martial traditions. If wetlands require substantial investments over time, it is equally unremarkable to find settled hierarchies and complex rights and obligations. Similarly, if monsoon conditions require a large labour force but only for short seasons, then socioeconomic command over subordinated workers may well develop as an aspect of the more successful systems of production. All students of India will recognize these examples and others like them. For example, the south Bihar irrigation system of temporary dams, long channels, and local tanks demanded supralocal authorities to mobilize labour and capital and to secure cooperation over many square miles. Again in East Bengal, shifting rivers and extensions of cultivation placed an emphasis on reclamation, and so the tenurial forms often reflected a need for capital and enterprise (this issue is addressed in Chapter 4).

My arguments do not ignore these imperatives, but they note that they did not frame the colonial power of the British to the same extent as they did the power of earlier regimes. The British followed additional or contradictory influences as well: the urge for standardization; the fiscal requirements of 'modern' government; the demands of British capital and Britain's international trade; economic and social theories of mainly European origin; and so on. These extraneous impulses interacted with Indian conditions, sometimes with disastrous consequences. (Above all, I believe, they produced circumstances in which economic differentiation either increased or became more damaging in its effects.) At the same time, however, they helped produce new kinds of categorizations and spread new ideas, which led to different expressions of identity. Indeed, these two aspects worked together. The possibly transitional economic impact itself became a force for identity formation both for nationalists and for classes and communities. Solidarities drew powerfully on the idea of disadvantage for one defined group against others: Indians against Europeans; peasants against landlords; Muslims against Hindus; Dalits against castes; and so on. Colonial rule did not invent these differences, but it refocused them.

I shall now expand on these points by turning to the case of famine, a telling example that depends on the categorization of a condition rather than a group. I shall consider the nature and causes of famines only incidentally, though of course they are extremely important. I shall concentrate on the arguments that arose around famine.

A sorry tale can be seen repeated across India, not least in some peculiar features. Among them were the *incidence* of famines and their coincidence with epidemics. There seem to have been occasional acute famines over a very long time (well before colonial rule) bringing serious distress and starvation about once or twice in a generation, until the latter decades of the nineteenth century when there was a dramatic increase, after which the pattern of famine occurring only at longer intervals, if at all, reappeared. In regard to Bihar, for example, W.W. Hunter claimed in his *Annals* that a third of the population of Purnea died in 1769–70 and that Buxar in north-western Shahabad was 'the very centre of the most cruelly stricken districts'.[8] Disaster struck again in 1791 and in the mid-1860s, and then repeatedly in the following decades (1873–4, 1878–9, 1888–9, 1892–3, 1896–7, 1906, and 1908). These later famines

---

[8] W.W. Hunter, *The Annals of Rural Bengal*, London, 1868, pp. 19 ff. and Appendix B: General Letters from Bengal, 1770.

claimed 'excess deaths' numbered in hundreds of thousands. As said, a similar pattern could be seen in other parts of India.

Various explanations were and are given for the famines. They were acts of god (climate was to blame), though the mechanism was lack of work more than lack of food. Or they were the result of increased vulnerability. Notably, this was attributed to colonial exploitation: high revenue demand, unfair commercialization, or the transfer of food production on to poorer lands. Following Ramesh Chandra Datta,[9] it was said that the British took the entire economic rent or otherwise prevented capital accumulation; that the expansion of cultivation reduced output per acre; and that food exports continued even as food prices rose to famine levels. Alternatively, the breakdown of traditional society or village community was blamed: commercialism forcing out altruism, or individualism triumphing over collectivity. The role of epidemic diseases was also noted—even before these were well understood—whether from endemic conditions that were traced to ecological disruption and movements of population, or more specifically from famine migration and crowding together on relief works. More recent debates follow similar lines.

Our interpretations of these famines are based on contemporary reports that were far from neutral in character and based on specific socio-economic theories. It was assumed by nineteenth-century officials by and large that the underlying causes were climatic and demographic. If there was a social element, it was the supposed fatalism and apathy of the population. This implied that famines resulted from occasional dearth of food experienced by a local economy as a whole. The term 'scarcity' implied this insufficient food supply, as in John Strachey's report on Moradabad in 1861, taken as a guide by government in 1868 and reported on by the Famine Commission under Richard Strachey (appointed in 1878).[10] The remedies followed from this, including 'protective' improvements in water supply and communications as well as legal reforms to secure property and tenure, so that populations had the means to survive adverse seasons. Various experts had their favourites—canals, railways, forest protection, or tenancy law—but their uniform aim was to augment food and wealth through the encouragement of enterprise and the improvement or defeat of nature.

The 1880–1 Famine Commission report did recognize that distress resulted from a loss of work and wages rather than from a complete lack of food. But this was not an early version of Amartya Sen's concept of 'exchange

---

9 Around 1900, Dutt (Datta) wrote a series of letters to the Viceroy attributing poverty to a high revenue demand; Lord Curzon replied in *Land Revenue Policy of the Indian Government*, Calcutta, 1902.

10 Report of the Famine Commission, Appendix II, Cd 3086 (1882), pp. 18–23.

entitlement'.[11] The Famine Commission believed either that traders were generally capable of importing grain to famine areas if there was effective demand, or alternatively that grain often existed in the areas but was exported for want of local buyers or hoarded for profit or out of panic. This did not prevent the Commission from attributing the origin of the crises to particular shortfalls of food production. It was an unfortunate combination of ideas. It was convenient to emphasize exceptional local shortages of food or work and the effects of profiteering or panic. To do so was to avoid asking whether or not 'normal' food supply was adequate and to divert attention away from more fundamental questions about the distribution of wealth. It reinforced the colonial preference for technological and legal regulatory solutions and the colonial commitment to commercial agriculture and trade.

The lesson drawn by W.W. Hunter from the 1769 famine, but applicable to the later nineteenth century, illustrated three of the elements of this thinking. By his account, famine was a disorder arising from India's economic and social backwardness, which modernization would cure. Firstly, he believed the state's role should be limited to providing such enlightened government as would allow the operation of the 'ordinary laws' of political economy, though some intervention was justified when commercialization and modern civilization did not yet prevail. Secondly, the landed classes should be encouraged to invest in agriculture by the granting of secure property rights. Thirdly, only growing trade and commerce, especially an influx of British capital, could support a growing population.[12] In short, Hunter echoed the popular maxims on laissez-faire, property rights, and investment. The same economic laws treated capital and trade as the engines of improvement and regarded climatic disasters and food shortages as the causes of famine. One paradox was that interdependence was another axiom much invoked—Hunter referred to binding up 'the commonwealth by the ties of mutual transaction and common interest', and both officials and nationalists blamed famines on the destruction of village communities—and yet the preferred economic and legal remedies focused on the rights and wealth of individuals, and did so alongside reports of persistent, general and abject poverty among rural populations (for example, in Bihar). This made it inevitable that such success as the British had in reducing famines was achieved mainly through crisis management rather than systemic reform.[13]

---

11 See for example, 'Starvation and Exchange Entitlements: A General Approach and its Application to the Great Bengal Famine', *Cambridge Journal of Economics*, 1 (1977) or the summary in Jean Dreze and Amartya Sen, *Hunger and Public Action*, Oxford, 1989, pp. 1–17.

12 Hunter, *Annals*, pp. 19–56, 227–8, and 365–8.

13 This argument differs from the meliorist conclusions of Michelle Burge McAlpin, who claimed that the real puzzle was not the cluster of late nineteenth-century famines

Richard Temple, Bengal's Lieutenant Governor, reported on Bihar in 1874. He found that half the population of the Darbhanga and Madhubani subdivisions had had to be supported for four months on grain imported by the state. He had urged this unusual action because the local markets were depleted. All available grain had been exported and there was no incentive for private grain imports. Better communications would solve this problem in future, he believed. Yet the government had ended up with substantial stocks of grain. Temple now realized that, after a good season, much food remained 'in the possession of the people' and that Indian cultivators were ready to make 'considerable alterations in their agriculture for the sake of increasing the food-supply at the earliest possible moment'.[14] This flexibility encouraged the British version of the old policy of making government agricultural loans (*takavi*) to distressed areas, namely Act IV of 1884. Temple was also a notable exponent of the importance of 'moral prosperity', meaning the possession of defined rights, as the route to material well-being.[15] Attention to rights was effectively a substitute for attention to modes of production and the economic impact of agrarian relations. As Stokes put it, the law of rent was never dethroned and officials were able to advocate profit maximization through high-rent and high-revenue strategies, denying any link between rural taxation and poverty or between property rights and the oppression of the landless. The models of landlord enterprise or of substantial peasant families employing their own capital and labour (as in J.S. Mill) informed policies that did not give much weight to the capacity of the poor to survive in good years, let alone bad.[16]

Antony MacDonnell, not much over 30 and early in his distinguished career as an Indian administrator, was also dispatched to prepare a report on the food supply of north Bihar. Valuable though it was, it assessed the available subsistence on the basis of averages. On one hand, he found that households typically kept three months' supply of food, assuming a daily ration of three quarters of a seer per head. On the other hand, as others argued, about half the people had no reserves at all.[17] Much other evidence was gathered in the later nineteenth century about the sections of the rural people vulnerable to

---

but their relative absence in the twentieth century, which she attributed to relief policies and market-led improvements; see her *Subject to Famine*, Princeton, 1983.

14 *Report of the Famine Commission*, Cd 3086 (1882), pp. 25–8 and 47.

15 *Report of the Famine Commission*, Cd 2086 (1882), pp. 29 ff.

16 See J.S. Mill, *Principles of Political Economy*, 1848; E.T. Stokes, *The English Utilitarians and India*, Oxford, 1959, especially pp. 135–9; and Curzon's *Land Revenue Policy*.

17 A.P. MacDonnell, *Report on the Food Grain Supply and Statistical Review of the Relief Operations in the Distressed Districts of Bihar and Bengal during the Famine of 1873–4*, Calcutta, 1876.

famine, but it too was defective. It used categories such as tenurial status and caste or religion, which were not identical with economic standing. It showed relatively little interest in the minutiae of agricultural production or labour deployment. Michael Finucane, Bengal's Director of Agriculture, one of the stronger advocates of agrarian reform and government intervention to improve agriculture, ruffled feathers in the 1890s by arguing that the vast majority of those on relief were not landless but poor cultivators, which he considered proved that the problem was not high prices but the inability of most raiyats to survive harvest failure.[18]

In Bihar, labourers were accustomed to reduced demand for their services between April and July; but in a poor season following a poor rabi harvest this downturn would bite hard. Wages and other outgoings were frequently paid in kind, in harvest shares, or at piece rates. Poorer cultivators relied in turn on advances of seed, grain, and money between harvests. Thus basic subsistence was soon at risk when production and credit systems were interrupted. It does seem then that the late nineteenth century famines resulted, as the officials thought, from the cessation of agricultural activities. In 1892, for example, the death rate and the attendance at government relief works both responded dramatically to the rainfall. Lack or excess of water halted cultivation; but once ploughing could begin, private and public credit was readily deployed for the next harvest, and food and money would begin to circulate.[19]

MacDonnell's food supply calculations inadvertently revealed the forms of exchange that lay at the heart of the Bihar countryside. At the end of each season, most people did not retain enough agricultural capital to finance the next harvest; often they did not have enough to feed themselves for more than short periods. But villages or communities as a whole did have stores that could be lent and shared. In short, the rich were able to sustain the poor when it suited them, at whatever level of suffering or sufficiency would maintain the labour supply and satisfy the social requirements of deference and prestige. What suited the rich changed over time—for example, from the effects of British rule and the growth of international trade. Famine revealed this inequal system; it did not disrupt a normal balance. Though some middling families

18 See Finucane's note, 8 May 1897, responding to H.E.M. James (Vice Chairman, Indian Famine Charitable Relief Fund Committee), 24 April 1897, R&A Famine C16–20, May 1897. Finucane's work was admired, but only strong pleading from Denzil Ibbetson prevented his being publicly censured for intemperate advocacy of a relief scheme put forward by the planter W. Hudson, who proposed using government loans to import grain. See R&A Famine A71–81, January 1897, and A54–7, March 1897.

19 See Peter Robb, 'State, Peasant and Moneylender in Late Nineteenth-century Bihar' in Peter Robb (ed.), *Rural India: Land, Power and Society under British Rule*, London, 1983; New Delhi, 1992.

had sufficiency on their own resources, most households both great and small were interdependent. Thus famine was understandable to those who suffered it not so much as a single event to be personified and propitiated (as with the smallpox goddess), but rather as an interruption of a cycle that already expressed hierarchy and dependency. Ploughing, planting, and harvest ceremonies, and all the rituals and offerings of the agricultural calendar, were designed not so much to ward off rare disasters as to ensure the continuity of the existing system of production and of society. Colonial officials called the recognition of this interdependence 'fatalism' or 'lethargy'.

There had always been a range of responses to famine—individual and collective, and indeed religious, political, and social—and these continued. But I wish to draw attention to reactions of a different order. Regardless of any arguments about the causes of colonial famines, it is certain that *awareness* of their incidence and severity in the late nineteenth century was a product of British rule. Increasingly, and especially after 1881, famine came to be defined by price rises and death rates according to local information collected by the state. This means that famines were identified by colonial measurements, typically statistics, that provided a definitive, official gauge of their occurrence. The standard was set high. Under the Bengal guidelines, food prices had to be 40 per cent above normal, or rather 67 per cent as the calculation of price was by weight; intervention was required and a famine would be declared when a rupee bought only 60 per cent of the normal quantity of staple grain.[20] A better but unmanageable measure would have been the distress of a given proportion of the population. MacDonnell claimed that he had tried to set the level of relief contributions on that basis in Bihar in 1896–7, but admitted that it sounded too dangerous a doctrine to make into a rule.[21] Indeed: it would have required a scrutiny of the proportion of the population 'normally' in distress.

The official definitions of famine implied firstly that the relevant measure was access to food, though it was admitted that this was affected in turn by the availability of work. Secondly, they implied that the vulnerable acquired their food by purchase. Thirdly, they implied that famine was a variation from the norm, in particular a crisis of the markets for food and labour. We noted in Chapter 2 the limitations of such views of India. The norm was assumed to be a sufficiency of work and food within a market economy, both as an ideal for human society and as the practical yardstick for administration. If it is by such measures that we know that 'famine' was specially frequent in the last 40 years or so of the nineteenth century, then by the same token they do

20 R&A Famine, A16–18, March 1906.
21 R&A Famine, A17–23, September 1901.

not tell us much about the comparative frequency of 'famine' over the preceding centuries. Nor do they tell us anything directly about the levels of endemic scarcity in the years after 1880, even though the frequency of 'famine' was regarded (inconsistently) as indicating the level of general impoverishment.

This idea of famine downplayed the importance of collective social action to remedy or mitigate social and economic ills. It removed or reduced the concept of unmanageable fate, whether natural or supernatural. This 'famine' was not a wilful goddess, not a divine scourge, not a punishment, not an inevitable facet of human suffering. It was a remediable failure of comprehensible systems. State policies followed from this process of definition. Famines would be ameliorated by work camps where workers were paid (usually in kind) at marginal rates as a test of 'need' and to avoid 'unnecessary' expenditure, or by gratuitous food relief for those unable to work; and by agricultural loans to kickstart the cycle of agricultural employment. Future famines could be prevented by development, by targeted investment, by better production and transport—in short, by improved policies for generating and distributing wealth. Political positions were thus produced; there was a rhetoric of famine. Officials used famine (as defined) alongside the fear of famine-related disorder as a means to advance other policies—with regard to budget conventions or priorities and to data collection, as well as to revenue and political policy, local government, communications, agriculture, commerce, credit, and so on. Indian politicians also took the package as a whole. They argued that famine indicted colonial rule and that famine could be relieved by policy. They suggested changes to the land revenue system, better laws, government by Indians, and so on. This assumed the state's responsibility for the work and food supply of the 'nation'.

This was not just famine that was experienced. It was famine defined and explained. Therefore, 'famine' produced debates about the duties of government; it generated economic nationalism; it established arguments for the proper entitlements of workers; and at the same time it was subject to scientific theories and standards. Moreover, its use was as selective as it was instrumental. A focus on the crisis of famine was sometimes a *substitute* for concern with wider issues of endemic poverty. It could allow an official to develop strategies for improvement without questioning colonialism and it could encourage economic nationalism in a caste Hindu who thought Dalits should be kept in their place. While nationalist accounts of famine obviously had the intention of condemning colonial policy and foreign rule, the government's reports had the inevitable aim of mounting a defence of policy when it came to assessing causes and attributing blame, while also emphasizing the importance of famines so as to underline the need for whatever policies were in favour. Famine was thus political in definition, in explanation, and in influence.

By serving a polemical purpose, famine was obviously one of the crises or scandals that would energize critics and force the government into action. When famine struck Company territories, for example, high officials asserted the pre-eminence of the free market and of land revenue. Some even argued that state interference would prevent the operation of a Malthusian check on population, which was to be preferred in the long run to the endless growth of unproductive mouths. Others, closer to the people, had to hear the demands for help and the public criticism that Indians' poverty and suffering proved the selfishness and inadequacy of colonial rule. Sooner rather than later, officials had to devise justifications for intervention. They had to re-interpret both their duty and their theories of statecraft and political economy. Moreover, once again, Indians understood what they had to do to be heard.[22]

A reified and politicized famine was of a piece with most other elements of life as it was now perceived. The nineteenth-century colonial 'famine' is an example of a way of seeing the world. It influences historical and political interpretations to the present day. We have seen how colonial rule affected the structure of identities; but a process was needed to turn categories into interests. Famine illustrated that process. It affected the agenda of government and inflamed its critics. It also forged interests by creating issues, defining debates, and encouraging confrontation. Moreover, the controversies over famine were about its nature and its causes and cure, which were matters for investigation and interpretation. Thus we come back again to the influence of science, which had changed the idea of government in the first place. Famine was an acute example, but also typical.

Arguably, in colonial India endemic impoverishment, malnourishment, and morbidity were more serious and widespread than the awful crises of deprivation and disease that struck some regions and classes at certain times. My arguments are in no way intended to belittle either kind of suffering. My purpose was to show how much flowed from definition, in this case setting the boundary between 'normal' and 'famine' conditions. I suggested that it was the process of categorization that encouraged the politicization of the issues of scarcity and poverty. The same lesson may be applied to almost any category. *Liberalism* also looked at political and administrative boundaries and at bounded languages. Earlier parts of this volume have considered tenurial categories and classes. Many more instances could be given. They are parallel in their character and effects. Under colonial rule, India experienced a politicization of the everyday.

22 Sanjay Sharma, *Famine, Philanthropy and the Colonial State: North India in the Early Nineteenth Century*, New Delhi, 2000.

Getting it Wrong

The operation of distinctions and borders meant that certain rules were applied on principle by the British officials. They would not support, say, religious endowments; they would not provide gratuitous relief in famines so as to interrupt trade; they would not permit dues to be collected in restraint of trade; and so on. The list is endless. And just as long is the story of exceptions to the rules in practice and of Indian pressure on the rulers to overlook their own guidelines. Every market was permitted in practice to impose its own taxes and tariffs. Local officials found ways of supporting religious endowments when it was politically expedient to do so. In famine relief, as already noted, they provided money aid, forbade hoarding, and even imported grain (at least in the early nineteenth century) on occasions when such action was asked for by Indians who defined it as a normal function of the ruler. Only later did the higher authorities enforce their doctrine of not interfering with merchants, being neutral in religion, or forbidding local tariffs and taxes. And in many of these instances, as already said, policy gradually shifted nearer what seemed to be the original Indian expectation. The fixed border between what the state would do and what it would not proved to be moveable. Perhaps this helps explain why, for example, free trade and laissez-faire were *espoused* more thoroughly than they were *applied* in India. Surprisingly many policies were prompted by Indian demand—petitions, protests, campaigns—at all levels of society, from princes and merchants anxious to protect their privileges to beggars lobbying local officers for relief in times of scarcity. British concessions and alliances even foreshadowed the special privileges for military, commercial, and administrative elites that have been such an important part of the economic and political condition of independent India as well as Pakistan.

But I do not draw the conclusion that colonial government was shallow. I draw the conclusion that it provided many points of entry and for many possible impacts. The statements of borders or rules influenced policies and hence expectations, and, as also suggested, the very fact that they were negotiable in practice made them political. Another point already touched upon is that of the negative consequences of colonial rule. There were many instances of crises during British rule in India, some of them certainly attributable to the changes ushered in by the British. Collectively these too may be regarded as creating a pressure that forced different responses on government.

The more that was done, the more relevant it is to ask how far Western categorizations distorted India. There was (and is) a misuse of history and an application of pseudo-science. The administrator-historians of India, like subsequent polemicists, too often broke the rules. Their transgression was the more serious because they claimed rationality and objectivity while concealing a multitude of pernicious assumptions. It is now a cliché to note that subjectivity is unavoidable, contributing to choices of subject and model-building, and that objective reality (assuming it exists) cannot even be approached except through our own concerns and language. But this does not mean that European observers of India (or anyone else) cannot be judged for different degrees of bias. Considerations of data may be either more or less ideological. A line is crossed when concepts and *a priori* notions no longer merely stimulate inquiries or order and help communicate knowledge, but replace and prevent the specific interpretation of information. Nineteenth-century officials certainly produced much that did not transgress by these criteria, but at key points they were limited by their preconceptions and prejudice.

Elsewhere I have discussed at length some of the damage caused by such follies and arrogance,[23] and I have plenty of company in drawing those conclusions. Considering empire and identity, however, it might be more interesting to think once again about more positive consequences of error. Though there was much probing of India, European theories were often based on acute observations of *European* society. Adam Smith related technological improvement to a rational man's desire to save labour and improve wealth. Marx emphasized the political implications of different roles in production and exchange. Though Darwin derived his notion of evolution partly from observations in nature, social theorists in Europe soon applied it to human societies. Of course new and often wrong-headed explanations therefore arose that purported to explain India, especially to the West. The most important, however, was perhaps not the usual farrago of racist denigrations but the powerful idea of universal progress.

Just as James Mill had dominated the early years of British dominion, in the later nineteenth century a key figure was Henry Maine, who erected a theory around the social factor as expressed in law in his *Ancient Law* (1861) and his *Village Communities of East and West* (1871). He was perhaps the single most important influence on British-Indian officials, given the prominence of legal and agrarian questions. For a generation, his work crystallized a gamut of intellectual change into a single compelling explanation of Indian society and history: the well-known distinction between status (whereby people were subjected to custom and collective will) and contract (which regulated behaviour only as a general body of civil legislation based on the integrity of the individual decision). Thus it was that the supreme importance of a contract supported by law came to be regarded as a universal measure of the level of civilization in preference to the sanctions of religion or custom. But this implied an assumption that societies evolve in one direction,

---

[23] For example in Peter Robb, *Ancient Rights and Future Comfort: Bihar, the Bengal Tenancy Act of 1885 and British Rule in India*, Richmond, Surrey, 1997.

and hence that social laws could be discovered and exploited. The idea that all of humankind is essentially the same was probably more important and indeed more imperialist than the equally ancient notion that there are tribes or races that differ fundamentally. The see-saw between these two poles constituted a basic debate of social theory and in the nineteenth century it was concentrated in no small part upon India. The consequences of the idea for India's national ambitions were far-reaching. Basically, in yet another instance of selective borrowing, nationalists rejected the comparison but claimed the progress.

Maine had encouraged the belief that earlier social forms survived in India but that they were universal or at least Indo-European, and hence capable of evolution towards 'modernity', towards a single 'rational' law, if suitably encouraged. This both explained and justified foreign rule. It did so better, or with a more optimistic and liberal gloss, than the alternative notion of Asia's essential difference and inferiority. But such a general presumption demanded new categories, or at least forged new understandings of existing ones. Emphases were changed, new social ideas reformulated. Why not turn the same argument into a denunciation of empire and an acclamation of national destiny?

Maine's influence was most potent when combined with fears and doubts (to which he also contributed) about the pace and cost—if not the direction and inevitability—of change. The supposedly indigenous was also privileged. The late-nineteenth century accounts believed in science and evolution and modernity, but shared in the alternative romanticism which privileged the past and the community—as much, ironically, in the minds of conservative administrators as in the claims of nationalists. The origins of this thinking lay not only in the classifications of rationality but in far earlier notions of 'Nature', hierarchy, and pastoralism (the very ones challenged by the scientific and technological revolution). British officials, alongside other historicists, regretted some of the consequences in Europe of industrialization, market forces, and urbanization, and feared the social and political impact of the division of labour that these changes forced upon peasant communities in India as defined by Maine. These views were both nostalgic and teleological. The idealized peasant was a foil for the wage labourer of the 'dark Satanic mills', and even the despotism under which peasants lived could be regretted in the face of ever more bureaucratic systems of power. In autocracy could be found a role for heroes and gentlemen and for chivalry and *noblesse oblige*, all of which were smuggled into the British conception of their role in India. To add the Christian gloss upon this, one might note John Bunyan's portrayal, as both origin and goal, of a purer, isolated, equitable society, in a *City of God* exactly contrary to Hobbes' *Leviathan*. Punjab officials, for example, sometimes sounded as if they thought they had found the remnants or prospect of this godly society in the region under their rule, in the form of the village community, the martial castes, or the sturdy peasant proprietor—and not least when trying to export these social models to Bengal and other parts of India.

Thus the habit of justifying policy on a historical basis also was ingrained by the late nineteenth century, and indeed characteristic of British and European thought. To devise present-day remedies, it was believed necessary to appreciate the development of institutions. The tendency had already found expression in the analyses of Philip Francis and his followers in the 1770s, and thus also in the Permanent Settlement of Bengal. There are ways in which it can be seen in Munro's descriptions of society. But historicist ideas, along with criticisms of classical political economy, played a particularly crucial part in administrative strategies from the 1870s.[24] They became the current orthodoxy and were embodied in an outpouring of official histories, settlement reports, studies of castes and tribes, and treatises upon rural and agrarian history. Though some of these were more polemical than others, all contributed to the definition and hence control of India. Their function was partly to contribute to intellectual debates centred upon Europe, notably with Henry Maine for example. It was also to regulate the opinions and actions of British officials by defining the people over whom they ruled, as was the motivation of such works as Baden-Powell's or W.W. Hunter's.[25] In this respect, the studies were not conservative but the most complete expression of a continual process of colonial rule, a stage with its own features and preoccupations. The process built upon descriptions of the Mughal zamindar and his accretions of hereditary rights in the eighteenth century, of the village community as in James Mill's *History* and the Fifth Report, and of religion and caste, including studies that sought to define the settled cultivator as the model subject and citizen, as Sleeman did in relation to *thagi*.[26]

Elsewhere, I have shown how the historical appreciation of agrarian conditions in Bihar and Bengal depended on ideological assumptions of mixed

24 See Clive Dewey, 'Images of the Village Community', *Modern Asian Studies*, 6(3), 1972.

25 See Chapter 1 for a fuller discussion and references for this point and others in this paragraph. See also Burton Stein (ed.), *The Making of Agrarian Policy in British India, 1770–1990*, New Delhi, 1992 and B.H. Baden Powell, *The Land System of British India*, 3 vols, Calcutta 1882.

26 The example of Sleeman reflects the work of Sanjay Nigam when preparing his London PhD. See also Thomas R. Metcalf, *Ideologies of the Raj*, Cambridge, 1994. Note, however, that he regards Maine as having established 'difference' above all in terms of an India that was supposed to be medieval and feudal. Perhaps for this reason Metcalf presents only the aristocratic model among the 'created constituencies' of the Raj, pp. 66–80 and 185–99.

ancestry.[27] These appeared repeatedly in the official and popular writings of the period. In the standard legal commentary on the Bengal Tenancy Act of 1885, the introduction began by referring to the code of Manu and its ambiguity about the ownership of the soil.[28] Some authorities concluded, from the fact that revenue was due to the king, that the king owned the land; others believed that there was a property residing in the portion of the agrarian surplus not owed to the state and that this descended from the rights of original settlement, as surmised in Field's *Digest* of tenancy law.[29] But such conclusions were deductive in origin, deriving from theoretical notions of property formation. Sahajanand had followed a similar thought process.

For our present purposes, it matters that the distortions meant that colonial rule never merely perpetuated or replicated pre-existing Indian institutions. Rather it re-invented them. Colonial officials, like some latter-day social scientists, tended to apply to India taxonomies derived from Europe. There are good arguments against doing this. Many of them were advanced by heretical officials at the time. But the prevailing theories nonetheless took Europe as their reference point. By the nineteenth century, with the extension of European empires and the improvements in communications, it seemed obvious that many parts of the world were experiencing similar changes, especially in trade, in relations of production, and in subjection to centralized, bureaucratic states and international trends. Certainly, though change was not straightforward, some such 'modernization' occurred in India too. The dominance of Western ideas and influence did mean that some of the story, even in India, began with the legacy of the Enlightenment and with new notions of categorization, of history, and of social science.

Even before and without Marx's conceptualization, hard categories or classes were defined according to their proper traits. The elements were often misrepresented or particular to dominant sections of the people, but they were not wholly invented. Actual experiences limited the range of possible representations. For that reason, languages were important. They had long been consciously related to community on the model of the Babylonian dispersal, and hence of family trees. Hence biological or cultural associations were implied. Race or identity were imagined in ways analogous to language despite the observable fact that they need not be coterminous. Then, as has been widely understood, standardizations occurred through socio-economic activity, scientific description, literature, and print. Such linguistic orthodoxies

---

27 Notably in *Ancient Rights*.
28 M. Finucane and B.F. Rampini, *The Bengal Tenancy Act being Act VIII of 1885...*, Calcutta, 1886.
29 C.D. Field, *A Digest of the Law of Landlord and Tenant in the Provinces Subject to the Lieutenant-Governor of Bengal*, Calcutta, 1879.

helped create nations. Though each language was always plural in actuality, each could be used to unite as well as to divide. Ranade described the Maratha confederacy as a 'process of nation-making', whereby people 'strongly bound together by the common affinities of language, race, religion and literature' were enabled to seek 'further solidarity by a common independent political existence'.[30] The choice of 'affinities' was not accidental; rather it was axiomatic in the later nineteenth century. They were the elements of colonial analysis. As Surendranath Banerjea also illustrated in his autobiography, nations were built from such connections or from the icons, metaphors, and histories in which they were embedded.

Moreover, contests between different categories and ideologies reinforced the linked identifications (of language, race, culture, and community) and gave a legitimizing role to original forms. It is difficult to imagine any story of origins—even unadorned genealogy—that contains no element of explanation. But the authority of the 'earliest' form became ever greater, despite the model of dispersal and difference, because of each category's need to define 'proper' characteristics and to defend possession and privilege. In such ways, languages were delineated and ranked, castes or religious communities treated as primordial races. Histories were devised on the basis of such assumptions, for example, about the Aryan 'invasions' or the Dravidian 'subjugation'. Communities acquired and were defined by their institutional 'memories', which languages in part expressed.

Two further points may be drawn from this discussion. First, there were both conservative and radical, Western and Orientalist approaches to India. Second, these new visions were powerful and persistent, and they changed perceptions. Both, for example, contributed to Indian nationalist discourse—from Gandhi's sentimentality about village India, equitable caste society, and bread labour or spinning, to Nehru's insistence on industrialization and the salience of modern economic class over 'feudal' ties. The confusions of the officials were repeated in the different voices of the nationalists. Perhaps this was because both British and Indians drew on both Western and Indian experience and concepts.

This ambiguity parallels another raised by the editors of *Krsi-parāsara* in respect of the agricultural knowledge presented in that text, already discussed in Chapter 2.[31] They contrasted the 'accuracy of observations...tested...in the proper scientific manner' with the text's 'superstitious ideas' and emphasis on 'rites and ceremonies', a comparison that might (they said) 'brand the work

---

30 M.G. Ranade, *Rise of the Maratha Power*, Bombay, 1900, pp. 6–7. I owe this reference to a seminar paper by Sudhir Chandra and ideas he put forward in the School of Oriental and African Studies (SOAS), London, April 1997.

31 See Chapter 2, note 1.

as a priestly manual'. They admitted that 'religious practices were closely interwoven into the texture of life', even in 'such practical things as agriculture'. But, they went on, the text also contained 'valuable instructions' regarding agriculture. Accordingly they posed the question: 'in this modern age, when the world is proud of various scientific achievements, what material advance has been made...[upon] rules...laid down in remote antiquity...?' Their text, they claimed, should be an 'eye-opener to those who decry the study of Sanskrit as having no practical utility'. However, the point was not really that it provided a sufficient manual for agriculture. Rather it showed (they claimed) that it was 'time that we dived deep into this literature and rescued the indigenous materials of national importance from unmerited oblivion and saw the India of our own in the proper perspective'.[32] The implication was that there was an indigenous knowledge that was somehow more useful or relevant or *satisfying* in India than the knowledge of 'science'. Like its recent echoes in India (or France), this was defensive and anti-colonial, but also essentializing and nativist. It was a reaction in that the 'shame' of colonialism helped create the 'pride' in the indigenous—it was re-evaluation but not re-categorization.

Identities in modern India were thus forged out of a range of materials, but in a mould shaped by the colonial experience. Put in the opposite way, modern forms were introduced because of foreign rule, trade, and technology, but based on a mix of external and indigenous elements. Hence class (or indeed 'national') awareness existed in India in forms often quite comparable to those emerging in the West, but with their own character, especially in regard to what Pinch means by religion (not communalism).[33] During the colonial era, some of the influences—technological and economic change, industrialization, 'modern' rhetoric and law—that had produced classes and nations in Europe *were* also felt in India. Indian versions of such identities appeared in response. But of course identities did not develop exactly in the ways they developed elsewhere.

The sadhus are one reason. Forms of identity—or knowledge—that appear to be the same may in fact differ markedly in their means, ideology, and function.[34] This allows space for an argument compatible with that of Pinch to the effect that the weight of Western categorization and enumeration and the institutional and economic change ushered in during colonial rule suborned some 'indigenous' forms, but merely modified or complemented others. From

32 *Krsi-parāsara*, introduction, pp. xvii–viii.
33 Pinch, *Peasants and Monks*.
34 With regard to agricultural knowledge, this is a possible reply to Bhaskar Mukhopadhyay when (in private conversation) he cites *Krsi-parāsara* as a refutation of arguments in David Ludden's essay in Robb, *Meanings of Agriculture*.

the nineteenth century, Indian social and political identities then became another complex amalgam of different influences.

I return to the points made in introducing this work. In *Liberalism* it was shown, as its Preface put it, that 'liberal rhetoric and modern technology and governance' led to 'the reinforcement of bounded categories and to a discourse of rights'. The Preface to this second volume claimed that the colonial era provided new definitions of 'place, time, task, reward, power, and organization'. Colonial rule defined both 'government and law, by identifying their responsibilities', and identified 'employers and employees' and hence other identities 'by defining their rights'. Such processes, it was claimed, assumed a concept of national society and economy in their purposes and rationale. They depended upon skills and technologies, and reinforced—and, indeed, were reinforced by—many comparable and parallel trends and categorizations. Inevitably, the categories created by these processes spawned identities, with organizations to represent them and claim their rights.

II

Law, Economic Change, Interest Groups, and Rights

4. Agrarian Structure and Economic Development[1]

This essay questions the nature of economic development in general (including a cursory comparison with Japan) by considering the changing meanings of terms relating to producers and factors of production, by assessing the roles of the state and of trade, and finally by analysing class-related changes in eastern India in the late nineteenth century.

In the 1980s, India's slow economic development was often contrasted with the Japanese economic 'miracle'. More recently, the travails of the Japanese have been compared with buoyant rates of growth in India. Whatever the perspective, it will be remembered that, for all its social, political, and managerial problems, Japan is still very rich because of its rapid industrialization and the development of a skilled workforce; India, despite its remarkable economic progress, continues to battle with long-term constraints of infrastructure, education, and governance. The intellectual interest of the comparison remains, and it is important to wide-ranging debates about the means and mode of economic development. It raises questions about universal conditions for development and about empirical features such as the links between land and power or the role of usury in different societies. It seems, too, that some explanations of the Indian case rely on assumptions about the origins of development that are no longer widely accepted.

Two stories are usually told. One concerns the decline of the East and the other the rise of the West (and then of Japan). The old picture is of declining continental empires superseded by vigorous, maritime, exporting powers. It has been modified by an emphasis upon prior developments in trade, class formation, even 'proto-capitalism' well beyond the industrializing regions.

---

[1] This is a revised version of an essay first published in Peter Robb, Kaoru Sugihara, and Rajat Datta, *Agrarian Structure and Economic Development: Landed Property in Bengal and Theories of Capitalism in Japan*, Occasional Papers in Third-World Economic History, vol. 4, London, 1992. It discussed the accompanying papers by Datta and Sugihara, but now has been given a more general focus. See also Rajat Datta, *Society, Economy, and the Market: Commercialization in Rural Bengal, c. 1760–1800*, New Delhi, 2000.

According to one version of this model, India experienced increasing monetization and commercialization in the seventeenth and eighteenth centuries, a development it shared with a wide band of territories from North Africa to South-East Asia. The impulse came from fiscal pressure, the growth of trade and import of silver, a rise in population, and the extension of consumption due to the emergence of merchant and service elites. Another suggestion relates the decline of the old land empires to a failure to accommodate the political and economic changes that inter-regional trade had encouraged. They succumbed to more vigorous regional states, whose characteristics provide another list of the means for development. The states were involved with merchants and commerce. They encouraged the growth of towns and urban control of the countryside, the settling of nomadic peoples, the creation of peasantries, and the strengthening of local identities and ideologies.[2]

Japanese capitalism is very differently understood according to political stance, which strongly influences the very chronology of Japanese economic history. All admit the importance of the state, though the agricultural sector also contributed to Japan's early and successful industrialization, and one argument has it that 'semi-feudal' elements survived to explain features of Japanese politics and economics into the twentieth century.[3] The state is evident in India as well. A parallel historiography has debated feudalism and the mode of production, but indigenous development is often supposed to have been thwarted by imperialist pillage. The implication is that colonialism forced significant changes in the Indian countryside, which is obviously true in some respects, but in others requires investigation. The debate is not just about India, but also about capitalism and development.

One set of issues concerns the starting point. The 'pre-capitalist' economy has been characterized by its petty production units under indirect and socio-economic control. Production was both for use and for the market.[4] Surplus was extracted mainly through rent. Important transactions were imperfectly monetized. Both the Japanese and Indian economies had long and deep involvement in marketing on such terms as these. Some therefore see development simply as the overcoming of such obstacles to growth. Others

2 See for example C.A. Bayly, *Rulers, Townsmen and Bazaars*, Cambridge, 1983; *Indian Society and the Making of the British Empire*, Cambridge, 1988.
3 Sugihara (see note 1) describes how from the 1920s, the Marxist Rono school stressed the 'backwardness' of Japan, contradicting others, the Koza-ha school, which emphasized the dynamism and hegemony of capitalism; the Kushida school analysed the 'non-feudal' origin and function of apparently feudal survivals.
4 See note 2 above and Rajat Datta, 'Agricultural Production, Social Participation and Domination in Late Eighteenth-century Bengal', *Journal of Peasant Studies*, 17(1), 1989.

regard the 'pre-capitalist' features as transitional.[5] Yet others suppose that similar forms came to serve different functions. It is recognized that similar conditions continued over time, despite or even because of capitalism. Nineteenth-century observers described Asian societies as having isolated villages, peasant production, and feudal polities. But it is now generally agreed that the villages were not unchanging (in character or boundaries), nor autarkic, nor undifferentiated, even before the putative revolutions of the seventeenth and eighteenth centuries. Rather, they were involved in trade and to some extent integrated with broad political, economic, and social systems through intermediate forces and institutions. Some fixed elements or cohesive forces, such as the territorial village and its ties (caste, kinship, bondage, or debt), have needed to be reinterpreted. Either they applied only to some levels of the society or they were largely created during the nineteenth century.

Ryozo Yamasaki (so I understand) stated that the debate on whether or not landlordism was 'feudalistic' is irrelevant to an understanding of the 'class' basis of the Emperor system. He argued that landlordism in Japan cannot be termed feudal and that both survivals and new modes of land control or specific modes adjacent to cities or on newly developed land are traceable from the early modern period to the twentieth century, amidst the development of the money system, commoditization, and tenancy disputes.[6] For India, Rajat Datta has stressed the importance of markets and of enterprising intermediaries in eighteenth-century Bengal—I shall return to this below. In another example, Jan Breman argued that great mobility, by individuals as well as groups, was an 'essential part of the rural system' in pre-colonial Asia and that consequently rural elites acted as rural entrepreneurs while a 'proto-proletariat' had some bargaining power in seeking employment.[7] But he also claims that South Asian labour, being consistently mobile but unfree, was restricted by the 'sedentarization' policies of colonial rulers following but exceeding the example of their predecessors. Labour then became migratory again, under more regulated conditions, when workers were recruited over long distances for capitalist enterprises.[8]

5 For example, Frank Perlin, 'Proto-industrialization and Pre-colonial South Asia', *Past and Present*, vol. xcviii, 1983.

6 Ryozo Yamasaki, 'An Historical Approach to Landlordism' in *Kindai Nihan Keizai-shi no Kihon Mondai (Fundamental Issues in Modern Japanese Economic History)*, Kyoto, 1989. I am indebted for its translation to Kaoru Sugihara.

7 Jan Breman, *The Shattered Image: Construction and Deconstruction of the Village in Colonial Asia*, Centre for Asian Studies Amsterdam (CASA), Comparative Asian Studies, vol. 2, Dordrecht, 1988.

8 Jan Breman, *Labour Migration and Rural Transformation in Colonial Asia*, CASA, Comparative Asian Studies, vol. 5, Dordrecht, 1990.

It might be concluded from this that there are idiosyncracies and continuities that contrast with a 'universal' framework in the form of the supposed shift from one kind of economy to another, notably from 'feudal' to 'capitalist'. Certainly some 'pre-capitalist' features persisted into the 'capitalist' twentieth century. Did India transform itself or did it stagnate; or did it do both?

Semantics

For answering these questions, more recent scholarship on South Asia represents a great advance on the old revenue histories. Their worst feature was an uncritical listing of regulations, without regard to their enforcement, and the use of revenue categories as if they were 'real'. Some words in the vocabulary applied to Bengal seem to be if not empty shells then incapable of carrying the burden that has been placed upon them. Under this heading fall many of the revenue and landholding terms—both British-Indian and Mughal—including such concepts as *khudkasht* (resident or privileged) or *pahikasht* (non-resident), which cause problems not only by being obscure and ambiguous, but by implying too great a certainty about the 'village' as a social and land-holding unit. These terms do have significance with regard to recognized rights and status in various spheres, but they do not seem to have been general in character or effect. The khudkasht raiyat was not the same as the rich one; the landholder-zamindar was not necessarily the greatest holder of land.

These problems do not apply less acutely to 'indigenous' than to 'foreign' words, those with a special function for outsiders (which would include 'zamindar' and 'raiyat'). The term 'malik', for example, meaning a local magnate or a powerful man, may seem less partial and more organic in its connotations than the rather artificial terms that served the external administrators. But it too is vague outside its mainly political and social connotation of prestige; there is no catechism of legal rights due to a malik. Within the revenue system, a term such as 'zamindar' or 'malguzar' had a very definite import. It meant one responsible for collecting land revenue and additionally, for the British, one who had legal title to the land, being a tenant-in-chief or freeholder. But the roles and rights were accorded to very diverse kinds and levels of people, so that—a mirror image to 'malik'—the revenue terms were often administratively clear but socially imprecise. Worse, identification of a particular actor did not mean that he and he alone performed his role. The travelling merchants and others described as moneylenders were not the only people who traded and lent, and the zamindars (revenue-collecting landowners) were not the only ones who held land.

The revenue and other terms may be treated, I suggest, as 'notional norms'. They are ideas around which a variety of practices existed. Thus, they are susceptible to changes in meaning corresponding to changes in practice—

susceptible, that is, to modifications in the socio-economic fields within which people operated. An excessive interest in terminology in its own right has often obscured these special conditionalities.

In India, there were various levels and arenas of decision-making. Production decisions have to be disaggregated. Some were taken by cultivators, some by landlords, and some by merchants.[9] Moreover, in addition to ecological, social, political, and economic constraints, there were different strategies for cash-cropping, for wet or occasional cultivation, and for subsistence and risk aversion. All of these imply different perspectives (and identities?) even with regard to agriculture.

This does not mean ignoring terminology. Revenue terms may provide a bad fit with more relevant ways of categorizing society; but that criticism applies also to concepts such as class.[10] In the end, the problem is not with the categories themselves. The problem, as said, is with seeing them as encompassing and explanatory when they represent only modes of description, one identity among a complex of other overlapping identities. Some categories certainly existed contemporaneously for particular purposes or from particular perspectives. They were related to common roles or interests. They help us appreciate how these arose and were consolidated. For example, landholding terminology may enable us to see what was happening in Bengal, and in particular to assess the level of involvement of agrarian elites. It may enable us to understand the means and the role of marketing, the part played by elites in agricultural production, and the availability of 'profit' to cultivators.

In short, despite the complexities, it is after all possible to differentiate roles. Eighteenth-century landed proprietors in Bengal possessed a range of different kinds of property right and holdings of varied sizes and, even before colonialism, some directly encouraged production. There was also a well-developed system of regional markets in which landlords were closely involved. Rajat Datta has drawn attention to the creation of privileged and intermediary rights over land, which he claims were intended to provide for particular tasks, namely the extension of cultivation and the management of production. The elites were acting in ways expected of them. They extended cultivation either through such sub-proprietary and revenue-free holdings or by engaging sharecroppers.

On the other hand, harvest loans were also an important means of extracting surplus from the general mass of tenantry, and these were not only

9 See below Chapters 5 and 6, and 'Ideas in Agrarian History', *Journal of the Royal Asiatic Society*, vol. 1, 1990.

10 On the imposition of categories, see Karl Marx, *Pre-capitalist Economic Formations*, (translated by Jack Cohen, edited by E.J. Hobsbawm), London, 1964, p. 132.

or not primarily provided by landlords. Here were other roles or a confusion in possible 'class' interests. The ubiquitous systems of advance payment were devices to secure the supply of certain crops and labour so as to manage availability and depress the prices paid for produce and services. It has been suggested that these systems grew, or indeed appeared, under colonial rule as a feature of newly commercial agriculture and of newly capitalist labour relations. But Datta finds that they were widely prevalent in the eighteenth century, for example, from intermediary landholder (taluqdars) to cultivators in Murshidabad and 24-Parganas.[11] Be that as it may, the prevalence of such arrangements by the eighteenth century implied that the rural controllers included merchants or rural moneylenders as well as landholders. In many villages, such elites not landlords acted as managers of production and controllers of marketing.

Landed Property

This lays open to scrutiny some of the assumptions about the modes of production that in one form or other lie at the heart of descriptions of modern economic change and class formation. Of all the factors of production, land-as-property has been most often discussed in the past with regard to India, since the eighteenth century. Scholars used to agree that colonial rule transformed the nature of landholding in India, and indeed that modernization required the institution of distinct and individual property rights. In Britain, enclosures were regarded as a part of an agrarian revolution. Thus personal land rights dissolved communal and feudal land relations. A transformation is clear enough, though not absolute or uniform, where laws of settlement were imposed on nomadic migratory or pastoral peoples. They often did have small areas under personal control for cultivation, but they did not in the main divide land into individual holdings. In the Americas, in Africa, and in Australasia, and generally among pastoralists and migrants, therefore, we may speak of dispossession. Indigenous people lost out from changes in land use, backed by laws that recognized only one kind of ownership in land and promoted settled agriculture through definite boundaries and titles. Somewhat similar points may be made in South Asia with regard to the extension of settled agriculture into areas once used informally, in rotation or indeed for slash-and-burn cultivation, hunting, or gathering.

But such is the story told, too, by subsequent critics of the permanent settlement of land revenue in Bengal in 1793. This revenue system was derided

---

11 See note 1. Sources cited were the *Proceedings of the Provincial Council of Revenue*, Murshidabad, 23(21), January 1779, and the Board of Revenue, p/72/6, 1 August 1792.

for its preconceptions about property—its aristocratic prejudice, as James Mill called it, on the grounds that it was intended to replicate in India the very social model that Mill and the Utilitarians rejected for Europe. However, dispossession alone could not have been at issue on the great bulk of the lands to which the Bengal regulations of 1793 were applied, where complex landholding arrangements already existed. Dwelling upon the alleged conflict between Western and non-Western ideas of land and property seriously overestimates the pace and extent of Company influence, and at the same time misrepresents pre-colonial conditions.

On the first point, take revenue-free holding—for example *la-kharaj* (revenue-free land). It was clearly a derogation (in terms of sovereignty) from the state's claims to surplus, and hence was often closely restricted—certainly by those would-be centralizers, the British. Yet it took the East India Company some 80 years or more to regulate it fully in Bengal, and thereby to re-establish a supremacy claimed by the Indian state, in theory at least, in the seventeenth century. Time and effort were needed to give effect to legislation. Many such imperfections of sovereignty—degrees of negotiation or consent—existed under the Company, as in all states. In eighteenth-century Bengal, the zamindar himself represented such an interruption insofar as he was an independent chief and not a revenue officer; the same was true perforce of sub-proprietors, to some of whom the Company extended further recognition in the early nineteenth century in its so-called 'pattidari' regulations. Even the tax net varied in effectiveness for different levels and areas. In addition, there were differential rent rates for high castes. Such customs also qualified state sovereignty. Many other limits on power could readily be substantiated.

Secondly, consider the concepts of ownership already defined by previous regimes. The existence of pre-colonial property rights has been debated as a question of whether or not, or when, a land market existed in India. It used to be thought axiomatic that there was none before British rule because there was no exclusive legal title in land or because, given high and arbitrary revenue demands, there was no economic value in land. There has been interesting work on the social and cultural inhibitions upon the development of land markets. Attention has been paid to collective and intermixed notions of ownership or use or control, with regard to land and the feebleness of the British challenge to these contradictions of private property.[12] And of course, on the other hand, great consequences have been attributed to the

12 See Jacques Pouchepadass, 'Land, Power and Market' in Peter Robb (ed.), *Rural India: Land Power and Society under British Rule*, London, 1983, and D.A. Washbrook, 'Law, State and Agrarian Society in Colonial India', *Modern Asian Studies*, 15(3), 1981.

transformation of land through colonial laws and capitalism into a commodity to be owned, bought, and sold. Yet, with regard to India, it is now increasingly realized that, well before British rule, there were means of transferring land (or rights over land), that these included sale, and that by the eighteenth century considerable quantities of land changed hands in this way.

What does it mean to say that there was no land 'market' in the eighteenth century? At one level this is a question of what we understand by the term 'market'. We could defend the original statement that a land market did not exist by saying that the conditions of the exchange, the manner of the fixing of the price, and so on, differ between different times and places and that we will reserve the word 'market' for one commercial kind of transaction. To do so, however, may be to set up a misleading impression of 'progress'. In the eastern region of India, there was a variety of forms of land control (fitting uneasily with the usual terminology), which included concepts of 'ownership' as well as of 'shares'. These need not be seen as the opposite ends of a process of transition.[13] The old disputes about private property shrivel to inconsequence before the detail of many transactions, as indeed do a great many assumptions about original proprietary forms in India. The question is not whether, but what manner of, private property in land existed at different times. To ask that is to chip away at one of the supports of far grander evolutionary assumptions.

Intermediaries between district and village were also accommodated in the administrative and tenurial systems. Two seemingly contradictory features of eighteenth-century Bengal were the entrenching of local power through the inheritance of offices, and the increase in land revenue, mainly to meet military expenditure or tribute. The increase was achieved partly through the use of revenue contractors or farmers, which has also been noticed in other regions, but local power was allowed for also in the fact that the farmers seem often to have been drawn from the intermediate elites who had already been consolidating their local position. Indeed, the inheritance of land rights may be seen in one sense as a reversion, in style and quite frequently in personnel as well, to local power brokerage, resting on control of followers, social prestige, and so on, which had preceded and then co-existed with the Mughal system. The farming of revenue thus represents not a breakdown so much as a new means of maintaining the old relationship between the local elites and the state. The land revenue transaction had often been a kind of bargain between the parties. Having revenue farmers made this overt, rather than subsuming it under codes of law and administration that only appeared to impose an external order on the countryside.

13 See Robb, *Rural India*, introduction.

Local power was derived both from below and from above, that is, from standing with followers or clients and with patrons or the state. The relative importance of each of these would vary. In the Bengal area, the role of the Mughal state is usually thought to have been stronger overall in the seventeenth than in the eighteenth centuries; but it always differed from place to place as well. It was generally stronger, for example, in south Bihar and weaker in the north. The increasing independence of Bengal *subah* (province) during the eighteenth century thus may appear from outside to be an assertion of regional dynamism. However, it depended itself on accommodation to varying degrees with more local forces, and sometimes (as Robert Clive understood only too well) with combinations which competed for control of the subah. This is not the old bipolar world of the 'village community' and 'Asiatic feudalism'. This is a world riven through with structures of power. It seems accurate in such a context to talk of 'ownership' (possession) of land and of various but effective ways of deciding on cultivation and commanding surplus, even though these might fall short of an absolute capacity to regulate use and access.[14]

The kinds of criticism that were levelled at the Bengal system are now also being made with regard to temporary and raiyatwari settlements applied by the Company elsewhere in India.[15] Taken in conjunction with the nature of power and landed property in Bengal, this implies that the Permanent Settlement was derived not only from ignorance and prejudice but also from pragmatism. In Bengal there was a gradual indirect takeover of working institutions. The existing systems were modified, even when property rights and a permanent settlement of the revenue demand were established in 1793. By contrast, in Madras and the Maratha territories of west and central India, there was a more warlike overthrow and consequently a felt need to 'cut down the tall poppies'.[16] In Bengal, the British were ready to endorse the form, while if necessary coercing the person, of the larger landholding intermediaries. Elsewhere they were anxious not to give strength to possible opponents among the magnates of ousted regimes. They preferred settlements based on a different

---

14 Compare the distinction between 'title' and 'effective possession' alongside assertions on modes of production—for capitalism, 'the crucial function of the system of commodity circulation in the mechanism of extraction of surplus-labour'— in Barry Hindess and Paul Q. Hurst, *Pre-Capitalist Modes of Production*, London, 1975, pp. 234–5 and 290.

15 Burton Stein, *Thomas Munro: The Origins of the Colonial State and his Vision of Empire*, Delhi, 1989, and 'Idiom and Ideology in Early Nineteenth-century South India' in Robb, *Rural India*.

16 In addition to this political argument, there were administrative and social ones, in favour of closer government and widespread landownership; see T.H. Beaglehole, *Thomas Munro and the Development of Administrative Policy in Madras, 1792–1818*, Cambridge, 1966, e.g. p. 8.

aspect of previous arrangements, the village-level revenue structures. After all, then, the Company did investigate rights of property and did attempt to codify what was there, or only to modify what had been standardized already, within limits posed by political considerations. The idea that they were wrong about agrarian structure, though partly true, underestimates their desire not to disturb. They also codified systems as required by their assumptions and political economy, but they were not the first to do so.

The State

This brings us back to the question of state influence on economic change. We need to describe colonial impact differently. It is not that there were no changes. What occurred—and this explains similarities across the areas conquered by Europeans—was in essence a matter of sovereignty, of the successful establishment of a residual, superordinate authority vested in the state. The British governments in India, like other states depending on settled agriculture, advanced a concept of territoriality. They claimed to inherit a role as tenants-in-chief of all land; they arrogated the concept 'public' to themselves, taking it away from any lesser collectivities or localities; and they set out constitutive as well as regulative rules of conduct (the 'what' as well as the 'how').

A more convincing charge against the East India Company (than the idea that it distorted the operation of property) is the suggestion that it failed comprehensively to understand the production system: the role of zamindars, of revenue-free lands, and of labour. Unlike their predecessors, the British in Bengal distanced themselves and the operation of revenue collection from the details of agriculture, credit, and markets. For that matter, even with regard to property law and revenue policy it can be argued that the British misunderstood land as a factor of production. Western law and administration failed, for example, to recognize the roles of various kinds of 'waste' land (revenue-free tenures, commons, fallows, forests, or grazing lands), which were all placed under a single concept of landownership. A conflict of views and of land use existed with regard to so-called forests and waste land, a conflict between peripatetic and settled agriculture. Informal or extensive land use was regarded as 'useless' by an influential strand in nineteenth-century British thought, and perhaps by older regimes too, in their search for land revenue. Hence waste and forests were restricted or appropriated through state regulation or through 'developmental' tenures.[17] This affected 'marginal' peoples and pastoralists. But it also affected peasant communities. Earlier

17 This preceded Company rule, but accelerated through the nineteenth century. Compare Stein, *Munro*, pp. 102–41 and 195–6, and 'Idiom and Ideology'; and Eric Stokes, 'Privileged Land Tenure in Village India in the Early Nineteenth Century' in *The Peasant and the Raj*, Cambridge, 1978.

ambiguities of landholding had provided for risk aversion and flexible responses, rotations and grazing, alternative incomes and agricultural extension. They allowed, in south and north-western India, migratory cultivation that was often mandatory in dry or politically disturbed areas. They accommodated, on the great deltas of Bengal, climatic variability, frontier opportunities, and the mobility of river channels. It was no wonder that in Bengal a persistently high proportion of land was held on special tenures, for they facilitated the work of reclamation: clearance, drainage, protection, and development.

Similar differences of perception existed even with regard to lands devoted to commercial crops. In Bihar, an indigo planter claiming a proportion of the land in many holdings for his factory crops entered into a contest with (*inter alia*) customary ideas of land use. These ideas were based on a complex of social and ritual expectations as well as agricultural choices. In part, they concerned economic strategies (say, the comparative returns on rice, sugar, or indigo); but even the crops themselves had a moral as well as a monetary value. Above all, the colonial government did not seem to understand how production occurred. Like many development analysts to this day, they thought in terms of simple production units taking decisions about capital investment and marketing strategies. They did not grasp, or at least did not allow for, the fact that agricultural decision-making was complex and hedged in by features peculiar to Indian conditions. These persistent failures to understand may be attributed to imported ideas of laissez-faire, for example, in succession to the influence of physiocratic thinking.

Or consider another argument—that policies were 'inappropriate'. The Permanent Settlement of Bengal was said to have encouraged property-owning without ensuring investment. It was implied that a 'pre-modern' (static, irrational) society was being asked to perform a 'modern' (dynamic, maximizing) task. We now find that improvement was already a strong motive among the landholders. This raises the possibility of an accidental fit between policy and imperatives of production. A radical hypothesis would be that the Permanent Settlement was quite well calculated to achieve increases in output. There was after all an appreciable expansion of cultivation, especially in more valuable crops, during the nineteenth century. Similarly, it has been shown that the East India Company's salt monopoly permitted and even (partly from its imperfections) encouraged the development of salt producers, merchants, and importers.[18] Despite all that has been written to the contrary, it is not certain that the land experiment in Bengal was markedly less successful at

---

18 Sayako Miki, 'Merchants, Markets and the Monopoly of the East India Company: The Salt Trade in Bengal under Colonial Control, c.1790–1836', PhD Thesis, University of London, 2005.

this stage than the alternative measures advanced by the followers of James Mill, Munro, or the Punjab peasant school. The point of such arguments is that they imply endogenous trends in production and exchange, and hence that different economic amalgams are necessary, indeed unavoidable, in different conditions. The 1885 Bengal Tenancy Act might be taken to show—for example in Bihar—that belief in the universal rationality and efficiency of free peasant proprietors was of little relevance to places where few of them were to be found.

This is not an argument that the colonial state was irrelevant. On the contrary, it assumes that states define some of the variables in economic change because they differ between cultures and over time, in the ways conceptual as well as physical boundaries are drawn, in the forms or levels of political control, and in the extent of 'public' activity. At its base too are distinctions not only in terms of character and capacity, but in the ideas people have of what a state is—indeed, whether or not they have any idea of a state at all. 'State' now implies a distinct authority over territory and people, and hence, as a separate idea, a national economy. Neither of these conceptual separations was clearly applicable in eighteenth-century Bengal, even in the minds of East India Company servants. The idea in Britain, in reaction against European mercantilism, was that an economy was a 'natural' process in which the state should not intervene. As a corollary, it was a process in which the stance of the state mattered. Inevitably, as in British India, official economic goals expanded—from facilitating through infrastructure and law, to 'assisting' in production and trade, to protecting society or sections of it. State responsibility widened gradually until it embraced the economic well-being of regions as a whole. They edged from guarantee, through subsidy, towards control (such as over prices, wages, or interest rates) and management, even planning. Colonialism and nationalist critiques both encouraged the development. Never entirely reversible, it represented successive re-definitions of the state, with the effect that economic life fell under the sway successively of other preponderant ideas: for example, that the market alone would provide, that export trade was the key to progress, or that living standards were (or were not) the best criteria for measuring economic success.

Trade and Urbanization

A more neglected area is trade and urbanization. Here too the emphasis has been upon European intervention rather than indigenous tendencies. We have noted that commercial intermediaries also played a crucial part alongside the landed and caste elites in the agrarian economy of India. These lay behind the pockets of economic growth in India existing at the same time as the expansion of Europe and also behind the growing extraction of surplus that permitted a growth of consumption—spending on warfare, government, and items of trade. The growth was specific in character to the places where it occurred and had no necessary outcome or direction. However, from mid-century (if not before), Bengal became ever more closely linked to wider systems. The tribute it paid to the Marathas or to the East India Company increased the wealth of new or old elites in areas far removed from Bengal as well as locally, and arguably this increased demand on producers was why Bengal and Bihar suffered several economic catastrophes over the period in areas under close control and others where central power was weak.

It is very well known that colonial India then became deeply involved in the production of large quantities of relatively low quality and value—whether in wheat, cotton, or manufactured goods—as part of a worldwide system of trade. It was one in which there was often no or insufficient premium to the primary producer for better quality products. Colonial trade developed partly as a result of agricultural extension rather than intensification. It attracted capital, much of which continued to be expended on risk aversion and manpower. Economic disparities widened between regions and people. Indigenous traders and moneylenders gained in strength and reach alongside European capitalists. There are mixed messages, but the evolution of capitalism permeates accounts of India's economic history and development. Often details of production and exchange are largely absent. For example, 'third world' poverty is new, argues Willem van Schlendel. It resulted from capitalism directly or from its imperfect penetration. Poverty as it exists today is not a problem of scarcity, but of social and political structures; it is determined not by the ratio of resources (including technology and capital) to population, but by unequal relations between regions and social groups.[19] On the now familiar argument of Amartya Sen, it is a problem of distribution or effective entitlement. There are many illustrations of this fact at particular points, but fewer accounts that trace the local conditions that would have produced it over a long period.

There are limits to the hegemony of capitalism, moreover. The existence of trading networks or capitalist investment does not wholly determine the character of an economy. Not everything follows from markets. Just as a market system often requires a visible hand in order to operate effectively, so too it can readily coexist with non-market practices. To put it another way, there is always some division of labour and hence some exchange, so that the existence of even large and established markets does not imply a system dominated by a single 'market' rationale. This is the fallacy contained in the hope that economic development is merely a matter of replication. Circumstances differ.

19 Willem van Schlendel, *Three Deltas*, Delhi, 1990.

In seventeenth- and eighteenth-century Japan, the expansion of markets in agricultural produce depended primarily upon self-cultivating landholders working perhaps 4–10 hectares, at the lower limit using family labour and at the upper employing others as well. The village communities aided development, organizing as cooperatives to sell produce. In Bengal in the same period, as we have noted, there were extensive trading networks that carried produce to townsmen, artisans, soldiers and treasuries. As a result there was some specialization of production. There were extensive merchant houses, mostly combining a range of commercial and financial tasks, in some respects allied self-interestedly with the Company state (as over the monopoly in salt). There was quite extensive trading in some products over long distances well before European involvement. Such mercantile activities existed within hierarchies of control and were also sustained alongside more localized exchange at small markets and in the form of rents, patronage, customary and village dues, and credit relations. Later, Bengal did become dependent on imported rice, but in the eighteenth century a vigorous market coexisted with a good deal of subsistence, if that means meeting most normal food requirements through non-specialized production in each locality (rather than necessarily each household). Moreover, markets operated within a distinctive formation of society and production in which they were not the only or the main determinant of relations. If such conditions are common, economies can hardly be subject to a single law of behaviour.

This was an economy with regional market networks that contained a degree of commercial management and knowledge without being fully integrated. In Bengal, a system of trade and a related system of revenue collection were managed by magnates, moneylenders, and agents (systems interestingly different from those operating in Japan in the same period). Office was a significant resource, and revenue-related office was more valuable in 1790 than 1920; rent (with a broad definition) and also debt were key levers of control. Village-level power, based also on landholding, followers, and social prestige, was one stay on which the system rested. Others were the town bazaars and village markets, and the agencies of various kinds that managed the markets in different commodities.

It seems certain therefore that elites in eighteenth-century Bengal controlled certain aspects of production, but chiefly those aspects that required capital in the widest sense. By this means, the society as a whole could cope with all but the most severe seasonal differences. Variable strategies were made possible in different seasons—cultivation could move as required by climatic or riverine changes; production could expand by means of irrigation or reclamation. Thus, too, larger holdings of land could be managed by allocation as small holdings without the need to employ unfamiliar strategies of large-scale cultivation.

Labour, though a scarce resource, could be deployed as required by the dominant ideas of status as well as by economic needs, thus at the same time being kept under constraint. Revenue and other cash needs, and indeed the market, could be supplied despite the fragmentation of production units. The whole effect was neatly interdependent. It seems to have lasted in very different political and economic environments precisely because it did a number of jobs fairly well. Petty cultivators generally required elite intervention to ensure the continuation of agricultural production from season to season. The elites needed the traders not just to transmit tribute and turn crops into cash, but also to provide them with credit to meet the many demands (personal, social, fiscal, and military) that occurred out of step with their fluctuating and seasonal income. Units of production were dispersed. There was relatively limited specialization and local capacity for subsistence. The producers were potentially mobile, but there were physical, instrumental, or ideological barriers to communications. In all these factors, one finds a match with such social and economic features as the harvest loans and also an explanation for the layers of intermediaries, the practice of alienating rights in order to extend cultivation, and the attempts to coopt or coerce cultivators through khudkasht privileges or pahikasht deals.

It will be noticed that this description makes little or no reference to so-called fundamentals. It hardly needs saying that physical environment, climate, man : land ratios, communications, and so on are all extremely important. But they do not operate consistently as independent variables. They have a different impact according to context, a context that of course they continually conspire with others to create.

Nineteenth-century Changes

Chitta Panda argues that in the Midnapur district of Bengal, the zamindars declined during the nineteenth century, being challenged by affluent peasants.[20] Panda provides explanations for zamindari weakness in the horizontal and vertical partition of zamindari rights, in the rising expenditure of zamindari families, and in the difficulties of rent collection. He sees evidence of hardship in increasing revenue arrears, in budget estimates of selected families, and in debt incurred for legal and social expenses. Yet in the later nineteenth century, with a run of good harvests and favourable rainfall, the region as a whole benefited from higher profits from agriculture, over and above the burden of taxation. Improving conditions were implied by the growing size and value

20 Chitta Panda, 'Decline of the Bengal Zamindars, Midnapore 1870–1930', DPhil. Thesis, University of Oxford, 1989. See also Panda, *The Decline of the Bengal Zamindars: Midnapore, 1870–1920*, Delhi, 1996.

of surpluses of exported crops, especially paddy. Why should landlords not have reaped the bulk of these returns?

According to Panda, benefits for peasants rather than rent receivers were suggested in acquisitions of land (less than 5 per cent of transfers going to 'zamindars'), and in a many-fold increase in agrarian disputes heard before the courts. The tendency of rents to standardize (a possible consequence of tenancy legislation after 1859) suggested an initial increase but a subsequent stickiness in total returns, as against a secular inflation of prices and costs. The peasants of Midnapur, however, were strongly differentiated, many being very small semi-landless cultivators and a few being substantial farmers. Early in the twentieth century, 38 per cent of holdings were below 2 acres, and 65 per cent below 4 acres; and, while 90 per cent of holdings paid less than Rs 20 in rent, the remainder paid nearly 40 per cent of the total. This pattern is not unusual in nineteenth-century India. Some of the peasants were able to acquire control over more land, for example by acquiring additional holdings or plots, by providing usufructuary mortgages to zamindars, or, where there was little competition from external moneylenders, by financing the agriculture of others, and later through manipulations of the cooperative movement. Panda calls these people affluent peasants and sees them as shading into those whom the 1885 Tenancy Act assumed were 'tenure-holders', that is, secondary rent receivers holding more than 100 bighas (about 80 acres). These were the people, by his account, who gained most from the changing economic fortunes of Midnapur.

A crisis of 'landlords' and the rise of 'peasants' may be more typical of eastern India in the late nineteenth century than is sometimes supposed. My present concern is not with the regional variations that have been identified.[21] Nor is the earlier 'rise of the jotedar' at issue, as that intermediary role was effectively that of a smaller local landlord, whatever the tenurial niceties. The question is rather of the existence of change, as against those arguing for continuity and even 'semi-feudalism'.[22] Even Binay Chaudhuri, the doyen of

21 See Partha Chatterjee, 'Agrarian Structure in Pre-Partition Bengal', in Asok Sen, Partha Chatterjee, and Sugata Mukherjee, *Perspectives in Social Science 2: Three Studies on the Agrarian Structure of Bengal*, Calcutta, 1982, and Sugata Bose, *Agrarian Bengal: Economy, Social Structure and Politics, 1991–1947*, Cambridge, 1986.

22 Ratnalekha Ray's thesis on jotedars (see note 28) and B.B. Chaudhuri's discussions of 'de-peasantization' ('The Process of Depeasantization in Bengal and Bihar, 1885–1947', *Indian Historical Review*, 2(1), 1975) both in their different ways imply long-term continuities, which for his part Partha Chatterjee defined as 'semi-feudal' even in the twentieth century (note 21 above). My concerns have been to explain the limits of commercialization and the continuities of structure without falling into the trap of denying change (given the enormous alterations in external environment) or assuming that what is apparently similar (names, structures, relations of production) was in practice identical over time.

these studies and a sceptic when it comes to downplaying zamindari dominance, has written of the 'reduced powers of zamindars', 'the increasing consciousness of peasants', and the 'complex... distribution of power within the village'. He treats the late-nineteenth century challenge to the landowners as the result in part of rival groups gaining direct control over the peasants. He notes direct zamindari investment as 'positive in several regions' and the indirect incentives they provided through estate management, but sees these as being weakened generally by personal or institutional shortcomings and as suffering a decline during the nineteenth century.[23] Panda's account gains modified support also from Pouchepadass' *Paysans de la Plaine du Gange*, which refers to the increase in stature of some enterprising and hardworking agricultural castes in Champaran district, north Bihar.[24] I have made a similar assessment of Gangetic Bihar.[25]

It seems plain that there were changes that favoured those who effectively managed cultivation for the market and who negotiated the perils and opportunities of markets in land and tenancies. Nariako Nakazato has shown this convincingly in his study of eastern Bengal, which describes what he calls a new type of landlordism at the lower levels of the zamindari system, among the most successful of a more stratified tenantry and at the expense of superior landholders, though not of the often interdependent land-controlling classes taken as a whole.[26] Even Akinobu Kawai, a dissenter who dates the decline in rental incomes and zamindari power only from the economic depression of the 1930s, shows the complex array of forces that needed to be balanced in order for any player to succeed in the Bengal countryside. He also focuses on

---

23 B.B. Chaudhuri, 'Rural Power Structure and Agricultural Productivity in Eastern India, 1757–1947' in Meghnad Desai, Susanne Hoeber Rudolph, and Ashok Rudra (eds), *Agrarian Power and Agricultural Productivity in South Asia*, Berkeley, 1984. The non-productive zamindar is also castigated in Rajat Ray, 'The Crisis of Bengal Agriculture, 1870–1927', *Indian Economic and Social History Review*, 10(3), 1973.

24 Jacques Pouchepadass, *Paysans de la Plaine du Gange*, Paris, 1989; see pp. 284–92, Chapter X, part III, and pp. 594–7. This book has been published in English as *Land, Power and Market: A Bihar District under Colonial Rule, 1860–1947*, New Delhi, 2000.

25 See Peter Robb, *Ancient Rights and Future Comfort: Bihar, the Bengal Tenancy Act of 1885 and British Rule in India*, Richmond, Surrey, 1997, chapters 9 and 10.

26 Nariako Nakazato, 'Agrarian Structure in the Dacca Division of Eastern Bengal, c.1870–1910' (manuscript courtesy of the author); see also *Agrarian System in Eastern Bengal, c. 1870–1910*, Calcutta, 1994. He explains that methods of control, especially over sharecroppers, were 'feudal' in the sense of being socio-political rather than only legal or economic, but insists that society was *not* 'feudal' because of capitalist and colonial pressures. He also stresses the common interests of the potentially opposed agrarian managers and controllers.

estates that came under the Court of Wards, an experience that usually *followed* some kind of crisis and led to the regulation of intermediaries and records and to improvements in management and income.[27]

Such changes are not failures of the colonial state or of capitalism—they are attributed to new laws and the spread of commercial agriculture. But they are also manifestly incomplete and imperfect, for those forces do not penetrate fully and transform all the institutions of power and commerce. Agricultural produce was increasingly marketed while markets in the main factors of production remained sluggish, unfree, or marginal. The conditions do not fit the usual attributions of development to new forms of land control and land use, to state intervention, or to capitalism. In short, they do not support the argument that even though capitalism may spread unevenly through an economy, it is the capitalistic elements that provide dynamism. Moreover, the changes do not wholly match the complementary assumption that new forms of production and exchange impoverished all the primary producers and led to de-peasantization, the formation of a rural proletariat, and capitalist labour relations in agriculture.

For analysing these conditions, the categories of landlord and tenant or of zamindar and peasant are inadequate. At least four roles need to be considered: those of rentier, production manager, independent cultivator, and labourer. It is not certain that these should be called 'classes' in the eighteenth and nineteenth centuries, because, as I have already said, the roles overlapped. More important, there was a tendency in eastern India for independent cultivators to become production managers (moneylenders or brokers) whenever possible. This was probably because of the density of population and the multiplicity of rights in land. Once they acquired a surplus of land or income and especially if they were high in social status—the countryside was full of would-be or had-been lords—they would become moneylenders to their fellows, produce brokers, sub-letters, and employers of labour. These were the expected fruits of independence. Its threshold, for a peasant, was an ability to manage and retain the profits of production. That ability varied from time to time and place to place depending on soil fertility, the need for capital inputs, and the value of output.

Certainly there was greater impoverishment of the swollen majorities whose resources, independence, and options were eroded during colonial rule. But there were also successful agrarian controllers and intermediaries. This implies three effective roles, none of which fitted exactly with tenurial categories nor

27 Akinobu Kawai, *'Landlords' and Imperial Rule: Change in Bengal Agrarian Society, c.1885–1940*, 2 volumes, Institute for the Study of Languages and Cultures of Asia and Africa, Tokyo, 1986 and 1987.

was performed exclusively by all members of one group. What then was the nature of the change? Was it structural? These categories of rural people seem to have been as plain in the eighteenth century as the late nineteenth, as was the involvement of rural elites both with agricultural production and with trade and government. Of course different fortunes may be traced for each role. In the early nineteenth century, the rentier seems to have had an easier time, while the rural manager was to the fore in the late eighteenth and nineteenth centuries. But contrary to the implication that might be read into Panda's account, there was not a generalized past when the zamindar's position was consistently all-powerful and unchallenged. This is the message of Rajat Datta's work and of the re-thinking by Ratna and Rajat Ray, in their discussions of Bengali 'jotedars' (generically redefined by Chaudhuri as any true land controlling group involved at village level in reclamation).[28]

It may be argued on the other hand that, in the early twentieth century, peasant societies or the Indian National Congress in Midnapur under B.S. Sasmal represented the growing political importance of a section of dominant villagers. There was pressure from the large scale of commercial production and from the greater definition of legal rights by the state. These changes seem to have made the categories gradually harder, more exclusive, and more self-aware. By the mid-twentieth century, some assertiveness could be found among poor peasants as well. Was this not a development of classes? Was there also a slow transformation of rural broker and village elite into capitalist farmer? These identities are hard to categorize because of the ambiguities of the economic transformation itself.

There are, at base, two major traditions for understanding the role of capitalism: the free market, trade-focused model derived from Adam Smith and the production relations-oriented, class-focused model derived from Marx and found (for example) in the work of Brenner or in the Indian 'mode of production' debates.[29] Yet empirical studies have increasingly thrown up economies that do not fit. There are examples of capitalist exchange alongside non-capitalist relations of production, and of peasantries subordinated to but not destroyed by the market. These conditions tend to be regarded as hybrid or transitional. But (as argued above) that conclusion is driven by typology rather than observation. Do the hybrids exist because of capitalism? Does the form of intermixed control associated with harvest loans or with

---

[28] See summary and conclusions in Rajat Kanta Ray, 'The Retreat of the Jotedar?', *Indian Economic and Social History Review*, 25(2), 1988; and also Ratnalekha Ray, *Change in Bengal Agrarian Society, c.1760–1860*, Delhi, 1979.

[29] See note 32, and Utsa Patnak (ed.), *Agrarian Relations and Accumulation: The 'Mode of Production' Debate in India*, Bombay, 1990.

sharecropping, for example, result from the demand made by European capital and Western markets upon traditional small-holding producers.[30] Or should 'capitalism' be regarded not as a system but as a process? If conditions result not from one influence but from a balance of rival processes, then the 'world system', as a description of economic modes, is challenged by particularist forms. There are relative degrees of integration rather than homogeneity. In that case, we might expect to find—as we do—that the solidarities of Indian peasants are as complex as their economic and political positions. In India as in Japan (to quote Sugihara), a key problem is 'reconciling the notion of... universality...with the need to differentiate'.[31]

A second set of difficulties with explanations based upon hegemonic capitalism concerns the exogenous influences upon its development in Europe and the existence of 'indigenous' capitalism outside or prior to that of the West. The implication, often admitted but seldom followed through, is that there are *capitalisms*—that the term is after all like all other terms and defines a core of characteristics around which lies a penumbra of associated features. Accordingly, one might argue that there were market systems in eighteenth-century Bengal that were broadly capitalist and that were as or more influential in determining the character of subsequent Indian capitalism as any experience of Europe or any expansion in worldwide trade. We need not regard these features as 'proto'-capitalist, or 'semi-feudal', or representing transitions between one economic state and another. On the contrary, elite participation in reclamation or the socio-economic command of the harvest loan represent persistent features of an indigenous system. They are not distortions imposed on a non-capitalist economy by capitalism.

Similarly, with regard to the evolution of property rights, eighteenth-century circumstances encourage scepticism over the two-classes, two-rights model for Bengal that was the framework for the debates about Bengal tenancy. It is possible to argue that the changes in India parallel Brenner's analysis of changes in European agriculture (the shift from rent-based towards production-based appropriation, where 'lords' were strong enough to dispossess 'peasants' and to institute leasehold and market rents alongside direct management of production). But in practice, 'survivals' may be as important as 'innovations'.[32] Indian class identities also mixed new and inherited elements. This helps explain the complexities of the social and political systems that emerged during

30 See Chapter 6.
31 Robb, Sugihara, and Datta, *Agrarian Structure*, p. 32.
32 See K. Brenner, 'Agrarian Class Structure and Economic Development in Pre-industrial Europe' in T.H. Ashton and C.H.E. Philpin, *The Brenner Debate: Agrarian Class Structure and Economic Development in Pre-industrial Europe*, Cambridge, 1988.

colonial rule. There were certainly 'class' interests, whether for zamindars, merchants, richer peasants, sharecroppers, or bonded labourers. Organizations and ideologies developed to represent each of these constituencies. But there was also a fluid and contradictory intermixing in the forces that determined status and defined the conditions of life for individuals and groups, just as they decided the terms of labour, production, and trade. Above all, there were overlying and interwoven social and religious allegiances. These too were as influenced by 'capitalism' as by 'tradition'.

5. Law and Agrarian Society in India*
The Case of Bihar and the Nineteenth-century Tenancy Debate

This essay, some of which is included in revised form in Peter Robb, Ancient Rights and Future Comfort, *summarizes some of that book's arguments on tenancy laws for convenience in this volume and supplements those of Chapter 1. It also discusses features of village life and economic conditions in Bihar, the better to understand the colonial impact on society and on social differentiation.*

David Washbrook's original treatment of the question of law and society to which the title of the present paper refers has not stimulated the response that might have been expected.[1] It is a wide-ranging study and only part of it will be taken up in this paper, namely its arguments about landed property rights in the nineteenth century. Washbrook states that in the first half of the century, private property in land remained a 'pure farce' in India because of continued state involvement in the economy, excessive revenue demands, the persistence of personal law (as codified), and the weakness of the system of courts. He emphasizes the political implications of the cooption of dominant groups for revenue collection and other purposes of British administration. For the second half of the century, Washbrook proposes an improvement in the position of landed and powerful interests as the law at last 'beat back the frontier' of personal law and disentangled private property rights from family and communal fetters.

This paper will not dispute the main lines of Washbrook's case, but it does begin from a sense that his account of property law seems exaggerated when seen from the perspective of the Lower Provinces of the Bengal Presidency. In particular, Washbrook seems first to underestimate the impact of European

---

* First published in *Modern Asian Studies*, 22(2), 1988, pp. 319–54.

1 D.A. Washbrook, 'Law, State and Agrarian Society in Colonial India', *Modern Asian Studies*, 15(3), 1981, pp. 649–721. On landed property, see also Jacques Pouchepadass, 'Land, Power and Market: The Rise of the Land Market in Gangetic India' in Peter Robb (ed.), *Rural India: Land, Power and Society under British Rule*, London, 1983, pp. 76–105.

jurisprudential ideas on the nature of landed property and later to overestimate their impact on agrarian relations. It is usually accepted that landed property began to increase in value one or two decades after the Permanent Settlement of the land revenue in 1793. Revenue sales generated information about prices, which appeared to relate to general economic considerations even though a 'true' market in land was slow to appear. Individual as opposed to collective ownership of estates was also increasingly sought and achieved, a match between the opportunity provided by law and the pressures of economic and demographic growth. Certainly landowning rested upon much earlier developments. Certainly, too, no legal enactment transforms a society at a stroke, even for governments better equipped than that of the British in nineteenth-century Bengal. But neither is law without influence. Washbrook claims that the rulers added an apparent lack of will to their incapacity of means despite protestations in favour of private property; but this seems a strained interpretation for the Cornwallis system. It seems to underplay the ideological and political need for the British to *settle* the population—to hold their Indian subjects in defined spaces, within definite categories and roles. They had strong motives to promote agriculture as the norm and to order land and people, by force if necessary. There were means enough to encourage private property; there were sales laws, resumption proceedings, and a pro-landlord bias in government. Interests in land had clearly been multiple and diverse; but the regulations of the 1790s defined what estates were in law, and thereafter they were gradually defined in reality as well. The means included surveys and physical demarcation, revenue demands and records, and courts. In all these cases, an estate was treated as a discrete, individual item of transferable property. That was the image of an estate from outside. Internally, it might well still be complex and represent collective interests, as may any kind of so-called individual property; but an essential change was being wrought in its external character. It was assisted by, but not dependent upon, the separation of collective ownership through partition, as also such influences on value as the expansion of cultivation and marketing and the falling real rate of agrarian taxation.

Washbrook's interpretation makes much of the fact that civil courts heard few property cases. This argument seems weakened even in areas that were temporarily settled because such cases were intended to be heard mainly by revenue officers; it also ignores the impact of repeated revenue settlements. In Bengal, the civil courts were far more active, as Washbrook concedes, though revenue officers were responsible even there initially, until 1869. (And no sooner did they lose the role than attempts were made under north-Indian influence to have it restored.) Bengal did not, of course, enjoy local agencies of government as effective as those maintained for revenue purposes where the settlement was temporary. On the other hand, this very omission made it even more important that the revenue estate should be established as private property, at risk for arrears and supportive of social order. It is safe to conclude that throughout India the law was administered within restrictions placed by different circumstances, but also that there were common assumptions that the British did not escape, for political as well as intellectual reasons. One of these was the Western concept of property in land.

Washbrook believes that this notion of private property was effectively delayed until the later nineteenth century. But for Bengal and Bihar, it seems possible to trace an earlier grafting of Western concepts onto longer-term forms of land control. Washbrook also stresses the suffering of subordinate groups as the landed interest asserted itself. Here, too, matters seem more complex in the north-east. The zamindari settlement did not, according to the best of recent treatments, subject the bulk of the population to a uniform oppression. This revision of older views depends partly on a more complete picture of pre-existing society and partly on empirical research into realities in place of reliance upon legal enactments. It fits well with these necessarily complicated ideas not to exaggerate the changes as property right strengthened. Even late in the century, competitive rents were not widespread in many areas. Moreover, as Washbrook argues, deliberate efforts were then made to use law to reverse distortions supposedly introduced by absolute legal principles, particularly of contract, and by excessive partiality to landlords. Yet this protection was itself flawed. The Bengal Tenancy Acts were not mere devices to improve rent collection; but nor were they straightforward shackles on change.

All is not well with current interpretations of the revenue and tenancy history of the permanently settled areas. There is much to be learnt from Washbrook's revision, given that the introduction of a law is not the same as the revolution of practice. But if we accept much of Washbrook and his periodization, we are led to look seriously at the assumptions and assertions that the British themselves made. With regard to landed property, clarifying definitions helps pinpoint what was novel and influential. We then find as much social distortion as preservation in late-nineteenth century tenancy laws in Bengal. Secondly, if Washbrook shows that law should not be treated in isolation, this implies a complex mix with the pre-existing systems. Hence in this paper, which will focus particularly on Bihar, an example of conceptual analysis will be followed by a broad survey of economy and trade.

The Law and Tenancy

A useful window onto these questions is provided by the great rent law debate of the 1870s and 1880s. Questions of revenue, property-in-land, and tenancy were continually discussed throughout British rule, but the most sustained and wide-reaching dispute occurred, for Bengal, during the decade or so preceding the Tenancy Act of 1885. To no part of the Presidency was this debate more relevant than to Bihar. Protagonists in the debate, which produced mountains of documentation and publications, were divided in their history and political economy. They read eighteenth-century conditions differently; they were opposed in their impressions of the present; and they disagreed about the best policy to ensure general well-being. For convenience, they may be divided into two camps: one of which professed to favour the interests of raiyats and the other of which made a case for the zamindars. In this essay, a brief examination will be made of the pro-raiyat case, which will be assessed in terms of agrarian conditions in Bihar.[2]

All statements of theory and principle in support of policy may be regarded, no doubt, more or less as rationalizations. In obvious or indirect ways, participants in the great rent law debate were using specific analyses to justify positions taken on more general, even subliminal grounds. The officials who supported the pro-raiyat position delved into regulations and memoranda of the 1790s and were not surprised to find justifications for a system of proprietary cultivators. They believed it essential for prosperity and economic progress. The Bengal government under Ashley Eden, the high point for the local influence of the pro-raiyat school, was equally persuaded that official experience (from the days of George Campbell, at least) represented a connected and consistent movement towards the same opinion.

Alexander Mackenzie, while Chief Secretary to the government, wrote a long and not very memorable minute to prove this case.[3] At times, such rationalizations were disingenuous or deluded. An obvious example was the more extreme formulation put forward in the Rent Law Commission of 1880

---

2 These questions have been discussed in Robb, *Ancient Rights*. The present paper is closely related also to Peter Robb, 'In Search of Dominant Peasants: Notes on the Implementation in Bihar of the Bengal Tenancy Act 1885' in C.J. Dewey (ed.), *Arrested Development in India: The Historical Perspective*, Riverhead and Delhi, 1988. Some of the questions are also raised in 'Land and Society: The British "Transformation" in India' and 'State, Peasant and Moneylender in Late Nineteenth-century Bihar: Some Colonial Inputs' in Robb, *Rural India*, pp. 1–22 and 106–48, and 'Ideas in Agrarian History: Some Observations on the British and Nineteenth-century Bihar', *Journal of the Rural Asiatic Society*, vol. 1, 1990, pp. 17–43.

3 A. M[ackenzie], 'Memorandum on the History of the Rent Question in Bengal since the passing of Act X of 1859' in *Report of the Government of Bengal on the Proposed Amendment of the Law of Landlord and Tenant in the Province with the revised Bill and Appendices*, vol. I, Calcutta, 1881. The sources for a discussion of the rent law debate are exceptionally voluminous, including many published collections of official papers. In this essay, references will be provided only for specific points or quotations.

to the effect that the Permanent Settlement had intended to endorse the raiyat's 'property' in land as it had supposedly existed in the eighteenth century.[4] Thus Mackenzie and his leading ally on the Commission, J. O'Kinealy, could argue that the word 'let' was used loosely in Regulation VIII of 1793, because the relationship between zamindar and resident raiyat was not one of landlord and tenant and was not intended to become so. Opponents could retort that 'let' meant what it usually means, which supported their contention that zamindars had or had acquired proprietary rights of an exclusive kind.[5]

Yet rationalizations also reveal underlying assumptions and may be part of a process of forming and changing views. The digest of rent law made by C.D. Field and the report of the Rent Law Commission itself were major events in this sense, informing opinions on the nature of agrarian relations over a quarter of a century and beyond. They fulfilled a role similar to that of the classics among north Indian settlement reports or the Famine Commission reports of the same period. The 1880 famine report in particular was obviously from the same stable as that of the Rent Law Commission and, with the report of 1901, may be said to have delineated a particular period in British rule. Moreover, a kind of personal and political alliance developed among those who advocated reforms to create or benefit tenant 'proprietors' and for constructive official interference with agriculture. It stretched from E.C. Buck, Secretary of the Government of India's Revenue and Agriculture Department, to Michael Finucane, Secretary to the Rent Law Commission and Bengal's first Director of Land Records and Agriculture. A key figure was a personal friend of both Buck and Finucane, namely A.P. MacDonnell, whose own early hopes of advancement were encouraged at a time when he was writing a long memorandum on the Rent Bill in 1885 and who was to see himself in 1893 (when Acting Lieutenant Governor of Bengal) as defending the reformers' legacy against subservience to the landlords on the part of Charles Elliott. In 1906, Finucane was still appealing to the true path of protecting the raiyats. It was a path set, as far as Bengal was concerned, by outsiders, specifically by the ideas of Henry Maine and the experience of the Punjab. As MacDonnell put it, quoting Maine (in another context, while advocating the gradual extension of the elective principle in India), it was not until the 'warlike people' of the north-west had been subjugated that the true proprietary unit of India

---

4 See the evidence and report volumes in *Report of the Rent Law Commission*, Calcutta, 1880. The best-known version of the extreme case is otherwise *The Zemindary Settlement of Bengal*, 2 vols, Calcutta, 1879, published anonymously by a minor official.

5 See Ashutosh Mookerjea, 'The Proposed New Rent Law for Bengal and Bihar', *Calcutta Review*, October 1880; reprint Calcutta, 1880.

was discovered. He meant the 'village republic', made up of proprietary cultivators.

But even within Bengal, over a 20 year period from the time of Ripon to that of Curzon, taking a pro-raiyat stance proved an aid to advancement in the service; it was also a factor in isolating some officials from their fellows. The bitter public row in the 1880s between Alexander MacKenzie and the Bengal Chief Justice, Richard Garth, was the most notorious instance, but Elliott's relations with MacDonnell in 1893 were almost as hostile, while O'Kinealy was still reported at that time as being estranged from his colleagues on the High Court bench over tenancy questions.[6]

The radical core of the pro-raiyat stance was the idea, already mentioned, of coextensive rights of property, that is, the interest in land divided into different aspects between landlord and cultivator. It was argued, as the Bengal government put it, that raiyats had and should have 'substantial rights of a proprietary character', expressed in security of occupation, and rents that took account of their 'beneficial interest' in the soil.[7] Rent-receiving rights, it was said, ought to be qualified by this property in the cultivation. The idea has its roots in theories of Asiatic or Indian social formation, polity, and production, and has become familiar not just to readers of Henry Maine but to those of Richard Jones, Karl Marx, and more recent historiography. But the idea itself (though not its Hegelian underpinnings) was novel in official and public circles in Bengal in the 1870s and 1880s. It was introduced by officials such as the group already mentioned. They had been alerted by agrarian conditions in Bihar; they proposed north Indian remedies.

For all the inventive readings in the records, the idea would have been unintelligible to the officials' eighteenth-century predecessors. At that time, although the elements for the construction of such a theory were arguably present, even the best minds did not fully grasp the possibility of a redefinition of real property. They believed in two models: in one, ownership was derived

---

6 The MacDonnell Collection in the Bodleian Library, Oxford, gives some impression of the situation among officials; see his letters to his wife, 'Sunday evening' and 28 August 1885, Mss. Eng. hist. d. 215, and his other correspondence, ibid., d. 235 *passim*; and Finucane's memorandum on the 1906 Amendment Act, ibid., c. 368. See also C.D. Field, *A Digest of the Law of Landlord and Tenant in the Provinces subject to the Lieutenant Governor of Bengal*, Calcutta, 1879. Other useful sources drawn on for this essay show the practice of the courts on land and tenancy questions: M. Finucane and B.F. Rampini, *The Bengal Tenancy Act being Act VIII of 1885*, Calcutta, 1886, and M. Finucane and Syed Ameer Ali, *A Commentary on the Bengal Tenancy Act (Act VIII of 1885)*, second edition, edited by J. Byrne, Calcutta, [1911].

7 Government of Bengal to Government of India, Revenue and Agriculture Department, 27 July 1881, in *Report of the Government of Bengal*. The notion can be traced back to the early nineteenth century.

from sovereignty and in the other sovereignty was derived from ownership. Both of these were thought indivisible.

In India, as the British seemed unable to find individual ownership, they concluded that the state owned the land and granted subordinate rights in it. This seemed to them a primitive state of affairs, one which the British nation had eschewed with great consequences for economic and social progress. They resolved therefore to do away with it in Bengal. They offered absolute rights in landed property, subject only to the payment of revenue, and sought to strengthen or create an aristocracy on what they thought the model of a well-regulated society. It is true that they intended an autocratic government for Bengal and therefore held on to the state's claim to original ownership and rights over surplus that justified land revenue demands. They also proposed that land law should be universal and that administration, though minimal, should be general and bureaucratic. Hence landlords could not be admitted to be ruling over little fiefdoms. But it did not occur to them to reserve some original property to the raiyats; they merely asked that the terms of voluntary alienations, contracts and leases should be equitable and certain, by agreement between the parties, so as not to disturb the peace or jeopardize the revenue. The state's renunciation of its own land rights was to set an example for moderate behaviour by the landlords.

By contrast, the radicals in the 1880s, while conceding that the rights of zamindars could not be confiscated, argued that it was the duty of the state to intervene to restore some of the position of the resident cultivators. On rent, therefore, they preferred Jones to Malthus or Ricardo. In seeking a theoretical basis for rates, they rejected the role of the market and of competition on better soils and instead argued for political intervention to fix levels that would secure a sufficiency of income to the tenants. Rent was not the necessary expression of factors creating a 'net product'; it was a variable traced originally to the power of the state. In the past, this power had regulated rents through fixing a 'pargana rate'; it was the inadvertent abandonment of this practice that had so impoverished the tenants and enriched the rentier class. The outcome included famine, subinfeudation, and political unrest. The role of the state had therefore to be reasserted. Here was a view of public policy whereby the government was required to arbitrate between the naturally selfish interests of its subjects. It contrasted with views of the state that expected it merely to provide conditions in which the beneficial influence of social and economic processes could flow.

The reformers adhered, in short, to general theories, many of which are still influential. But first and last, they clung to the 'magic' of property, the belief that ownership was a necessary engine of economic advance. They clung to it while arguing that the landlords of Bengal had failed to create prosperity.

They insisted that the ideal was for the owner and the producer to be combined. The landlord was a parasite, neither placed nor concerned to increase production. How unlike the peasant proprietor! He was the indigenous figure in the Indian landscape and his selfishness could be harnessed to the development of the economy, thus combining social harmony with prosperity. If he in turn should grow rapacious, as the reformers suggested at one awkward moment in their proposals (to a chorus of derision from their critics), then the government could intervene again and redress the balance. By such nimble footwork, a path was struck for an interventionist policy through the prevailing thicket of laissez-faire.

The ambivalence of these ideas contributed to some of what are now regarded as failures in the 1885 Act. The pro-raiyat school in Bengal was selective in its radicalism. It was inventive when it came to reinterpreting agrarian relations in the eighteenth century, but not when defining the nature of the property that was to be provided for the tenants. The intention, of course, was to give rights of occupancy to the vast majority of raiyats. But this property was not to be any inalienable good nor a right inherent in the cultivation of land. Such proposals foundered on the twin rocks of practical politics and incomplete theory. This property was to be an exclusive personal possession in precisely the sense in which the courts had hitherto usually supposed the landlord's estate to be. It was to be bought and sold because property, it was assumed, had to have value and marketability. In his digest, Field had accepted that 'alienability was not an ordinary incident of landed property in its early state', but had also argued that the tendency of development in any society was towards that end. Accordingly, the government, in supporting early drafts of the 1885 Act, set about investigations purporting to prove that the raiyats' holdings were in practice readily transferred throughout the Presidency, if only at the behest of landlords who sought to oust a defaulting tenant.[8] It was held to be wrong, therefore, to restrict transfer; it had already appeared in the natural course and in advance of any legislative interference.

Opponents retorted that transfer was mostly very uncommon, and certainly did not take place without the landlord's consent. To introduce it by legislation would thus be 'mischievous'. A little later, the desire to restrict land transfer would seem to be a fixture of the pro-peasant school of thought, part of an inheritance taken up chiefly by Denzil Ibbetson and to be found in published treatises on Indian law from at least as early as that of Raymond West in 1873. But in fact it was not essential. Both sides of the argument on transfer were adherents of the evolutionary ideas which Maine had expressed and both paid at least lip service to the ideal of appropriate rather than universal legislation.

8 Ibid.

It has been suggested that the consequence of allowing occupancy holdings to be bought and sold was to sever ownership from production once more, creating petty landlords who oppressed an ever more impoverished labouring class.[9] Just such an outcome was predicted by opponents of the 1885 Act and admitted by some of its defenders as early as the 1890s. Yet Eden's government in 1881 had aimed not only to 'encourage the growth of a substantial cultivating class', but also to 'discourage the conversion of men originally cultivators into mere middlemen, or speculators of rent'.[10] Here again evolutionary theory stood in the way. Eden's government went on to admit the impossibility of 'changing the face of the country by statute'. Rather (they thought) it would change by natural processes, as it had already from a community of subsistence peasants to a society marked by various classes and occupations. Thus social differentiation, like markets, resulted from change over time. It was the product of innovation and not part of the original fabric. And most of the change, according to the majority of such interpretations, was comparatively recent, resulting from Western government and influence. The objection, too, was not to the process itself, which was thought inevitable and (often enough) 'civilizing', but to distortions that had been introduced within it, sometimes by errors of British government. In the present case, for example, subletting would be objectionable, though impossible to avoid entirely; but transfer of land between occupancy raiyats would be welcomed as a sign of progress. It would create a class of well-to-do cultivators with larger-than-average holdings.

Legislation is bound to assume or seek to impose uniformity, a tendency extended when administration and courts are systems of record and precedent. With regard to landed property, the laws (including those from before British rule) represented progressive standardizations. The Permanent Settlement standardized the status of proprietors, especially when read with the enforcement of an initially high revenue demand and the analytical predilections of the courts. In Act X of 1859, the British believed they were resolving a conflict between proprietors and tenants and were codifying a wider range of relations in land. (At first, the courts, on assumptions that they assumed to be universal, still opined that all rights in land derived from its exclusive owner, the landlord.) In 1885, the attempt was no less than the regulation of an entire society. Four main categories were defined (proprietors,

---

9 For a recent statement of this view, see Asok Sen, Partha Chatterjee, and Saugata Mukherji, *Perspectives in Social Sciences 2: Three Studies on the Agrarian Structure in Bengal 1850–1947*, Calcutta, 1982. See also B.B. Chaudhuri, 'The Process of Depeasantisation in Bengal and Bihar 1885–1947', *Indian Historical Review*, 2(1), 1975, pp. 105–65.

10 See note 7.

intermediate rent-receivers, raiyats, and under-raiyats) and their characteristics and privileges set out.

Some aspects were left to 'custom' in 1885, but custom was assumed to be definite in nature and extent, so as to be susceptible to findings of fact in a court of law. Thus even when professing their sensitivity to Indian realities, the British were proposing general rules based on assumptions of uniformity. Indeed, they assumed that custom itself was a generalizing force. Of course they often appreciated the complexities and deployed them in argument; but they could not entertain them in policy overall, lest they preclude the making of laws. In the 1880s, for example, the Commissioner of Patna Division complained of draft proposals for setting out fair rents and in particular to the drawing up of tables of rates. 'These sections,' he complained, 'contain a Procrustian scheme of enforcing uniformity in matters in which, from the nature of things, no uniformity exists. The rates in a village are about as numerous as the fields of the ryots, and cannot be classified without an arbitrary disregard of actual facts.' The same Commissioner, however, supported the legal categorization of occupancy raiyats as well as most of the incidents of this status that the legislation proposed.[11] In short, where the British admitted diversity, they tried to manage it and present it as comprising definite sets of categories.

The categories were not, as is sometimes assumed, mere reflections of reality. They resulted from theory and discrimination. Even within the 1885 Act itself, it is possible to discern alternatives. It contains an imperfectly resolved contradiction between the four major headings and a distinction made between rent-payers of all kinds and rent-receivers (called 'landlords' in the Act whatever their legal status). Compared with the writings of the pro-raiyat group as a whole, the chosen terminology was notable for having obscured the original concern with the 'actual cultivator', code in this context for the peasant proprietor, as opposed to non-cultivating owners or landless cultivators.

Hence legislation occurred under the influence of ideas whose limitations it reproduced. Here we approach the nub of the question of law and society. Particular distortions can be traced to social theories and views of India that made up the mentality of the officials, whether large ideas with a wide currency or specific interpretations with a restricted appeal. Two of the larger ideas may be discerned in the examples already discussed. They are the alleged

11 The Commissioner (F.W. Halliday) was reporting the views of Collectors after a conference in July 1883. The remarks were later taken up by pro-landlord interests; see J. Dacosta, 'Remarks and Extracts from Official Reports on the Bengal Tenancy Bill', London, 1884. See also H.J. Reynolds, 'Memorandum on the Rent Bill', 18 May 1881, in *Report of the Government of Bengal*.

immobility and lack of social differentiation in rural India in pre-British times and the subsequent evolution towards dynamism and stratification. In the rent-law debates, these ideas clearly contributed to the notion of a uniform peasantry. The term used was 'resident raiyat'. We can now see that this notion was defective. It tried to describe conditions on the basis of speculation about the origins of property rights. There *was* a recognized eighteenth-century category of villagers with security of tenure, or rather an obligation to remain in the village. But this category was not eroded during the nineteenth century to be replaced by an unprecedented free-for-all. On the one hand, the status of permanent resident remained a powerful idea. In the 1880s, one of the arguments against expecting competitive rents was that on the whole men did not go about looking for holdings and that rents reflected very local demand for land.[12] On the other hand, landed interests had been complex long before the British appeared. They were influenced not only by customary expectations but also by ideological inputs and by commercial and political forces. There is abundant evidence that in the eighteenth century some people moved in order to sell their labour and to take up holdings as non-residents. The very concept of a non-resident cultivator implies this.[13] Clearly raiyats could compete, and even residence was an advantage of shifting import. If there were changes in these respects during the nineteenth century, they were a matter of degree and not of kind.

The assumption that there was a single category of peasant and that its natural state was one of stability helps explain the failure of the reformers in the 1880s to inquire more fully into the identity of the 'bona fide cultivator' who was to be protected. Implicitly, they relied on an ideal definition whereby those who collected rent could be wholly distinguished from those who cultivated using their own labour. Against all such standardization, we must place the multiplicity of relations on the land. By British accounts, someone who employed labour was an anomaly. This was admitted but not faced. Also anomalous was someone who sub-let part of his holding and cultivated another part. Accordingly, after 1885, officials uncovered hundreds of different types of relations and rights that they had to squeeze into the categories provided in the Tenancy Act. Not only were there rights that did not fit in; there were individuals who performed in several roles at the same time. Indigenous categories existed and they were legion, local, and subject to change.

12 This view was put forward by J. Phear in the Great Rent Case, Thakurani Dassee *v.* Bisheshur Mookerjee, Bengal Law Reports (BLR), Full Bench (FB), 326, June 1865, and adopted by the Government of Bengal in 1881 (see above, note 7).

13 For a discussion of the earlier period, see Aditee Nag Chowdhury-Zilly, *The Vagrant Peasant: Agrarian Distress and Desertion in Bengal 1770 to 1830*, Wiesbaden, 1982.

Obviously, one effect of the assumptions was to suppress the implications of evidence that was known to all. Indeed, this included information that provided part of the impulse for the 1885 Act. Thus, in 1878, the Collector of Patna wrote of visiting the houses of petty traders and cultivators—Telis, Banias, Gowallas (Ahirs), and Halwais—and seeing the manner in which they lived. He would not have believed their abject poverty, he said, if he had not witnessed it for himself. In Bihar, he argued, the specific problem was low wages; the general one was that the region was too poor to buy up its own harvests. Many of the cultivators farmed only two or three bighas (an acre or less) and 10 to 15 per cent of the population were landless labourers who were barely kept alive by those who held 10 or more bighas and wanted their labour.[14]

About the same time Antony MacDonnell attributed famine, more succinctly, to the 'inequitable distribution of the produce of the soil'.[15] Yet these conclusions were lost sight of in the more generalized assertions about oppressed raiyats and rapacious landlords. It was assumed in effect (even by MacDonnell) that he meant that zamindars were taking too much from tenants generally, rather than that various groups towards the bottom of society had too little to live on or were vulnerable to downturns in economic conditions. Explanations were sought in effects that might be supposed to impinge broadly (and that also relied on general theories): such factors as a rising population or the rapaciousness of the *mahajan*s.

It follows that law affected agrarian relations as a generalizing tendency in a situation of diversity. It has increasingly been recognized, but not yet much reflected in interpretations of revenue and tenancy law, that differentiation was the starting point and not the end product of the changes under British rule. Thus, to return to an example mentioned at the outset, the partition of estates indicated the impact of regulations favouring individual property rights, but it also occurred more in some places than in others and meant different things in different places.

In general, a proprietor was now being secured in his position by the state, substituting for the weight of the clan. With rising agricultural returns, it was inevitable that advantage would be taken of the mechanism provided in the revenue law to separate individual shares from collective property. There was a general incentive apparently in the economic advantages of undivided management and of recording an enhanced rent roll during the pre-partition

14 Patna Resolution for 1878–9, quoted in Mackenzie, 'Memorandum'.
15 MacDonnell's views arose out his work in famine relief as a district officer in Bihar and in preparing his Report on the Foodgrains Supply, Calcutta, 1876. This particular remark was quoted by Sir R. Temple in 1874–5 and again in Mackenzie, 'Memorandum'.

survey and settlement. But the consequences were not general at all. The incidence of partition was far greater in Bihar than elsewhere and was highest of all in some parts in north of the Ganges. In much of north Bihar, it was appropriate or necessary to slice up dominant and proprietorial interests vertically. In Bengal proper and also where there were very large estates in Bihar, such interests were more likely to be divided horizontally. In both cases, then, the resulting society was a mix of pre-existing conditions or long-term trends and the changing pressures of and chances under British rule.

Society and Trade

We have to examine the society in order to understand the impact of law on it. We will now consider some features of village conditions in Bihar, first as bearing on their diversity and then as defining the involvement of the locality with the wider world. To do this is to set the generalizing impulses of law against the relativity of actual institutions. It is also to qualify some descriptions and interpretations that still reflect the old British attitudes of the nineteenth century. Two opposing typologies are familiar in the current literature: of the village as self-sufficient, *sui generis*, and more or less independent, and of the village as a replication in miniature of the larger society to which it belongs. The failure to unravel this contradiction or to shed the assumptions on which the alternatives rely continues to bedevil many general interpretations of change and continuity in the Indian context. Nineteenth-century Bihar included places that were both distinct from and connected with their surroundings. By resolving this paradox, we come closer to understanding the limits and potential of the influence of law and British rule and also incidentally of other forces, such as international trade.[16]

We can identify four main features of the society. First come complexities of status. In land one found multiple and indefinite roles, and rights conditional upon those of others. There were variations in rent according to the tenant and not just the land, that is, by caste as well as by soil. There might be distinctions between actual and ritual employment. Agricultural practice varied in response to climate and conditions both from place to place and from time to time. Generally, contrary to what would be expected if villages were either homogeneous or wholly subordinate and hence levelled down,

[16] The information in the following paragraphs is not intended to be new or contentious, though an attempt is made at re-interpretation. Illustrations of readily available data may be found in the appropriate district gazetteers and settlement reports for Champaran, Darbhanga, Muzaffarpur, Saran, Shahabad, Patna, and Gaya; in the volumes covering these areas in W.W. Hunter, *A Statistical Account of Bengal*, Calcutta, 1876 etc.; and in the report and evidence volumes of the Bihar and Orissa Provincial Banking Enquiry Committee, Patna, 1930. Statistics may also be found in the Bengal Land Revenue Administration Reports, Calcutta, from 1847.

the differences could be minute; they could also be perpetuated and rationalized.

Nonetheless, a result in economic as in social behaviour was a higher degree of pragmatism, an adjustment to circumstances very unlike what was encoded in British laws with their insistence upon abstract, absolute principle and certainty. Of course, variations and ambiguities imply integration and interdependence, as anthropologists have shown. Each status was particular but described in comparative terms, for what was intrinsic to one was extrinsic to others, as for example, Brahmans implied non-Brahmans and castes implied outcastes. Together, they constituted a whole.

Then, too, production depended upon a division of labour that offered protection at the expense of 'efficiency'. Some high castes in north Bihar, for example, sold their standing tobacco crops to Koiris in order to avoid the effort and the social stigma of harvesting and preparation, at the cost of some redistribution of profit. Many occupations—the multitude of agents and brokers, for example, or some specialists such as ploughmen—seemed to exist mainly in order to delineate more exactly the status of the principals (their employers: the rulers, landowners, or merchants) and to incorporate at the same time a range of people who were seen to be otherwise distinct. If a high-caste member employed labourers or refrained from marketing produce, he was at once separating himself out from the mass and sharing himself with it. He was also merging aspects of his activities by combining social and economic relationships. He was expressing his involvement in the whole while asserting his separate identity.

The village was not one corporate unit of production; it was many that performed cooperatively. Moreover, the most common relationships were of dominance and dependence, concepts repeated endlessly in the state, the region, the village, the family, even with reference to the human body. In the village, the existence of difference also necessarily implied that poorer families worked for richer: notably (though this was not an invariable or solitary instance) the socially inferior for the ritually pure. The theory might propose that each person served the whole according to his dharma. The practice was that resources such as water or land were distributed by those who were locally powerful (admittedly within differing limits imposed by custom or, latterly by law) and usually in alliance with some outside authority (a clan or state) capable of influence over wider areas. Such was the case with the *pyne* and *ahara* irrigation systems (these were channels and reservoirs depending on temporary embankments and dams) of south Bihar.[17]

17 Information on this is summarized in Nirmal Sengupta, 'The Indigenous Irrigation Organization in South Bihar', *Indian Economic and Social History Review*, 17(2), 1980.

But the differentiation should not be thought of as originating from outside; it was apparent in the very ecology of the village. Nor in itself should it be related to a particular type of trading relationship or external control. Where division of labour occurs without the stimulus of specific technology, it is hardly surprising that it should express internal political factors. Nor is it surprising that locally generated difference should result in a system that was dispersed, risk-averting, redistributive, and incorporating. It is tempting to attribute it in Bihar to a rich but not entirely secure agriculture in conditions of dense population. It would also accommodate underemployment, arguably necessary where the pattern of agricultural work was at the mercy of the climate.

A third feature was the insulation of the locality from the outside world. This was not at all because, as used to be thought, the village was disconnected from its surroundings. It was because of the nature of its involvement. Some particular features follow from what has been said of internal characteristics. One is that outsiders were also susceptible to the mode of social and economic relations and, whatever their wider horizons, tended to approach the village or be perceived by it on the village's terms. Studies increasingly throw up this element, discrediting the static and autochthonous model of village society. But just as we need to abandon yet more of the old assumptions, so also we need to place the new findings carefully in context. The key is that consistently and over time, in different conditions, we find that, mediating between the village and regional elites who wanted to extract surplus, there stood the villages' own leaders and specialists—in Bihar, the maliks, *jeth-raiyat*s and *patwari*s (landowners, headmen, and accountants)—whose importance lay partly in this role interposed between village and region. Caste itself was an expression and a vehicle of such exchanges, each jati being a regulator of behaviour in the village and of outside relations through kinship and marriage. Superior castes, too, acted for and gained from associating with the great caste lords who dominated regional social life, as also from echoes of the Brahmanical tradition that were incorporated in village mores.

Perhaps most importantly, we find that intermediaries were as characteristic as 'big men' and dependents. In almost any transaction, they institutionalized the distance between parties. Of course the bulk of exchanges, as I have said, occurred between dominant and subordinate people. Village controllers could also corner the marketing of village produce. But if we consider the trading case further, we find how complex were the roles played by a wide range of intermediaries, and also once again that many of the features observable in the late nineteenth century were in long-term existence and were not innovations resulting from British rule and commercialization as is sometimes suggested. A funnelling of trade at the village level, for example, was to be expected whenever crops were bought separately, where most individual farmers had a various and small output. But why should there also have been networks of brokers who conducted transactions in bulk? Some produce intended for export ended up with a very few European agents and this was no doubt instrumental in the shaping of the 'colonial' economy. But every item of trade, like each stage in production, was capable of passing through hand after hand. Over the whole range of local trade, the overwhelming impression is of decentralization and of a multiplicity of different roles, each slightly differentiated in function. Similar roles were pervasive in other arenas too. Zamindars were ready to farm out the management of their rents, not least to indigo factories ready to pay highly for thikadari leases over villages whose production they wished to control. But far from applying a direct, centralized command over labour, the factories depended (as arguably the cultivators did also) upon a dispersed management by *amla*s (factory agents) and jeth-raiyats. (We may note that British officials who found the factories oppressive also thought they conformed to a 'traditional' Indian pattern.) Opium growers, too, were organized through *lambardar*s, who provided them with advances paid to them by agents of the Opium Department; the same lambardars arranged the final payments to cultivators after the crop had been delivered.

The chains of credit and marketing have yet to be fully researched. Some accounts have it that they depended upon external finance generated by international or at least long-distance trade; others that they were more or less sealed local systems based upon rural moneylending. Clearly they were used as much for new crops and by European agency as for established production, and may be assumed always to have had external input: in the past, for example, through the involvement of bankers and rural elites with revenue farming and the encouragement of cash crops. But just as obviously, they were altogether too important for local and inter-regional trade not to have had a large component of local capital, meaning, in the case of Bihar in the late nineteenth century, rice and seed as well as coin. It is best to see the system as an extension or another dimension of the relationships of credit and obligation within the village between those with stores of wealth and those who were semi-independent (or subject) producers and labourers. It was a system maintained in (not created by) a time when production for the market, the range of crops, and the speed of transport were all enhanced. Crucial was its ubiquity.

A cultural influence (or rationalization) seems to have been at work, perhaps a suspicion of transactions between equals in conditions of reciprocity. It has been supposed that an important strand of thought in South Asia has regarded the gift as superior to the exchange, the former gaining as an expression of duty.[18] Some of this seems to have had a resonance in Bihar, as in all the many

18 This suggestion was encouraged by a paper on Mauss *The Gift* given by T. Trautman at the School of Oriental and African Studies on 8 November 1985.

areas where comparable systems are found. Fictions appeared to be generated to disguise the mutuality of obligations. There was, for example, a notional separation of supply and payment, as in the harvest shares of village servants, in the advances paid to cultivators, or the intercession of agents at markets. Payment was separated from supply if village controllers fed labourers in famines when there was no work, or if it was suggested that there was no absolute requirement for a cultivator to sell his crop to the same broker who had advanced him the means to produce it, or if people incurred debt without expecting that repayment must inevitably follow. There is evidence of all these.[19] Perhaps it was separated, too, in the vagueness many tenants were alleged to display about rents, as if the possession of the land did not relate directly to the payment, and as if both were owed independently (a matter of status, duties, or rights). The usual explanation was that there were real variations in effective rent demands; but this seems rather to reinforce the suggestion than to contradict it. The variations were not solely related to land or production; even occasional remissions seemed to express a social obligation, as indeed the British argued when urging great zamindars to leniency. Behind rent lay rule.

The linkages between the village and its region were a species of the distancing that occurred in transactions in general. It occurred over space, as goods moved from hand to hand, and over time, because of the customs governing advances or services. It occurred, that is, both within and across the exchange systems: within them by separating payment from supply and across them by interpolating intermediaries. This amounted perhaps to an imperfect concept of value. It did not prevent purely economic relations including the sale of land, but it discouraged some transactions and clothed others in a tactful ambiguity. Nor was it a factor of monetization as such, though many transactions in Bihar were not, perhaps even had ceased to be, monetized at the end of the century. It was a factor of the way money was used or exchange carried out. (Is the poor cultivator participating in a money economy when he buys salt or millets at the local market? He is using up coins just received at a price from a broker in return for a bowlful of rice, which could itself have been obtained from the zamindar in return for work. This is an economy in which for some the value of money is notional, immediate, and local, as indeed was suggested more generally in the variations in the

---

19 Proceedings of the Government of India, Revenue and Agriculture Department, Agric., B 52–3, June 1895, National Archives of India. The tendency was for land rights to be regarded as surety for indefinite credit. This encouraged rather than prevented any tendency for land transfer. Land acquisition might in turn commend itself to richer cultivators, even on apparently uneconomic terms, as a convenient and safe outlet for money.

purchasing power of the rupee and the lack of integration shown even between larger markets in Bihar. The increasing use of smaller coins may tell us about transactions at higher levels and not prove the market was integrated overall.)

The final point arises from the other three, that the existing structures were devices of control as well as of redistribution and insulation. Thus was Bihar able to accommodate change; thus, too, was the course of change decided. With caste, the element of control is obvious, as it is with rent and land rights. But marketing also had a tendency to monopoly and command. The tactic was to capture the producer rather than to compete for his production. The same strategy existed for labour. Loans and indirect systems of exchange were the main economic weapons. An advance to a cultivator was an attempt to commit him to a particular intermediary and often a particular crop, playing on his need for credit between harvests. This system of advance payments has been noticed in many places. It is sometimes treated as if it were 'proto-industrial', or at least associated with some economic 'stage' or 'level'. But in Bihar, it was evidently of a type with many other kinds of credit relation. There were longer-term agreements guaranteed by formal loans and mortgages. These, too, could provide levers for social and trading influence. There were usufructuary mortgages, in which even greater control was achieved by taking over the rent collection from holdings or villages.

Except for reasons of social prestige, moneylenders proper were not generally interested in a complete control over land. If they had to foreclose on a holding, they often kept on the former tenant to work it; and even this overcommitted their capital to the fortunes of a particular place. Yet it is obvious that many moneylenders of all kinds were chiefly concerned to control crops. This was most obvious where would-be intermediaries lent to zamindars at a loss in order to gain long usufructuary leases. We have already noted that indigo planters did so to ensure supply of indigo at monopoly prices. In the 1890s, along with north Bihari zamindars, they were vociferous in seeking to obstruct the maintenance of a public record of land rights and to prevent the free transfer of raiyati holdings. The reason, as many officials noted at the time, was their wish to exercise control over cultivation. Parallel to this was a persistent wish to command labour even outside agriculture. Thus, later, this demand led coal mines in south Bihar to buy up bankrupt villages.[20]

The pressures on the cultivators were surely growing as the likely rewards increased, but the pattern seems an old one, namely that debt was a major instrument of coercion. Sometimes it was part of a broader tenurial relationship, the debt being in the form of rent arrears, real or contrived. Most

20 The land records issue was extensively discussed by MacDonnell (see above, note 6). On coal mines, see D. Rothermund and D.C. Wadha, *Zamindars, Mines and Peasants*, New Delhi, 1978, for example p. 8.

of all, the cultivator borrowed for food and production costs within a single harvest. After a harvest failure had prevented repayment or on the occasion of social expenditure, he might enter into a formal loan. For many families, therefore, debt was not an aspect of involvement in the money economy, which assisted but was not essential to the system. For many, debt was merely a version of other systems of control to which it was closely allied.

One consequence was a restriction of direct involvement in the market. Of course the subordinated producer secured some advantages from his capture because (following the familiar 'feudal' explanations) he found the means to meet immediate liabilities, a possible hedge against risk, and a single known tyranny rather than multiple depredations. But the result was neither market exclusion (subsistence strategies) nor market orientation (maximizing strategies). It was market asymmetry, in which the goal of the producer was sufficiency, the minimum required to meet the demands of others, but the controller's and the merchant's interests were commercial. The latter's demands (among others) could redefine the minimum without taking into account the needs of the producer.

Hence new crops and so-called commercialization did not necessarily open up wider market involvement for the majority. The growers could be confined to a relation with a specialist broker or a village controller, often (as with indigo) in conditions of exploitation. Some, such as the lower castes who grew the opium poppy, were doubly insulated: that is, by social as well as economic subservience. But advance-payments were not a qualification of a system that was otherwise increasingly 'commercial' according to some abstract notion; rather, they typified the system as it existed. By the same token, the normal manner of economic relations was indicated, and it was not a shortfall from some marketing ideal when in the late nineteenth century an agricultural labourer's wages (however calculated) were often not paid in cash and when the major local trade, in rice, was still conducted largely in kind.

What can be said of trade may be applied, *pari passu*, to social institutions. Hence a second consequence of the emphasis upon control was that features of society were reinforced rather than undermined by increasing trade and improved communications. This is not to say that change had to occur within existing structures or that institutions necessarily resisted change. It is to explain why state and economic inputs seemed to leave methods of production and patterns of social dominance little altered, when we are used to assuming that the quantity of exchange had implications for its form and social impact, and that the extent of governmental interference will determine its manner and influence.

In the past there have been essentially two explanations, both of them really re-statements of the problem. One claims that the inputs were not, after all, very great. The 1885 Tenancy Act, for example, has been taken to show that the government did not have the capacity to protect interests other than those of the zamindars. It is noted, too, that prevailing poverty meant that few consumed the new imports, while crops for the export trade continued to occupy relatively small proportions of the land. In Bihar, as said, rice remained the principal crop entering trade for cash as well as consumption, except in hard times when it might be replaced by lesser grains (which fed the poor even in good seasons). Rice merchants were the main lenders of seed and money in 1900 as they had been in 1800; in the villages, rice remained a major store of wealth whereby elites controlled and rewarded subordinates. Such minimalism is a useful corrective to earlier assumptions about nineteenth-century change, and may well help to explain the limited extent of change in Bihar or form the basis of comparisons with other parts of India. Yet it would be quite disproportionate to pretend that laws and communications were not greatly changed during the nineteenth century even in Bihar. In such circumstances, we still need a substantive explanation for the marked continuities in social and economic life.

The second explanation represents these features as a new trend. Now British rule and an unequal international trade are once again thought to be extremely influential. They distorted the society. British laws produced ill effects by stratifying the people; the 1885 Tenancy Act was an attempt to redress the balance, but it failed. The result of foreign trade was 'de-industrialization', meaning a decline in the proportion of the population engaged in secondary industry. The implicit expectation in any such interpretations as applied to Bihar is that the region had certain features that were at risk from international trade and Western government. At root, even while a more 'industrialized' past is proclaimed, it is being assumed that Bihar was inward-looking and self-contained.[21] The chief problems with this transformation model are, first, its apparent exaggeration of the influence of nineteenth-century state and trade, and secondly, an implicit conflict with much of what is known of pre-colonial Bihar and with recent trends in eighteenth-century studies generally.

It is quite true that a surplus-exporting countryside was typical of largely rural societies under central states. Even in the 1890s, Bihar contained regions— Madhubani is a good example—that exported their surplus without stimulating inward trade. They were unlike other areas, which maintained networks not

---

21 Thus far, the controversy (currently associated mainly with A.K. Bagchi) stretches from Daniel Thorner, 'De-industrialization in India, 1881–1931' in Daniel and Alice Thorner, *Land and Labour in India*, Bombay, 1962, to J. Krishnamurty, 'Deindustrialisation in Gangetic Bihar during the Nineteenth Century: Another Look at the Evidence', *Indian Economic and Social History Review*, 22(4), 1985.

only to extract but to import commodities. But it is a mistake to regard Madhubani therefore as a fossil, revealing the nature of the pre-colonial economy. There was not a necessary progression from 'closed' to 'open' societies, from total isolation to tribute-paying to market integration. The condition of a particular region in this regard depended upon a range of circumstances that could be patchy or spasmodic: political stability and ease of communications were probably the most important. In Bihar, north of the Ganges even more than to the south, political and economic power seems to have been notably decentralized even at the height of Mughal dominion, implying a countryside that contained consumers as well as producers for items of trade. Conversely, under British rule, production for long-distance trade remained *as an activity* in many senses peripheral for the bulk of the population, whatever its importance in relations with those who commanded the society.

Clearly, without challenging the elaborations of some theoretical studies, a very general distinction may be made. On one hand, there were decentralized elites based upon place, that is, on localized command and extraction of surplus. On the other hand, there were elites, either concentrated in cities or dispersed as magnates and officials, who were dependent upon extra-local authority and networks, that is, exchange. In practice, however, both these forms of control would be found in combination, with the proportions of each varying, perhaps even cyclically. Indeed, in a sense, they are distinctions not of type but of the unit of analysis, a measure of the relative extensiveness of command and exchange systems. This is because there is no absolute dichotomy in terms of surplus extraction between, say, an ascetic religious foundation supported by donations (which the value system enforced) and an elaborate temple complex depending upon land control; nor, for that matter, between an official supported directly by a land grant and one dependent upon a state salary. The inevitable dependence of consumers upon producers, and their dominance over them, imply that no elite could be set apart from the society. The more successful the elite was, the more involved it would be institutionally and politically.

Hence the persistent features that we have been discussing—we may call them flexibility, specialization, and competition. It is flexibility that partly undermines the 'deindustrialization' thesis, not because there were no changes in occupational structure under British rule but because production and division of labour worked less rigidly than the thesis requires. It was not new that artisans should cultivate on small patches of land or that patterns of production should reflect a fluctuating demand. It was not new either that agriculturists should process some of their crops. (That partial 'industrialization' *increased* in the nineteenth century with the expansion of sugar, tobacco, and opium.) Such flexibility rested ultimately on the variety of the seasons and the range of cultivating possibilities.

For the same reason, some specialization expressed in varying concentrations of production was probably as old as agriculture itself, if only in what was demanded by the environment and the distinction between wet and dry crops. In Bihar, by the late nineteenth century, there were occupational clusters of weavers and oil-pressers; there was localized production of hides, timber, and saltpetre with castes to match; there were Rajputs, Bhumihars, and Brahmans whose distribution was equally occupational in part. These were not sudden distortions introduced by the colonial economy; they were long-term and evolving differences. It follows that exchange was always needed: not only to make payments of tribute but to transfer commodities and skills at all levels of society. In the 1880s, we find an area such as Tajpur in north Bihar growing wheat in exchange for rice, using an ecological aptitude to meet a regional demand. But the networks thus implied must have been of great antiquity, as witnessed by the cities and great monasteries of ancient times.

And finally, to varying degrees, all production was competitive. One cash crop competed with another and with the staple, rice. A cultivator had to meet his rent and was disposed therefore to grow crops for sale on his best and most secure land. But dealers had also to stimulate production if, for example, they wanted to introduce opium, indigo, or sugar. The marketing system was neither incompatible with nor introduced by the late nineteenth-century economy. But it may well have evolved to encourage production for sale by those with a preference for subsistence.

Of course the argument that India had a long experience of both trade and state interference is hardly controversial; several aspects of the late nineteenth century as discussed here are also generally agreed. But the contention is that common ground between 'ancient' and 'modern' societies has tended to be overlooked while interpreting the period of British rule in India: in particular, despite short- and long-term cycles and secular trends, the importance of an *underlying continuum* in the modes and role of exchange, including long-distance trade. Thus the nature of rural society in nineteenth-century Bihar does not need to be explained either as a lack of change or as a transformation. Rather it is possible to see an intensification of existing conditions. As the range of potential crops widened and the rewards for selling them increased, how much more incentive there was to elaborate upon the marketing system! Thus an inherent flexibility paradoxically enhanced monopolies and an expansion of opportunity narrowed most people's options. Nineteenth-century trade built upon the foundations of an ancient exchange system and a long experience of cash cropping.

In social relations too, old dominance could continually re-form and find strength in some of the expanding economic activity. More particularly, the intrusion of state-based order also reinforced existing political linkages. The British state, like its predecessors, helped the extraction of surplus. It added its coercive powers and enforcement of public order to existing means of social control. Changes in an alternative direction, being insufficient for revolutionizing society, instead increased the need to maintain the existing institutions. Castes specialized in ways that reduced options for others; every village contained people who controlled or mediated in trade; even labour migration was focused on particular places, through agents, often building on situations in which family economies were already dependent on remittances.[22]

These descriptions are not intended as a way of minimizing change; they provide a means of describing it. They explain much that is otherwise puzzling about nineteenth-century Bihar. In particular, the example of trade provides a useful analogy if we are seeking to assess the impact of law. The Tenancy Acts too were no unprecedented imposition upon a region with no experience of state power; they were an enhancement of an influence long weakly felt and readily accommodated. More important still, law did not work in isolation. The existing society reflected economic and political forces in tandem; also, insofar as the 1885 Act influenced the local disposition of power and wealth, it did so in harness with the influence of economic change. In short, the conclusion is that law, like trade, worked upon a complex society, one that was already differentiated. Thus we pinpoint the means and the limits of change. The point is independent of whether we believe that the period saw unprecedented pressures or that their strength has been exaggerated. When the 1885 Act insisted, for example, on the category of occupancy raiyat, it did so on the assumption that there was no important difference between resident villagers. The outcome was enhanced security and certainty for the majority recognized as 'settled' raiyats, who had hitherto enjoyed continuity of residence and landholding de facto rather than de jure; but the outcome was also increased advantages for a minority among this number who were already privileged and strategically placed. The people

---

[22] The producers' options could increase by this argument, but not in proportion to improvements in communications and marketing. Hence specializations could become exaggerated for areas and people, just as records and communications have been said to make social and religious behaviour more, rather than less, 'orthodox'. On the other hand, the importance of particular resources or advantages could wax or wane over time—as discussed in Chapter 6—so that of course any dominant interest *could* lose out as circumstances changed. A possible decline in the rent-receiving and revenue-collecting roles is discussed below.

who were helped by expanding trade to capture petty producers in villages were likely to be the same people who could manipulate the opportunities offered by British laws. Indeed, this was all the more likely because of the law's standardizing impulses and its offer of state protection to the few who could seek its support.[23]

Land Law and Economic Change

This essay has tried to set out considerations relevant to an understanding of the impact of law on an agrarian society. For the Bengal Presidency, it was not helpful, we found, to treat the East India Company's rule merely as an *ancien régime* writ large, nor to regard the late nineteenth century simply as a time when landlords' power was enhanced. But Washbrook was surely right to stress continuities from the past as well as the gradualness of changes introduced by law. Indeed, a tendency to read back developments in time and to identify indigenous forces predating British influence distinguishes some of the most interesting of recent scholarship on India, from C.A. Bayly's revised periodization for the North to David Ludden's connected account of the Tamil country from earliest times.[24] In applying these lessons to the nineteenth century, we must of course relate economic changes to underlying trends. Thus we assess the importance of an expansion of cultivation under pressure from high revenue demand or market opportunities, or of an increase in the value of production due to new crops and rising prices. Change could also be effected by a greater certainty in landholding and security of title, following gradually on permanent settlement even if (as Washbrook contends) there was little development of a free land market and a lack of value in land. In Bengal and Bihar, the benefits of certainty extended under the influence of tenancy laws to dominant raiyats. These aspects, too, must be related to their context.

Under changing conditions, individual fortunes depended on opportunities that were in part embedded in the social system. The people who had a chance of advancement were those who had potential independence through a trade or moneylending and those cultivators or even labourers who were free to choose alternative sources of income. Many such people were still very poor,

---

23 See Robb, 'Dominant Peasants'. For an example of continuing zamindari control through intermediaries of a local market and industries, see also Robb, 'Town and Country: Economic Linkages and Political Mobilization in Bihar in the Late Nineteenth and Early Twentieth Centuries' in John L. Hill (ed.), *Debate on the Congress*, London and Wellesley Hills, MA, 1991.

24 C.A. Bayly, *Rulers, Townsmen and Bazaars: North Indian Society in the Age of British Expansion 1770–1870*, Cambridge, 1983, and David Ludden, *Peasant History in South India*, Princeton, 1985.

as the Patna Collector found; but perhaps the period of British rule may be said to have expanded their opportunities. Even in Bihar, there are references to growing wealth among a few of those very Telis, Banias, Halwais (or other artisans and traders) as well as Ahirs (or middling agricultural castes) whose general poverty the Collector noted on his visits. However, British rule did little for those who had no choice but to offer up their crop or their labour to the people to whom they were in thrall. One important reason is that British policy was based on imposed classifications which were seriously flawed. Above all, these had the effect of making poverty invisible in policy terms even while it was being admitted in a host of reports and studies. Indeed, any official who laid too much stress on the horror of rural conditions in Bihar was in danger of being ignored; efforts were made to demonstrate that the population did have enough food on which to live.

There are two explanations for this indifference, which are related to different aspects of our present discussion. One was the continuing British preoccupation with control. The debates of the period were not after all between sympathizers of the rich and supporters of the poor; they were between advocates of alternative modes of social dominance by zamindars or by peasant proprietors. The British had little choice but to acquiesce in local command systems because of their vested interest in 'order'. But secondly, there was also the kind of ideological myopia that allowed officials who were appalled at the condition of the poor to be satisfied with remedies directed towards occupancy raiyats. This mismatch was typical of British categorization. They consistently under-researched economic difference. Above all, when seeking to make more precise distinctions, they fell back upon caste, which certainly may have economic implications but which is not derived from them (at least in theory). Indeed, given that any caste was presumed to have a distinct function and could include a range of wealth, there was a sense in which the concept could mask or even justify the number and condition of the poor.

Does the case of Bihar have any wider significance? The remainder of this essay will consider land law and economic change in general in nineteenth-century India.[25] The choice between rent-receivers or controllers of cultivation

[25] The concluding pages of this essay are, once again, intended to do no more than suggest an interpretation of well-known materials, including those on rent questions from the earliest times gathered during the great rent-law debate. Most of the information may be found in Dharma Kumar (ed.), *The Cambridge Economic History of India*, vol. 2, Cambridge, 1983. Part of this section drawn out similarities in particular between Eric Stokes' contribution on northern India (see ibid., especially pp. 64–5 and 83–6) and my independent conclusions about Bihar. For other regions of India, see also pp. 199–206 and 236–41 of the same volume. Further reference may be made to books listed there on pp. 1035–9 or in Neil Charlesworth, *British Rule and the Indian Economy 1800–1914*, London, 1982. Among more recent studies

was not peculiar to Bihar or the 1885 Act; these were the two main strategies adopted before 1914 to protect and extend British power and revenues. The landlord strategy was expressed in the Permanent Settlement in Bengal, but also in a resurgence of pro-'aristocratic' thinking after the Great Rebellion of 1857. The peasant-proprietary model was associated with temporary or periodic settlements in the Madras and Bombay Presidencies and the northwest, but (as we have seen) also in part with Bengal tenancy laws, which imported it into the landlords' stronghold.

We may draw three conclusions about all these strategies: they changed the pre-existing legal framework; they contravened the complexities of agrarian relations through their uniformity of regulation; and they had some impact on behaviour and expectations, given relatively stable administration especially as the nineteenth century wore on. It mattered that there was, in effect, an imperfection in the official definition of tenancy. We have seen that British laws never contemplated anything less than exclusive property in land (except belatedly to reduce its transferability) and that when they tried to preserve a tenant right, it too was regarded as a kind of real estate. The British idea was that such rights subsumed all other rights. Landownership became *the* resource in terms of the law. Non-proprietors had at best an inferior right. They were tenants by actual or implied contract between the parties. Thus most subordinate land rights were ignored throughout the nineteenth century. In the landlord areas, the cause of the tenants was taken up from time to time under pro-peasant influence, yet (we found) the so-called tenancy legislation was effectively a charter for occupancy rather than a regulation of tenancy. In peasant-proprietary areas, tenants were hardly supposed to exist and were scarcely an issue before the twentieth century. Indeed, if tenancy legislation was intended to produce peasant-proprietors, it is hardly surprising that it was little favoured where they were believed to prevail already.

Certainly the outcome of legislation was progressively to create a legal category of protected tenancies that became, in effect, sub-proprietary. But to argue that imperial rule distorted the society by confiscating the rights of non-proprietors is to suggest that a pre-colonial system with definite features (a moral economy, the village community, and so on) was being superseded by

---

(not already cited above), see in particular Christopher John Baker, *An Indian Rural Economy 1880–1955: The Tamilnad Countryside*, Oxford, 1984; Neil Charlesworth, *Peasants and Imperial Rule: Agriculture and Agrarian Society in the Bombay Presidency, 1880–1935*, Cambridge, 1985; Sirajul Islam, *Bengal Land Tenure: The Origin and Growth of Intermediate Interests in the 19th Century*, Rotterdam, 1985; and K.N. Raj, Neeladri Bhattacharya, Sumit Guha, and Sakhi Padhi (eds), *Essays on the Commercialization of Indian Agriculture*, Delhi, 1985, especially the essays on the Punjab by Neeladri Bhattacharya and Mridula Mukherjee, pp. 51–162.

a new system that really mirrored what was provided by law. We have seen it was only historical interpretations of resident villagers as the original owners of the cultivation that convinced officials that a mass of would-be peasants was held down by zamindars. The 'village republic' was an *idea*. It follows that there could not be a 'natural' and even progression under British rule towards several property and social differentiation. Indeed, even as the doctrine of the village community was being devised, observers recognized an existing stratification. Land, manpower, cattle, water, and other resources were not evenly shared, but distributed according to 'ancestral rights' or by caste and power, which were anyway needed to make rights effective. Rights depended, that is, on economic and political forces as well as on custom and expectations, with the result that they were bound to be distributed differentially.

In general, several distinct and persistent roles can be distinguished. First, there was control over people, land, and other resources, which may be called the primary zamindari or, as in Bihar, the malik role, but which could be played equally by a clan, lineage, or 'brotherhood' as by an individual and his family.

Then there was a separate role of collecting land revenue, at least in Mughal times, that was known as malguzari. The holder is sometimes described as a secondary zamindar because he could operate from an area or regional base. But though malguzari was distinct in law it had at some stage to be combined or allied with the malik role. Just as central rulers, including the British, found it wise to accommodate and partially to incorporate regional magnates and chiefs into their state systems, so those regional powers in turn recruited or were linked with controllers at the village level.

Thirdly, below these superior roles, there was another distinction: between, on the one hand, resident or original, hereditary villagers (the Bengal term was khudkasht raiyats) and on the other hand, non-residents or outsiders (pahikasht raiyats). The difference was expressed in varying ways, but (as we have noted) the khudkasht raiyats were taken to have enhanced responsibility and claims within the village, while pahikasht raiyats included all families (including actual residents) who were not treated as original or full members of the community. It is safe to assume that before state law intervened (mainly under the British) the distinction was definite but not absolute over time.

Finally, though this has been a vexed issue, there were landless labourers. It was misleading of some early accounts to treat village society as comprised only of the landholders large and small. Labourers existed in villages among those with insufficient land as well as those with none: artisans, servants, and field workers. Their existence, as I argue with regard to Bihar, was not merely a factor of the man : land ratio, but attributable to the command system and exigencies of production. However, even these underprivileged people observed minute differences in status.

In considering British impact, the first point is thus pre-colonial stratification. But the second is that the system was far from rigid. Different roles might be played by the same people and might be ambiguous reflectors of relative power and wealth. They could change over time. A village could export people to farm on a pahikasht basis in other villages, or might be taken over by outsiders through fortune, conquest, or even purchase so that one layer of control was imposed on others. Relations and status occurred as a web of customs and obligations seldom exclusive to one kind of transaction.

None of this was quite as things were envisaged in British law. We need almost to reverse the old image of eighteenth-century stagnation and nineteenth-century dynamism, for British regulation—being impersonal—was inimical to diversity and flexibility. In all the revenue settlements, zamindari and malguzari roles were made legally inseparable, whether held by individuals or by groups. As we have noted, sales laws directed against the land replaced sanctions against the person in enforcing revenue demands. Raiyats too came progressively to be treated in law either as tenants or proprietors, without reference to khudkasht or pahikasht status; instead, anyone who was a resident in fact had legal advantages within each village in terms of establishing, if not necessarily of holding on to, rights. In promoting this change, the 1859 Tenancy Act confirmed a tendency initiated in Bengal in 1793.

Yet many of the features of the old systems continued under the British, bolstered up by the persistence of customs and institutions untouched by laws on revenue and land. Above all, 'tenancy' as the British defined it remained a legal and not a social or economic category, covering a broad range of rent-payers, from those who gained their livelihood by selling their labour, to others who received rent themselves. In north Bihar, for example, the legal terms confuse two patterns: one in which large zamindars had little land in direct cultivation and hence were true rent-receivers, and another in which small zamindars had a high proportion of the land in their own holdings and were really proprietary cultivators who employed labour and might also have tenants.

The most important continuity for this essay is that of raiyats as a group. Even before British rule, whatever the view taken by the state, most raiyats already approximated in status to tenants (whether under landlords or headmen) in the sense that when holding land they paid in cash, kind, or services. The rates might in theory be determined objectively outside the village, but in practice depended upon local transactions and authority. There were some areas with large 'zamindari' clans, but their egalitarianism depended upon how land and revenue payment were distributed; and even the clans could have their own 'tenants'. In the second place, the British definition of a tenant continued to run up against a residual variety of practice. It had to overlook the similarity still found between larger rent-payers and petty zamindars. It often had to exclude sub-tenants. It had to forget that individuals were not found exclusively in one role: even maliks might rent land as well as letting it out. It had to pretend that rents (whether paid to the landlord or the state) did not still vary on local grounds that were social as well as economic and that they did not still take into account caste and local power as well as soils and demand. Thanks to the confusion and secrecy of the local records, official and illegal cesses and opportunistic enhancements could be added to such demand to the benefit of those who distributed the burden and collected the payments. Dispositions of local power were challenged but not overturned by the British, as with previous state revenue systems.

Empirical study is undermining many of the generalizations about change in rural India. It is making terms such as 'feudalism' and 'de-peasantization' appear to depend upon crude overstatements of the break between British and pre-British times. If they remain powerful totems, it may be because they fit so well with more general theories. And yet, shorn of those deductive elements, many descriptions of the trends do cover similar ground. Two changes are often cited. In the light of what has been said about terminology, they seem to be identical in certain aspects. First, there is the growth of landlordism, implying a relegation of cultivator-owners to the status of tenants-at-will. Second, there is a polarization among tenants between the rich and the poor (sharecroppers and semi-landless labourers). Expressed differently, without the British categorization, both these descriptions imply a concentration of resources and the exploitation of a majority by a few. Once we regard such tendencies not as sudden by-products of imperialism but as developments within existing systems, we may find that we can go on to debate the nature and causation of an agreed process of change. We are assessing in particular the relative fortunes of two aspects of agrarian production: the control of surplus and the management of cultivation.

Three phases can be identified in terms of the increasing opportunities for marketing agricultural produce, which resulted from improved communications and rising prices. In the first phase, before the mid-nineteenth century, new crops and expanding cultivation represented (especially in some areas) a trend going back generations. Arguably the surplus was largely inspired and taken up by heavy revenue demands. The third phase followed the steep rise in population after about 1920. It is with the middle period that this paper is mainly concerned, a period when continued agricultural expansion and cash-cropping were mainly motivated by profit, though not necessarily that of the actual cultivator. This profit was increased by the relatively declining proportion of production taken as land revenue and the temporarily improving terms of trade for agriculture. The effect varied greatly according to the distribution of communications, crops, irrigation, and so on; but to some degree it was felt everywhere.

Rent-receivers benefited, but it is uncertain that real rents rose as a whole. There were official discussions on whether rents were or should be related to the revenue demand and there were suggestions that temporary settlements were raising them artificially. But, in general, except when poverty was being attributed to rack-renting, rents were considered to be 'sticky'. To a degree, also, they were increasingly regulated by government and law, both in the sense of limiting increases and in making tenants readier to resist additional cesses or illegal enhancement. By the early twentieth century, rates for settled and occupancy raiyats were probably increasing on average more slowly than prices. Unprotected, short-term rents, not everywhere so very different in the past, were by then less restrained.

In this middle period, therefore, there began to be a noticeable tendency away from control over surplus alone and towards more direct management of cultivation. Some large estates were able to set up bureaucratic management to replace the farming out of rents to intermediaries (thikadars in Bihar). Many smaller estates were partitioned between co-sharers, allowing closer supervision of tenants or cultivation. An increase in the number and a decrease in the average size of holdings concealed the increasing effectiveness of those whose acreage was large enough to support local dominance or permit independence, and allowed these fortunate people to control the remainder by substituting produce for money rents, or by marketing their produce, or by farming portions of their land. None of these measures was unprecedented, but there may well have been more of them and to greater effect. Successful landlords expanded the area of their own holdings, reduced their number, and farmed them directly or with sharecroppers on annual or even one-harvest leases.

Under these conditions, the larger, efficient cultivators would benefit in raiyatwari areas; but elsewhere too there are signs that some tenants were following the proprietors' example. It is interesting in this regard how rapidly tenancies rose in value in some areas as a consequence of laws protecting occupancy, giving clear title, and possibly stabilizing rents for the well-placed raiyat. An alternative strategy, partly to be seen in selective rent increases, was to let out more land to those willing to pay at higher rates—for example, agriculturists using family labour. This might indicate zamindari weakness or the influence of enterprising intermediaries, but always it implied close management of agrarian production and differences between cultivators. The result for the cultivator depended on how the crops were marketed. All the strategies could lead to confrontations and redistributions of power. But all had in common the fact that some form of cultivating possession (including sharecropping) was gradually becoming more valuable than rent-collecting *per se*.

What was the contribution of new law? The fixing and formalizing of landed property was a prerequisite for example for the partition of holdings, one of the instruments for widening social disparities. Arguably, too, individual property rights interrupted mechanisms that had maintained the integrity of some elites and their lands over generations. Under the British, while many large estates remained intact and middle-sized ones often stabilized at an economic size, the smallest came in the end to be multiplying endlessly, the victims perhaps of the discordance of Hindu laws of inheritance with British laws of property.

Among tenancies, similar patterns were observed. By the early 1900s, pressure of population was sufficient to swell the numbers without land or with too little of it, but the legal structure and economic opportunities seemed to be allowing others to exploit and even extend holdings of a viable size. These were the people—not all equally adept—who hoarded surplus, managed credit, provided work, entered the market freely, exchanged crops on behalf of others, and generally wielded social and political power. All over India, the range and number of exchanges within rural communities and between them and the wider world increased, the government playing its part along with trade. But these exchanges enhanced rather than reduced the control of the powerful over the weak. This seemed obvious in Bihar, but perhaps less so in more prosperous places—but there the beneficiaries were perhaps only more numerous, a feature that had provided the main component and the limit for their egalitarianism all along. Everywhere there were economic disparities and social controllers whom British rule assisted.

This was true even of debt, which was supposed to be restricted latterly by legislation—whether in 1879 for the Deccan or in 1900 for the Punjab. It is generally recognized (as in this essay) as a means of control and it was assisted over the longer term by the whole tenor of English law, with its emphasis on title and contract, and (even in the attempts at regulation) by the British reliance on watertight social categories and their unwillingness to notice, in policy, the fact that cultivators did not only cultivate nor only moneylenders lend. Credit might be offered by the old mahajans, bankers in local and intermediate markets. In the late nineteenth century, credit was also available from newcomers—travellers from other regions, European capitalists, or even (later) cooperative credit. But all these fitted in with existing norms; only the administrators of government loans tried to impose their own ways. And so too control by outsiders was matched by that of even more local elites: village moneylenders and dominant raiyats whom the British saw but overlooked.

In short, in the nineteenth century, there was almost everywhere a process whereby cultivation was becoming more profitable, but the benefits continued to be captured by a minority of the rural community. The change was not so much in agrarian structure as in the relative wealth and privilege of existing roles. For northern India, including eastern UP and Bihar, a distinction between absentee rent-receivers and cultivating landowners had some political importance in the twentieth century. But the key economic divide was between on the one hand cultivating landholders and the controllers of trade—often including the smaller 'gentry' who had become managers of cultivation—and, on the other hand the non-privileged sharecroppers and labourers. In Bengal too current interpretations draw attention to the village elites (jotedars) while 'depeasantization' implies poorer cultivators who laboured for others. In western India, a supposed increase in tenancy and the numbers of rich peasants can be translated as some proprietary raiyats proving more able to control cultivation using sharecroppers and labourers. A similar phenomenon is apparent in the South. One book has described how zamindars and village officers maintained or acquired wealth and status during the nineteenth century only to decay in the 1930s and 1940s in favour of 'new leaders... marked out by their involvement in agrarian production and commerce rather than... revenue collection'.[26]

We see then that, though different phases may be identified, in general trade and government strengthened channels along which they had long flowed. Perhaps they could do so because they were still peripheral in many areas well into this century. But though British government was always alien and relatively weak, it mattered that the government worked from wrong assumptions—for example, that peasant proprietors were original and hence appropriate in India or that all intermediaries were interlopers in a closed society. We need to replace these notions with a more dynamic model in which various forms of village community exist, but the so-called 'outsiders' are integral as well as integrating. On the other hand, we must not merely replace one set of assumptions with another. It is misleading, for example, to identify Indian social entities as classes; we need to admit the interlocking but cellular command structures of the society, for it was these above all which revealed the fallacy of the British categorizations. Thus we have found that the great rent-law debate postulated a fundamental divide between zamindar and raiyat, but that the reality was a broader and different set of distinctions between controller and controlled, and at the same time an interrelationship between them. Moreover, if the divide widened during the nineteenth century, this was explicable largely in the persistence of control.

26 Baker, *An Indian Rural Economy*, pp. 461–3.

The economic consequences were arguably serious. For wealth to spread through society, there would have to have been at the least a greater demand for the labour of the poor. It is uncertain that this generally occurred. Cities, plantations, and industry were relatively insignificant as alternative employers, especially against a rising population trend. Irrigation and double-cropping enabled the more efficient use of existing labour, and agricultural profits would have increased through prices and the expansion of higher-value crops even with a fixed input of labour. Paradoxically, the dominant minority was a brake on, rather than an instrument for, economic improvement precisely because in many places the dominant remained fairly numerous. If wealth was increasingly concentrated upon those who were already relatively rich, then the development of the internal market would be distorted or restricted. The attractiveness to capital of agriculture (and of hoarding or expenditure, which did not increase production) would be further increased, thus squandering India's favourable balance of trade and her imports of precious metals. And of course agriculture was comparatively profitable, in part because of international demand, which brings us back to the 'colonial' economy.

It has not been the intention of this paper to contribute to or even discuss general theories of agrarian change. But it may be thought to have some relevance to the familiar argument that a 'modern' world system emerged after the mid-nineteenth century. In some senses, this view is incontrovertible. But this paper reminds us that any 'system' is partly an explanatory construct from entity and context. In particular, it will contain elements 'foreign' or contrary to what are taken to be the system's defining characteristics. We need to resist substantialization, as even the advocates of general theory usually concede. For example, it is unwise to assume that a capitalist 'world system', in Wallerstein's sense, depended upon 'modern' state formation, 'modern' command of labour, and so on. Too often, general expositions seem to rest ultimately on an unreformed image of 'pre-capitalist' societies—either that they were more or less without exchange or that exchange was somehow peripheral to them and their social relations. It is as if merchants engaged in long-distance trade appeared only in 1750, or the cultivator never had to sell his produce in order to pay revenue, or the weaver never to produce for the intermediary who controlled him.

In this essay, by contrast, a major premise has been the inevitability of difference, even stratification, as featuring in exchange, state development, and so on. Notably, we have concluded that the advance payment system and other parallel means of control predated the expansion of European commerce and the emergence of unequal trade. How else could revenue farmers have enforced the extraction of marketable surplus? The concept of a colonial economy may fairly describe the international trade of India in the late nineteenth century. It does not follow that all relations and modes of production were accordingly transformed, nor that trade and law acted to generate wholly new conditions. Rather, they entered into a dialogue with a society that had continually been re-formed by similar transactions.[27]

27 Further work has appeared since this essay was written. On trading intermediaries, see Rajat Datta, 'Merchants and Peasants: A Study of the Structure of Local Trade in Late Eighteenth-century Bengal' and Kumkum Banerjee, 'Grain Traders and the East India Company: Patna and its Hinterland in the Late Eighteenth and Early Nineteenth Centuries', in *Indian Economic and Social History Review*, 23(4), 1986. For similar arguments (contrary to Washbrook) on the different impact of law and market forces, see Neeladri Bhattacharya, 'Colonial State and Agrarian Society' in Sabyasachi Bhattacharya and Romila Thapar (eds), *Situating Indian History*, Delhi, 1986. On Bengal land questions—defining social typologies on the management of production rather than of rent, a shift regarded in this essay as a change over time— see Sugata Bose, *Agrarian Bengal: Economy, Social Structure and Politics, 1919–1947*, Cambridge, 1986.

6. Peasants' Choices?*
Indian Agriculture and the Limits of Commercialization in Nineteenth-century Bihar

This essay outlines the socio-political conditions in which commercial production increased, the limitations of 'capitalist' transformation, the importance of non- or extra-economic influences, the ubiquity of intermediary roles, the resilience of existing concepts and practices, and consequently the difficulties of defining rural classes.

This essay discusses agricultural decision-making in one part of India: in Bihar, which was socio-economically 'backward' yet deeply involved in commercial production during the nineteenth century.[1] The combination of allegedly discordant characteristics is usually attributed to 'forced commercialization', the presumption being that the norm is free entry into the market. The term does not disturb the sway of most economic theories, which assume that capitalism was exported and closed systems were opened out as international trade expanded—a model which fits poorly with an agricultural system previously (but still incompletely) market-involved, as in much of India. Intellectually and in reality, we find here the imperialism of Western economics if 'empire' be understood as rule over diverse 'nations'. An enormous growth in trade obviously had major consequences, but not just from Western influence driven by Western demand and power. Generally India modified British ideas and institutions and allowed their adoption by Indians. Hence this article

* First published in *Economic History Review*, XLV(I), 1992, pp. 97–119. The original format of notes has been retained. See the References below, p. 147. These also include general works not cited in the notes.

1 Several of the discussions of the London Third World Economic History Group at the School of Oriental and African Studies (SOAS), London, have contributed to the ideas presented in this essay. Kaoru Sugihara's comments have been invaluable. A version of the paper was read to the Economic History Society at Exeter in 1989. See the References for general sources on the eighteenth century and commercialization outside Bihar and for works by authors mentioned without footnoting.

will question the idea that economic change has comprised a one-way traffic to a single destination and turned subsistence peasants into capitalist farmers or landless agricultural workers under the influence of the market, a picture now rejected by some economic historians of India. It will place a marker limiting the depth of commercialization and of capitalist development.

I

This approach is encouraged by current interpretations of eighteenth-century India that seek to replace the notions of political anarchy and economic decline with (at least for some areas) a picture of growing trade, developing merchant culture, and the involvement in agricultural production of territorial magnate-traders. The economy was characterized by a high degree of political and fiscal intervention.[2] Trade had given rise to various family firms and castes and to communities cutting across caste, which exchanged, insured, and transported money and goods. The pillar of indigenous mercantilism was the command of labour, of landed peasantry through rent, and more directly of large numbers of landless and dependent smallholders. To extract produce or stimulate production in order to match demand, the elites invested directly in irrigation or provided incentives to break in new land. But most characteristically, they lent money or seed at the time of ploughing and sowing, recovering the investment at the harvest. In the same way, they used food loans to secure seasonal labour. By such means too, a merchant could readily introduce a new cash crop or even bring new areas under the plough.

In describing this society, one should not expect a precise and exclusive functional definition for such words as 'landlord', 'tenant', 'peasant', 'banker', 'merchant', or 'state'.[3] In Bihar in the early 1800s, mixed occupations were common and perhaps the norm among artisans, so that (splitting actual and ritual concepts of labour) most of those whose caste names implied they would be working at a craft may have been engaged in agriculture. This suggests that demand was low and cultivation relatively more profitable than most trades, and also that labour would be available to the elites.[4] Conceptually,

2 Bayly, 'Indian Merchants', p. 178. Various papers read at SOAS by G.D. Sharma and Madhavi Bajkewal also contributed to this account. See Sharma, 'Urban Credit' in Austin and Sugihara (eds), *Local Supplies of Credit* and Subrahmanyam (ed.), *Merchants*.

3 See Robb, 'Ideas', pp. 18–23. Clearly these theoretical objections apply also to terms such as 'market', 'economic', 'social', and 'political', which are used here as analytical categories within which 'real' complexities are confined. By contrast, Ludden, 'Productive Power', seems to hope for greater certainty of terminology. The fact that such problems are not confined to the past is illustrated trenchantly by Polly Hill's writings.

4 See Buchanan, *Shahabad*. This volume is used here, but see also his volumes on Bihar and Purnea districts.

merchants, moneylenders, cultivators, and so on existed, but roles were often multiple, ambiguous, or overlapping. Even at the village level, though a few cultivators, artisans, and labourers followed their occupation exclusively, many dabbled in several roles.

The typical eighteenth-century merchant house too financed agriculture, farmed land revenue, lent out money, traded locally and at a distance, probably managed money transfers, and possibly took in deposits. But there was also, paradoxically, an unusually strong tendency for economic functions to be subdivided. The land- or revenue-focused power set up and taxed markets; it placed tolls upon roads, fords, ferries, landings, and gateways; but it also provided a host of specialized agents who exacted the taxes and fees and acted as go-betweens, adjudicators, weighers, and measurers, operating between the principals in commercial and financial transactions. The typical creature of the age was the *dalal*, or broker, who was not of one character but of many. Even in a small market, such apparently inseparable operations as introducing the parties to a bargain, setting a price, weighing or assessing the produce, verifying the payment, accepting it, and recording the deal might each be entrusted (even product by product) to a specialist intermediary who enjoyed a local monopoly backed by political power and paid for in cesses.

Generally, too, even without the impact of warfare there was quite a lot of mobility between villages during the eighteenth and early nineteenth centuries. The countryside was not full of neat, fixed settlements with measured fields and estates. Some areas *were* densely settled and carefully marked out; but in others, there were scattered or temporary dwellings and plots. Often people, especially the poor, were bonded to other people rather than to land, so that all would move together; others would escape from such ties and try to search out favourable terms for their labour. Many areas had traditions of military recruitment, especially among the poorer members of higher classes, and where families remained behind in the village they could be supported on army pay and booty. In the north, as the central authority of the Mughal empire weakened, migrant clans of military tribes or pastoralists moved from the hill lands across the plains and river valleys, setting up military kingdoms, settling in villages, and ousting or depressing some of the earlier elites. In south India, though the rich irrigated lands tended to be held by numerous shareholders who organized revenue payments and controlled labour for irrigation and agriculture, the drier lands were controlled by headmen and their followers (often of military origin and occupation) who were ready to move whole communities from season to season in search of land or water. And everywhere there were migrant traders and moneylenders.

This was not a peasant society in the sense of being typified by household production on smallholdings under strong but external political control. Above the village level, there were chiefs, landlords, military leaders, and officials, who claimed rights and dues from the villages. But also most villages contained dominant high status groups with above-average landholdings; subservient groups, with smaller holdings or no land, provided labour. Before the arrival of the British in the eighteenth century, there were distinctions between 'residents' and 'non-residents', 'permanent' and 'temporary' cultivators, shareholders and sharecroppers. The dominant groups usually held village office, managed most of the local resources, and controlled the village's contact with the outside world. Generally they took part in establishing or maintaining irrigation, in collecting land taxes, and in encouraging, managing, and taxing trade and markets.

In many places, sizeable proportions of the land were controlled by such groups, either without paying land revenue to the state or on very favourable terms. They employed others to cultivate their land whenever possible—as sharecroppers, tenants, labourers, or slaves—but would work in their own fields if necessary, for example if they were relatively numerous and each family's holdings were small. For example, in Tirunelvelli at the tip of India, a moderately rich area with a large export trade, where peasant cultivators were supposed to be the norm, 55 per cent of landholders in 1817 reportedly cultivated their own land (using slaves and other labour) while 38 per cent let their holdings to non-resident (unprivileged) tenants. In poorer, dry, inland Salem, the great majority of holdings were said to be cultivated using family labour; little produce was exported; but still there were to be found 'rich' families with 'five ploughs' and hence some tenancy, hired labour, and agrarian servitude.[5]

Exchanges of food, land, and labour as well as a degree of interdependence characterized the 'villages'. This could extend to the allocation of the land; the use of cattle, ploughs, and water; and the choice and harvesting of crops. Entrenched or customary rights existed for different social levels, and dominance relied on office, wealth, stores of grain, social prestige, or force of arms as well as on possession of land. The elites 'managed' village life, paying labourers in food and small plots of land and lending to poorer cultivators. Independent producers would sell directly to traders and also take a share of some of the crops of poorer farmers to whom they had given seed and food. They might take up and encourage the spread of particular crops. They were often associated with petty state building or with revenue-collecting rights, especially during the eighteenth century.

Since land revenue dues were calculated in money terms and, even if collected in kind, were paid in cash into the state's coffers, the produce of the

---

[5] Kumar, *Land and Caste*, pp. 19, 20, and 22–3; see also Ludden, *Peasant History*.

countryside from both farmers and artisans was naturally attracted to towns and over substantial distances. The revenues came not only from rich irrigated tracts, those most closely controlled and taxed by outsiders, but in varying degrees from all regions where there were revenue demands and rents. Most areas therefore had some experience of the complex and extensive trading networks that dealt in all the necessities of life—foodgrains, oilseeds, salt, cloth, utensils, timber, and livestock—and with their local representatives in the form of specialist traders or moneylenders. Thus three production strategies could exist together: crops were grown for use, they were sold for subsistence (including payments to others), and they were sold for gain.

But insofar as agricultural production was directed towards markets, it operated under close control and within constraints. The travelling merchants, who reached villages at harvest time, seldom set their prices competitively. Buyers attempted to monopolize access to the villages and to employ coercion in various forms in order to secure the crop. Advance payments provided the weapon of debt, but revenue and rent demands usually ensured that a sale would be agreed promptly at the harvest. One finds arrangements of these kinds all over India across a long timespan. From the seventeenth century, for example, most villages in western India had a trader who advanced seed and food (but rarely cash) and later took a share of the harvest. And a more extreme version was described in Ferozepur district in the Punjab in the 1830s: 'The Hindu merchants, from the command which they have of money, exercise a preponderating influence... The ryuts [cultivators], from their extreme poverty, are forced to mortgage their crops to provide themselves with seed and the necessary implements of husbandry. Money is advanced at an enormous rate of interest... The cattle and even the ploughs are the property of the merchants.'[6]

Such systems spread commodity production thinly, limiting the influence of the market even in the most commercially oriented regions and reducing the effective monetization of transactions at the village level. Payments of land or grain secured produce at minimal cost, but at the expense of a subcontracting system that isolated the long-distance trader and the producer from each other and did not necessarily involve the capitalist in actual production. Such systems have sometimes been identified with a specific stage of economic development. The present discussion asks if this was so or, to put it another way, what changed in the nineteenth century?

On the one hand is the picture of vigorous local trade. To Chaudhuri, Bengal's post-1770 recession seemed so deep that commercial agriculture could

---

[6] See Roseberry, *Imperial Rule*, p. 234; quoting from Mackeson's 'Journal', pp. 190–3.

develop only in response to international demand. Now instead we have Datta's account of the region's rice trade.[7] And even in poor, overtaxed south Bihar early in the nineteenth century, rice (and in smaller quantities barley, other grains, and pulses) were exported and imported. Wheat was exported in large quantities, as were various amounts of spices, oilseeds, oils, cotton cloth, blankets, paper, timber products, and some locally bred buffaloes. Tobacco, sugar, most culinary salt, cotton and cotton thread, iron, brass and other metal utensils, and most oxen were imported.[8] On the other hand, this is not to imply, as Datta does, a well-integrated monetized economy at all social levels, given the evidence of diverse weights and measures, transportation difficulties, payments and credit in kind, and other market imperfections. There was still much payment through land; a relatively small proportion of the cultivated area was devoted to marketed crops. Datta shows that rice, opium, and indigo were all extracted largely in association with advances to cultivators, but overlooks the fact that such crops occupied a part of very many holdings, necessitating intermediaries and social control over labour and poor cultivators.[9] Moreover, a similar situation obtained in late-nineteenth century Bihar, which was not thereby less commercialized; money was then more rather than less generally available.[10]

How do we define change while explaining these continuities? A possible answer is that cultivators had been 'using' merchants in order to spread risk by exploiting the system of advance payments. Later problems, revealed in famines, represent 'teething troubles' from incomplete changes in modes of production.[11] But from a Bihari perspective, it is difficult to endorse this analysis. The moneylender was often regarded as a social inferior, but most advance payments subordinated the borrower because he could (at best) only shift to another patron and seldom possessed the resources to operate independently. Even those in dominant positions, those who lent to others, often needed to employ intermediaries and kept afloat with help from moneylenders.

7 Chaudhuri (Chowdhury), *Commercial Agriculture* and *idem*, 'Agricultural Growth'; Datta, 'Merchants and Peasants'.

8 Buchanan, *Shahabad*.

9 Datta, 'Rural Bengal', esp. pp. 329–38.

10 Buchanan, *Shahabad*. Demonetization is suggested in Perlin, 'Proto-industrialisation', but in Shahabad in the early 1800s, though money was exchanged in several places including at some cloth dealers, bank notes could be changed for cash only at Arrah, the main town. Revenue had to be paid in the Company's silver coinage, but most instalments were managed by large moneylenders (much land revenue by just one banker in Arrah), who encouraged circulation of the less reliable and cheaper Banares silver. The Company's copper coinage was found only in Arrah, though other debased coins and cowrees were more widely used.

11 I owe this argument to Burton Stein, personal communication. It recalls the meliorist explanations of McAlpin, *Subject to Famine*.

II

Over most of the century, the British gradually regulated and bureaucratized the fiscal apparatus. By adding some real security and a clearer definition to landed property, they reduced the need for elites to extract surplus as revenue agents or as landowners or creditors. The British state also withdrew progressively from most attempts to control markets or monopolize trade. At the same time, India generally became more involved in external markets. Yet paradoxically, at the level of the agricultural producer and the immediate relations of production, almost all of the features just described for the eighteenth century apply perfectly well (at least in Bihar) at the end of the nineteenth. Some, including advance payments as a restriction of the producers' options, were encouraged by the expansion of trading opportunities. The central image remains one of dispersed or fragmented commercial production and of intermixed social and political controls (which the advance payments may exemplify). The agriculture of commerce was far from commercial, yet the 'peasant farm' was not an autonomous unit of production and decision-making. Pursuing these points, we will discover mutual or intrinsic as well as superordinate controls defining the orbit of peasants' choices, and indeed that commercial and political influences were themselves restricted to particular, appropriate means of managing production and securing surplus.

An excellent example of a surviving rent-based production system was irrigated cultivation in Gaya district, south Bihar, where the supply of water supposedly justified produce-sharing rents (*bhaoli*) to ensure and remunerate the input of the landlords.[12] Their 'earth-moving' (*gilandazi*), as it was called, was a capital investment in a technical sense and richly rewarding in those terms. But in large part the 'capital' comprised social prestige and organization to enlist an unpaid or low-paid local labour force, to strike and enforce agreements between villages, and so on. A consequence of bhaoli rents—in the nineteenth century as in the eighteenth—was that the landlord or intermediary leaseholder or thikadar was obliged to endorse a small army of village officials. On any estate, in addition to several kinds of cash rent, there were at least two forms of produce collection: actual crop division (*batai*) and appraisal (*danabandi*). The landlord needed an agent, watchmen to prevent pilferage before and during the harvest, an accountant (patwari), an assessor, a measurer, an arbitrator, a recording clerk or writer, and a headman. As with the *dalali* system in the local markets and for the same reasons (fragmentation of function and of points of 'taxation'), this rental system was highly interventionist. It not only extracted rent but redistributed produce within the village. Almost three

---

[12] Among many sources relating to this system and agriculture in Gaya, the most useful, from which the present account is mainly drawn, is Grierson, *Gaya*. See also Sengupta, 'Indigenous Irrigation'.

quarters of the population, whether as village servants, artisans, or labourers, received some perquisites from the harvests of others, under a collective supervision and mostly before division—that is, before any allocation of the produce into the private store of zamindar and raiyat (landlord and cultivator).

Hence 'peasants choices' about cropping and work depended upon a wide range of controls, related mainly to the extraction of rent but also to interdependence within the local community. Each cultivator's responsibility, even for his day-to-day activities, was circumscribed in various ways because neither his holding nor his methods of production existed in isolation from the political structures that surrounded him. He might be bound to provide labour for others; he hardly had a free market in which to obtain labour himself. His choice of cash crops would depend not only on his own judgement but also on patterns of land use and water supply beyond his immediate control. Nor could he always decide the methods or timing of his cultivation. Agricultural equipment was frequently shared and labour was bonded. In north Bihar, for example, the usual word for ploughman (*harwaha*) meant one who worked after taking advance payments; a different word (*uttha*) was used for a ploughman who worked without them.[13]

This was still very much the system as described early in the century by Buchanan,[14] when on a typical estate he found many small local intermediaries of the zamindar, who were permitted to collect rents and supposed to keep up reservoirs and other irrigation works, and many holders of rent-free lands and other privileged tenants, including some who claimed descent from former proprietors as well as village clerks, crop assessors, messengers, and watchmen. Most villages did not have headmen as such, but the term (here jeth-raiyat) was used generally for wealthy tenants who (in Buchanan's words) 'commonly assist their poor and ignorant neighbours in settling their accounts'. Of the villagers who controlled land and agriculture, he distinguished gentry (people of high caste or social status), artisans or traders who rented land, and 'ploughmen', a class which ranged from wage labourers and sharecroppers to rich cultivators who had sufficient surplus to be able to act as village 'traders'. The local name for the latter, *grihashta beopar*, meant 'householder-trader'; Buchanan called them 'trading farmers'. Such 'cultivators' had some capital and might keep bullocks to transport grain to market, but they dealt chiefly with their poorer neighbours, supporting them between harvests.

13 Grierson, *Behar Peasant Life*, pp. 177–9, 197–201, and 313–20. Also Proceedings of the GOI, R&A Dept., Agriculture Branch, C series, no. 2, May 1898, C2 October 1898; and C7 and 9, December 1898, National Archives of India, New Delhi.

14 Buchanan, *Shahabad*. Compare the volumes on these districts, in Hunter, *Statistical Account*, and the Report of the Bihar and Orissa Provincial Banking Enquiry Committee, 1929–30, 3 vols, Patna, 1930.

132 Peasants, Political Economy, and Law

Advances were made 'at a very usurious rate' of interest and repaid from the crop. Cultivation was carried on individually or sometimes by large bands working each other's fields in turn. A few 'slaves' were employed as well as ploughmen and day labourers, again bonded through small advances in money or by land grants for sharecropping. The local grain trade was in the hands of travelling merchants, and other products were exported or imported mainly by boatmen. In most respects, these conditions survived the arrival both of the British and of the railway and were still in evidence 80 years later.

III

However, by late in the nineteenth century, there were complaints that absentee landlords no longer ensured the irrigation works that had supported south Bihar throughout the ages, even though the evidence from government estates is that it remained in the interests of the landlord and his local representatives to maintain them. There was a strong tendency towards the commutation of produce rents.[15] It might be concluded that the old regime was being broken down by the influence of changing law and markets. Certainly, alongside the old and extensive trade in rice and oilseeds, three crops—sugar, opium, and indigo—were grown and sold in Bihar to a greatly increased extent during the nineteenth century. For the second and third of these, Bihari output was of global significance, managed in one case by the British state and in the other by European planters and export houses. Yet the most striking feature of the cultivation of these new crops was not new relations of production, but the persistence of indirect and intermixed (socio-political) methods of control.[16] In opium, for example, there was a huge increase in the value of the crop, while crude prices to the cultivator remained stable; but at the same time, between 1840 and 1880, the area under cultivation was extended by more than two-and-a-half times.

15 On the other hand, complaints of decay may have been perennial; they appear still in Singh and Kumar, *Monograph*, pp. 62–3.
16 See R&A, *Agriculture*, A17–18 January 1891; Kling, *Blue Mutiny*; Mishra, *Agrarian Problems*; Fisher, 'Planters and Peasants', and especially Pouchepadass, *Planteurs et Paysans*. The case of indigo was discussed in Chapter 2. For opium, see especially Wright, *Economic Problems*, pp. 106–65; *Selections from the Records of the Government of Bengal*, part 1, no. 33, part (1–3) Calcutta, 1860, especially *Report of a Commission Appointed by the Government of India to Enquire into the Working of the Opium Department in Bengal and the North-Western Provinces*; Colebrooke, *Husbandry*, p. 117; Ram Chand Pandit, joint opium contractor, in *Selections from the Duncan Records*, vol. II, no. 10, p. 166; A.C. Mangles (Opium Agent, Patna) to the Commissioner of Patna Division, 18 March 1883, Records of the Commissioner of Patna Division, Bihar State Archives, *basta* (bundle) 338, collection 7, file 84, 10 (1883–4), (hereafter PCR) and the Collector of Gaya to the Commissioner, ibid., 7/91. For the evidence before the opium commission, see PCR 364 29/8, 1895–6.

The key to production was an advance-payment system already established in its essentials during the eighteenth century and later embodied in Regulation VI of 1799. Its administration comprised three distinct levels above the cultivators. At the top was the Collector as Deputy Opium Agent and, in Bihar, his 11 sub-deputies. Next were minor officials, the *gomashta*s who received the opium and were paid a salary and commission, and the *ziladar*s, on salary only, who were responsible for groups of 20 or 30 villages. An important part of their function was to prevent the growers from retaining any of the opium or disposing of it privately. At the third level were the *khatadar*s—25,000 in the 1880s with an average of 32 cultivators each, whom they allegedly represented. The khatadar recruited the cultivators or *assami*s, signed the agreement that they supposedly made, arranged with the ziladar to receive and distribute cash advances on upto three occasions, organized irrigation loans and their repayment, in practice (though not in regulations) made the *taidad* or estimate of the crop that the gomashta presented in February or March to determine the amount of the second advance payment, and finally brought the assamis before the ziladar and gomashta and distributed the final payment for the opium. The khatadar was a relatively powerful and prosperous intermediary or 'principal cultivator', a village official or rich peasant.

Despite the criticisms from the time of Burke, it was sometimes said that the cultivators welcomed opium advances in preference to the exactions of landlords. A century later, in the 1880s, zamindars were still allegedly hostile to opium cultivation because it promoted independence. An opium cultivator was closely involved with agents of government. By the later nineteenth century, he tended to pay money rents on all his land, at a time when some zamindars were trying to extend their *zerat* (demesne land) and the arena of informal, unregulated rents so as to return to produce-sharing or sharecropping arrangements. Moreover, in many parts of Bihar, only limited areas were cropped with cereals of a quality suitable for marketing, and local prices were very responsive to harvest yield, greatly reducing the return to the cultivator from good harvests. Much of the rice, wheat, barley, and maize was poor and the majority of the millets and pulses were 'not much superior to the seeds of wild grasses', so that even in the dearest seasons, they had little market value.[17] By contrast, opium—though bought cheaply in relation to the price obtained by government—was very valuable locally, not least for being paid for at a fixed rate. It could provide a source of capital or credit for the development of other crops. Opium advances and improvement loans provided money for investment or expenditure on relatively favourable terms.

17 D.N. Reid (indigo planter of Saran) to Mangles, 30 December 1881, R&A Agriculture, B3, May 1899.

But it is plain that benefits were not evenly shared. Opium cultivation exhausted the soil and the cultivator. It was grown on the best land and was extravagant of manure; the poppies had to be watered continually until they were two or three inches high; and then had to be thinned two or three times. The harvest began with the removal of the petals and involved the repeated lancing of the opium pods, a process lasting over several weeks. The drug had to be dried in cloth—both the cloth and the liquid residue were collected by the opium agents. The flowers were made into opium cakes and packed in the leaves and stalks of the plant. There were petitions against opium cultivation as early as 1818; by the 1880s, as the crop became less and less attractive, it was said that unwilling growers were being coerced with the assistance of the native police and trumped-up charges. Officials would admit only that there were grievances, but the most compelling testimony is to the petty tyranny of the opium department's local subordinates. The khatadars were paid a small commission—so little, it was admitted, that they had to derive illegal income from their office; but no opium agent was ever successfully prosecuted in Bihar.

The claim that opium cultivation deepened the subjection of most cultivators is therefore justified. Yet firstly, this subjection was not absolute; secondly, it was not directly to the opium department; and thirdly, it was not uniform among a body of cultivators. Later in the century some shifted from opium to indigo or (near towns and railways) took to tobacco, potatoes, or other vegetables, either independently or at the behest of patrons and local magnates. Mounting protest chiefly reflected the extent to which opium was less advantageous to the khatadar than other crops. Similar arguments can be made about opposition to indigo, culminating in Gandhi's intervention in 1917. Finally, the subjection did not occur in the form that it did entirely because it was convenient and profitable for the British. As early as 1831 and several times thereafter, officials proposed to abandon advance payments and hence to bypass the local intermediary and his socio-political power. All these schemes were ruled impracticable. The same system, the British found, was used not just by mahajans (bankers) but 'even in private matters such as hiring a *palky* (carriage)'.[18] Similarly from the 1880s, indigo planters—under government pressure to introduce more 'commercial' methods—made various experiments in direct purchasing but fell back mainly upon varieties of advance payments, indirect management, and landlord-style coercion. The opium agents were obviously monopolists and creditors, but also allied with rent-collectors, great landlords, and dominant villagers; the planters were

18 Report on opium cultivation by Forbes, Commissioner of Patna Division, PCR 364 29/8, 1895/6.

leaseholders as well. But all were buyers who failed to establish a direct contact with their suppliers.

Unlike opium, sugar was not a monopoly, nor was it a product manufactured wholly by modern factory methods and for export, like indigo in Bihar. But it too was grown in a small way on a large number of holdings 'within a complex system of indebtedness and dependence' to benefit the profits of intermediaries, especially the processors and traders of refined sugar, 'a pretty wealthy class of people'.[19] Once again, the system was resilient. In Shahabad, south Bihar, the sugar manufacturers Thomson and Mylne concluded that it was impossible to institute a central factory system based on steam-driven machinery, partly because of the refusal of the raiyats to grow cane for them or sell their standing crops at a 'fair valuation'. The obstacles were the price paid under existing local arrangements and the obligations between the cultivators and the landlords or sugar factors.[20] In north Bihar by contrast, European sugar factories expanded in the early twentieth century (even though the natural conditions for cane were not as good as in the south) simply because the planters transferred their capital and hence their raiyats' cultivation from indigo to sugar. The factories acted as their own brokers, advancing seed and sometimes money short-term.[21] In the late 1930s, cane was still purchased through contractors, who prevented the establishment of cooperative sugarcane societies.[22]

IV

Fisher makes an interesting but perhaps overstated distinction between dedicated and general trade. In the case of indigo, or opium, or oilseeds, trade was carried on between known dealers at specific places; but in the case of rice, by cartmen in numerous short-range transactions. Only in this context

19 The quotations on sugar in this paragraph are from the Commissioner's report in PCR 364 29/8, 1895–6. The fullest modern account of the sugar industry is Amin, *Sugarcane*, and see also Whitcombe, *Agrarian Conditions*. This essay draws on Watt, *Economic Products*, vi, pp. 3–380; Grierson, *Behar Peasant Life*, pp. 50–60 and 232–7; B.C. Basu, 'Note on the Manufacture of Sugar and its Probable Improvements', R&A, Agriculture, A9–11, July 1892; the proceedings of the Agricultural Conference, October, 1893, R&A, Agriculture, A9 and 10, February 1894; and the *Report of the Royal Commission on Agriculture in India*, 1927, vol. viii (hereafter *RCA*). See also R&A Agriculture, A22, A27, and A29–30, February and A10, July 1890, and A9–11, July 1892.

20 R&A Land Revenue Branch, B52–3, June 1895.

21 See especially in *RCA* the evidence of J. Henry, Lohat Sugar Works, Darbhanga; C.G. Atkins, Dowlatpore Agricultural Concern; and N. Meyrick, Bihar Planters' Association, Motihari.

22 Director of Agriculture's letter, 28 April 1937, Bihar Development Department (Industries), nos 1–18, January, file 18/218, 1938, Bihar State Archives, Patna.

could raiyats hope to participate themselves, cutting out the middlemen. They sought to do so, from the 1860s at least, by owning their own carts and carrying on their own marketing. The missing element in this analysis is fuller information about the raiyats who were thus involved in trade. Some were becoming traders just as some were becoming moneylenders or rent-receivers. Such opportunities almost certainly widened, as also did the gap between rich and poor; but none of the changes—neither dedicated trade nor peasant-traders—constituted a sharp break with the past. Commercial agriculture in Bihar, far from overturning an antique style, adopted many features of eighteenth-century agrarian relations and of the rent-based model still found in nineteenth-century Gaya. And yet elites entered the market to dispose of produce they had themselves produced or which they had acquired from their control over others. Why did more cultivators not respond to the market directly? To do so required capital, independence, access to transport, and awareness—in a situation in which many were poor, dependent, and isolated. As a result, the cultivator was not necessarily an economic man, making agricultural decisions within parameters of need and opportunity determined by the state and merchants. This point has often been remarked. It is less common to remark that the traders also were not wholly free agents.

A more pertinent form of the question is this: Why did government, planters, and merchants alike continue (over such a very long period, in such different trading conditions) to adopt these 'pre-' or 'proto-capitalist' relations of production? Why do many of their successors continue to do so today? One obvious answer is profit. Socio-political and credit-based controls were devices for securing labour at artificially low cost, whether for the landlord who paid his field-workers in land as well as food or for the indigo planter or opium agent who largely avoided having to compete in order to attract cultivators. Concentration not on production but on credit and distribution, on processing and retailing, is a situation analogous to that observed in other areas of smallholding (or dispersed manufacturing).[23] Certainly there was coercion. Yet the lack of either direct production control or a wholesale market complicated the supply and arguably diverted profits to middlemen. Thus, if on one hand this was a pocket 'command' economy, on the other it was a costly and incomplete commercialization impeded from 'inside'. The cultivator was unable to break out of his subordination, but also the external market or the state was unable to prevail against the intermediary—and he in turn chose or was constrained to secure produce through intermixed control. Perhaps the system persisted because of specific features affecting agricultural decisions. Hence the need to locate the choices concerning production.

23 Friedman, 'World Market', and Harriss, *Rural Development*. The system was not at all confined to the nineteenth century—Raj, *Commercialization*, passim.

Chief among these features were the differentiation of the society, the intricacies of landholding, the complexities of land use and agriculture, and the resilience of custom. In villages, the most common exchanges of labour and goods were between patrons and clients. Also well before any European involvement, commerce had had to accommodate itself to all these conditions. By the nineteenth century, therefore, habits or institutions were already long established. There were independent producers in Bihar—landlords and planters using hired labour on their 'own' lands, small market-gardeners, and so on—but characteristically, 'commercial' farming was widely dispersed and indirectly controlled. Institutional impediments explain why there were so many producers: landholding patterns, dense population, and government interference. Imperfections in the market—considerable self-sufficiency among agriculturists, relatively low volumes, still difficult transportation, and the communications block of differing cultures and illiteracy—account for the difficulties for buyers in obtaining produce from the multitudes of cultivators. Interposed powers (landlords, village elites, and long-established traders) also made it hard to penetrate to the individual seller of crops. The answer was at hand: to use intermediaries as well as rental and debt bondage, to work with the social and political conditions rather than across them. Commercial agriculture had to be carried on in a small proportion of a large number of smallholdings. Produce extraction relied on complex, even parallel systems of control. It was no wonder that the 'eighteenth-century' way—command of manpower—should have commended itself to later entrepreneurs.

We cannot go into all these features in detail here. The continuing existence of hierarchies of control and the minute subdivisions of landed holdings are familiar aspects. Their great importance in this analysis may be accepted without further ado, as may that of habits produced by earlier involvement in trade. Other factors, such as fertility of soil, customs over land use, and village institutions could also be influential. A distinction may be drawn, for example, between high-value, marketable production and poorer foodgrains, despite 'command' through debt, landholding, or social prestige. Above all, it mattered that agricultural decision-making was fragmented, that various levels and areas of autonomy persisted. Even the lowliest cultivator made some of his own decisions. The raiyat might be left alone to decide on techniques and even to choose the crop on most of his lands. Subject to caste restrictions and the demands of superiors, he could manage his labour too. But then, for all the other resources he needed—credit, land, water, even implements and animals—he was more likely to depend on others. Even within each basic production unit, the allocation of tasks among family members or between them and employees or patrons might be subject to restrictions and agreements.

The typical sponsor of cash crops could seldom overturn this collective decision-making, which enabled villages or groups to observe distinctions in land use or decide on methods of cultivation. Hence traders and planters chiefly influenced production decisions only on a small part of the best land. In Saran district, fields could be classified generally in six ways—the pattern was more or less repeated everywhere under different names. There was *korar*, land adjacent to the *basti* (or settlement) and used for the main cash crops (poppy, indigo, and sugarcane); then the much larger area of general farmland or *chour*, cultivated with *bhadoi* and rabi (autumn and spring) crops (maize, barley, pulses) in ordinary years or with paddy when there was abundant rain; then *bharsi*, similar land even further from the village; then *choum*, low-lying land used only for the main winter rice crop (almost 35 per cent of the total acreage); *bagh* lands containing fruit and other trees; and finally *parti* (waste or pasture). Hence the planter competed mainly over the allocation of korar, but did not introduce its links with the market nor otherwise fundamentally alter land use.[24] Moreover we can distinguish the sponsorship of cash crops from that of methods of cultivation. Intermediaries tried—but usually unsuccessfully—to prevent practices whereby different crops were sown together, often to avert risk or to produce home supplies alongside cash crops. Such partnerships allowed gradual adjustments from year to year and also rapid changes of tactic within each season. For example, cotton was generally grown with *arhar* (a pulse), linseed in rows with gram (chickpea) or as a border to mixed plots of wheat and barley, and the latter broadcast with rapeseed. The rather tender oilseed sesamum, or *til*, was universally grown as a border or mixed crop to provide household supplies of oil.[25] Nor could commercial pressures immediately unravel the many agreements over labour and implements, which persisted throughout the century and beyond. Labour sharing was called *badlaiya*, *palta*, or *painch*; agreement to plough fields in turn was generally called *bhanj*. These systems, usually regarded as reciprocal, were also strongly hierarchial.[26] Thus interdependence and subordination wove a web in which agricultural decisions were caught.

So-called commercialization differs case by case therefore, because modes of production evolve within specific cultural and technical parameters. The

24 G. Roy, Deputy Collector, to Saran Collector, 30 September/October 1889, PCR 350, 2/472, 1889–90.

25 See D.N. Mukherjee, 'Wheat Survey of Bengal', R&A Agriculture, A45–7, February 1908; R&A Agriculture, A7, May 1890; R&A Agriculture, A20–2, January 1891; R&A Agriculture, C35, September 1893 (experimental cultivation of Buxar and other wheats); R&A Agriculture, C5, February 1899 (on cotton).

26 Grierson, *Behar Peasant Life*, pp. 177–8.

system in Gaya, for example, depended on interrelated physical and political conditions. First, stiff clayey soils and the undulation of a succession of broad river valleys allowed the building of banks across the drainage lines and longer channels to divert water from rivers. Flow irrigation, necessarily preferred, implied high-level reservoirs so that, as the river beds were usually 8–10 feet below the gradually sloping countryside, most channels were several miles long and fed a number of reservoirs in turn. Such conditions demanded the close involvement of landlords and their agents. Secondly, by contrast, the lands on which cash rather than produce rents prevailed included poor plots that received no irrigation, as well as cultivable waste when first brought under the plough, but also lands irrigated from wells, often near rivers.[27] Similarly, different crops or combinations of crops might also impose particular agricultural regimes. The imperatives of oilseeds grown incidentally as a border to other crops and processed simply, locally, and at any time during the year were clearly very different from those of sugarcane, tying up land over several harvests, demanding irrigation, having to be guarded, needing complex processing as soon as possible, and producing high returns per acre.[28] There was a bewildering array of factors at work: ecology, location, soil type, technology, tenures, rentals, cropping patterns, and economic considerations—the field within which 'choices' were made in agriculture.

V

The findings of this paper modify some of the more sweeping interpretations of 'capitalism' and of 'development'. First, they contradict the idea that poorer, 'less commercial' areas took little part in commerce and experienced little occupational diversity, as well as the opposite idea that commercialization necessarily implies economic advance. We may note the very wide range of productive, artistic, ceremonial, and religious professions and the various and extensive trade even in rather depressed areas of Bihar in the early nineteenth century. Equally, the range of activities cited to indicate the dynamism of a small Punjabi centre in the 1920s and 1930s could be replicated in a similar

27 The reservoirs (ahars) were three-sided areas (some very large and on average covering about 100 acres) built out from a high point of land and fed by a channel (*pain*). Well water was usually raised by hand from shallow, temporary wells and was applied particularly to poppy cultivation, but also to wheat and sugarcane. See note 12 above.

28 Accordingly in Gaya, areas devoted to particular crops—most notably sugarcane—under a system of rotation, were customarily divided in each village into three parts shared between the different holdings. When sugarcane was cultivated, often followed by opium, the tenant paid a cash rent. In the third year, provided rice was grown and hence pain and ahara irrigation applied, a bhaoli rent was paid—the system was called *paran*.

large village in moribund Bihar in the 1870s.[29] This is not to say that all economies are the same. In Buchanan's Bihar, the high proportion of 'service' occupations tells us of the large local expenditure on manpower, rather than commodities, for display and ceremonies. Nor should the economic upheavals that (by contrast) occurred in India later in the nineteenth century be underestimated. The changes included new crops, enlarged cultivation, new agriculturists (from military, service, pastoral, 'tribal' people, and artisans), new routes and management for trade, reduced transactional cost (better communications and fewer local tolls and duties), new urban centres, increased and redirected exports, and changing organization and deployments of capital. Most of these raise problems of interpretation. Some were economically beneficial, some favoured certain areas or people, some had immediate or delayed ill effects. In agriculture, despite massive investment and rising returns (and applying the anachronistic notion of a 'national economy'), the issues to be considered include the loss of a particular sort of compact between state capital, agricultural development, and trade; the deflationary effects of some East India Company policies; the subsequent limits on state investment and the weakness of public institutions of capital; the diversion of investment into agriculture and away from manufacture (though not all processing); the concentration on low-value production in bulk; the discouragement of certain established local patterns of demand; the emphasis upon export trade (a model of economic advance perhaps less than apt for India) whenever state intervention and the development of the infrastructure took place; and the capture of large parts of the export trade by European investors and managers. But it is precisely because change was so marked in many respects that the lack of change at the lower levels of commercial production is of such interest.

Secondly, therefore, one can see that the oppressive social conditions in some regions were not in any simple sense the result of recent commercial expansion. They existed because of a colloquy amongst a range of conditions, including trade. The capitalist was often the chief beneficiary of the system of production; but he alone did not invent it, nor could he change it at will. One is reminded of Chayanov's pluralism, his reference to the inhibition of proletarianization in nineteenth-century Russia: 'While *in a production sense* concentration in agriculture is scarcely reflected in the foundation of new large-scale undertakings, *in an economic sense* capitalism as a general economic system makes great headway in agriculture.' The difference is that Chayanov shared with much Marxist and developmentalist thought the idea of rural non-

---

29 Compare Dewey, 'Consequences' and Robb, *Evolution*; see also Datta, 'Merchants and Peasants'. Presumably economic advance derived more from the level and rapidity of exchange and from profitability than from the range or type of activity.

capitalist production as essentially passive—family farm sectors subordinated to the 'hegemony' of capitalist relations[30]—and also transitional, following from the assumption by Marx that there must be a dominant mode to provide the 'law of motion' and 'a general illumination', whereby for example in the feudal Middle Ages, all capital (including artisans' tools) had a 'landed-property character' and in bourgeois society, agriculture is more and more 'a branch of industry...entirely dominated by capital'.[31] But in Bihar, it is far from clear that the localized command economy was subordinated to capitalism as a determinant of the mode of production, remaking it in its own image; almost the reverse was true. The elites did not newly *become* capitalist and their commercial dominance was mediated through pre-capitalist relations. This is a 'firm historical location', as called for by Byres, but an uncomfortable one.[32]

It will be noticed that these arguments also offer a critique of entrenched attitudes to 'pre-modern' production and the 'village community'. They accord with many of the descriptions by Indian anthropologists, which though concentrated to a misleading degree on the village as an isolate or exemplum, nonetheless repeatedly record its wider involvement, its interdependence, and its hierarchies as they influence agricultural production.[33] The assumption has been that these conditions are 'modern', largely because such recent observations contrast with assertions, from Aristotle to Polanyi, that subsistence and market cultivation are different in kind, even though the former may predominate in different units of production (feudal estate or peasant smallholding) and also survive peripheral contact with the market. Subsistence agriculture developed as household or family farm production-for-use. Supposedly, the peasant was self-sufficient both in labour and in consumption and naturally his activities could not be described in terms of capital or profit. The same features are central to Chayanov's definitions. It is the fact that the peasant farm ordinarily employs no labour that above all singles it out as a category, an enterprise making 'non-capitalist' decisions. It may indeed be found in some parts of India or at some social levels. But the idea of a *society* of egalitarian villages is now mostly abandoned, for the more distant as well as the recent past, even for its *fons et origo*, the Punjab. In the

30 Chayanov, 'Peasant Farm Organization', pp. 225 and 257.
31 Marx, *Grundrisse*, pp. 106–7.
32 Byres, 'Modes of Production', to which this paragraph is indebted. Compare Dobb, *Capitalism*, p. 11, on 'the preponderating influence of a single, more or less homogeneous economic form'.
33 See, for example, Mandelbaum, *Society in India*, pp. 327–45 and chapter 22; Béteille, *Caste, Class and Power*; Srinivas, *Remembered Village*, esp. pp. 128–9; Mayer, *Caste and Kinship*, p. 86 and chapter 5, 6, and 7.

canal colonies—the most favourable condition—peasant family farming extended at best only over about half the cultivated area.[34]

When we talk of peasants, it is hard not to think of a community that is undifferentiated, little involved in trade, and controlled from outside. We tend to assume that peasants change by *becoming* stratified or *beginning* to produce for the market. Yet there are no agrarian societies that are wholly egalitarian and isolated with no experience of exchange. We do not need to deal in absolutes. Degrees of self-sufficiency exist within families, within villages, within regions. At each level, some exchange is implied. Similarly, among many degrees of market orientation, even the strongest need not rule out some subsistence production. The important differences between economies are found in forms and structures of connection and hierarchy and in the manner as well as the degree of trade.

The experience of Indian peasants under colonial rule illustrates these points. The farmers of north India had been involved in commerce for millenia. Rural producers and (to a lesser extent) consumers took part in lively and various regional trade. By the eighteenth and in the nineteenth century, the cultivators' produce was entering the market in two main ways: through relationships of either rent or debt. And we have found the autonomy of the Indian village was inherently hierarchical, the concomitant barriers paradoxically the occasion for a tyranny made all the sterner by the accommodation they demanded. For a majority of the peasantry in Bihar, family farm independence was not possible. Indeed, since the social hierarchy developed from military-, caste-, and state-based structures, it is difficult to imagine when the golden age of peasant production could have been. Only the rich were their own masters, and their production drew on the labour of the poor. Commercialization increased this interdependence. It was easiest to supplement a certain amount of direct production using wage labour with a larger amount of what amounted to contracting out. Though more dramatic changes of production methods occurred at the margins of established Indian agriculture, with the central plantation and migrant wage labour systems adopted in the production of such important crops as tea and coffee, and though other large-scale and apparently disruptive investments were made in irrigation and transportation, most of the agricultural growth resulted from quasi- or 'forced' commercialization within prevailing norms, rather than from a capitalist transformation.[35]

The result has been said to be a mixed form of production, a 'coexistence of multiple modes', and attributed to the differentiation of the peasantry and

---

34 Ali, *Punjab*, p. 204; also Bhattacharya, 'Agricultural Labour'. But contrast Kessinger, *Vilyatpur*.
35 But contrast Dewey, 'Consequences', and Epstein, *Earthy Soil*.

consequent market imperfections. The idea seems traceable to a seminal article by Bagchi, which observed the 'symbiotic relationship between precapitalist and capitalist modes of production' with reference to the use of 'non-market coercion' by European planters and government opium agents.[36] Subsequently, Bhaduri theorized on the growing importance of forced commercial production in comparison with rent as a means of extracting surplus, on the fact that primitive accumulation relies on 'compulsions such as that created by the mechanism of debt' rather than competition on the basis of the relative efficiency of large and small farms, and on the detrimental developmental consequences of 'involuntary market involvement'.[37]

Such analyses usually contain some connected assumptions: (1) The direction of economic development is universal and linear, by means of changes in a unitary or predominant mode of production, and towards or through 'capitalism' and 'industrialization'—this despite Althusser's revisionism.[38] (2) India's economic misfortunes result particularly from economic *reversal*, chiefly a failure to continue to industrialize.[39] (3) Indian agricultural production and producers were therefore subordinated to foreign capitalists, and a rural proletariat was created. (4) The colonial state and its laws were largely responsible. Thus Das, distinguishing between structures of work and exploitation, with the latter changing from rack-renting to usury and wage labour, describes 'a distorted economy based on a distorted commercialisation'.[40] Mishra, seeing the permanent revenue settlement of 1793 as a crucial divide in the agrarian history of Bihar, argues that marketing was stimulated because cash rents were demanded to meet the higher tax and because the new status for zamindars damaged non-zamindari land rights and permitted intermediary tenures (which in Champaran explained the success of the indigo planters).

The present essay, without necessarily challenging all these conclusions, begins outside the prescriptions about history and social structures that underlie them. It suggests a more fundamental revision. Clearly by the early 1800s, or even earlier, some local producers already experienced competition from imported commodities; others suffered from a paucity of local demand when so many goods and services were exchanged through credit transactions, reflecting social prestige or in accordance with village custom. Moreover, on the one hand, free peasant production was possible but only for some, with its incidence having little to do with markets; on the other, commercial agriculture

36 Bharadwaj, 'Commercialisation', pp. 10–11, quoting Bagchi.
37 Bhaduri, *Backward Agriculture*, pp. 8–9, 26–7, and 100.
38 Thorner, 'Semi-feudalism or Capitalism'.
39 For a recent summary of the debate, see C. Krishnamurty, 'Deindustrialization'.
40 Das, *Agrarian Unrest*, pp. 1–78; Chaudhuri, 'Depeasantization'.

was in large part controlled by intermediaries or by 'peasants' acting instead of capitalists. When we examine the experience of Bihar, we find areas of rural self-sufficiency and areas of commerce that were only part of a complex array of forces influencing the modes of production and precluding *any* easy typologies. As a result, we abandon any attempt to resolve the heated and irreconcilable confusions among those trying to explain India in theoretical or Marxist terms, and understand why they tend to produce hybrid terms (such as 'quasi-feudal', 'trans-class', or 'false consciousness').

VI

What model of village autonomy are we left with if the old village community of family farm producers is unacceptable and yet the capitalist cannot wholly transform it through trade? One repository of village autonomy is custom and belief, which delineate local traditions. They represent not a fixed agenda, but an orbit for subjective negotiations and choices. In that sense, a Bihari cultivator's decisions were hedged in by his own experience and customs. He operated, as revealed in a contemporary linguistic record, within a rich tapestry of distinctions, implying standards of behaviour as well as ecological norms. The many hundreds of names of soils were not just descriptive but prescriptive.[41] Agricultural processes too had a clear framework in language, for example in the distinct words for first, second, third, and fourth ploughings; for several kinds of re-ploughing after sowing; and for styles of ploughing (straight, diagonal, circular, cross, and so on). Such terminology seems not only to describe but almost to generate actions. Thus the same word might generally be used for hoeing and for weeding, but there was a range of words for particular kinds of both activities.[42] Conversely, a restriction of vocabulary would mark a greater control over the environment. The Bihari lexicon seems more than technical; it is like snapshots of an attitude of mind.

In proverbs too one finds, more directly, a set of perceptions and value judgements. Many sayings recorded agricultural information. Behind such popular wisdom lay a broader corpus of belief. The agricultural calendar embodied memories that circumscribed practice—not simply that winter rice should be sown after the first fall of rain in Jeth (May–June), but that transplanting should begin after a special festival on the fifth day of Sawan (July–August). Religious observations and sacred texts added to the sense of an unavoidable rhythm shared by the heavens, by time, by the seasons, by the cycle of crops, and hence by man. The divisions of time were imagined as

---

[41] The following discussion is based on Grierson, *Behar Peasant Life*, especially division III.

[42] For example, for deep or superficial weedings, or for the first hoeing for sugarcane in January–February, or for the special hoeing in June–May.

so many rajas bestowing gifts. The recipient—or sufferer—was defined by his part in this transaction. A cultivator was not just one who grew crops, but one who performed certain agricultural functions according to the norms. In a host of customs and rhymes, the cultivator was reminded of the expected character of the season; he was provided with a timetable according to which he could anticipate heat or rainfall and carry out particular tasks, at once social, religious, and agricultural.[43] He was offered the impression of predictability in—and hence an ability to respond to—the environment amid variable seasons. For this reason also, agricultural decisions must be seen as taking place within a value system. Even crops were perceived as existing in a social as well as an economic hierarchy. Rice was a power in the land, its numerous varieties compared with the clans of the Rajputs or the Babhans, the dominant castes; but the millets were associated with poverty and lowliness.[44] If food were a major and visible illustration of status, cropping decisions could hardly be socially neutral or easily imposed by outsiders.

Despite these very different conditions, nineteenth-century tenancy debates, pleas for state intervention, and popular protests were (and are) all sustained on European models such as industrialization's defeat of 'community' or the exploitation of 'workers' by individual property and capital. Such arguments distorted India's past and its present. An imposed economic change did not need a Weberian reform of custom, Marxian classes, or suppression of skill *à la* Andrew Ure. Hence specialist intermediaries still had to operate various coercive levers and, at village level, were not dislodged; indeed, tenancy or contract laws and trade increased their hold. Produce for marketing outside the locality was still secured almost entirely by itinerants (*bepari*s), by general or specialist traders and agents who dealt on the one hand in the villages with cultivators or local controllers and on the other hand in the towns with merchants. Direct links between village and exporter were still rare, though reported to be increasing late in the century. Usually any increase in marketing from within villages may be presumed to have represented a few villagers, including *bania*s, expanding their mercantile activities. The expansion was not so great as to suggest that it was undertaken by ordinary raiyats. Moreover, the bepari as an institution was still alive and well in the 1920s, while the growing number of carts—given the increasing scale of trade, roads, and population—does not prove a widening of direct popular access to the market, even in rice.

43 Here, too, the labels were complex and precise. The year was divided not only into 12 months, each with a light and a dark half, but also into 27 lunar asterisms, each associated with some important agricultural activity. See Grierson, *Behar Peasant Life*, division vi.
44 Ibid., p. 216.

Scholars are understandably uncertain about classes in rural Bihar. Bhaduri compounds intermediaries and long-distance traders, and concentrates on 'direct agricultural producers, mostly small peasants' with a right of occupancy.[45] But Pouchepadass notes in north Bihar:

des districts...qui sont...presqu'entièrement la propriété d'un ou de quelques très grands *zamīndār*, et où il n'existe pratiquement pas de paysans propriétaires. On y trouve, certes, une abondante population de tenanciers de rang moyen. Mais comment dire de ces paysans moyens qu'ils jouissent [sic] d'une sécurité particulière, alors qu'il [sic] sont soumis en permanence aux menaces et aux formes très diverses de contrainte extra-économique liées à leur situation semi-féodale?[46]

'Middle peasants' may be expected by theory; but empirically further disaggregations are needed. As village autonomy was inherently hierarchical, this is a tale not only of capitalists—or even *kulaks*—and peasants. At different levels, people repeatedly gained control over others. There was no one distinct class lording it over a depressed peasantry or rural proletariat. Rent- and credit-based controls were repeated in small ways throughout the society, in village-wide arrangements, and between even slightly richer and slightly poorer villagers. Thus central to the argument are the pre-existence of mutual dependence, the chains of command, and a fragmentation of decision-making. Authorities at different levels successively controlled elements of tenurial and economic power. Labour too was variously controlled. Even so-called harvest shares—for agricultural, religious, and other village services, or for artisans—were as much expressions of finely graded hierarchy as of community. The intermediary was therefore not one category of individual, but many. The sugar factor, the opium agent, the village headman, and the richer cultivator represent together a multiplicity of brokers, all of them within as well as outside the village. They link different parts of the picture; but they also penetrate them, deconstructing the elements (peasant, lord, village, trader) we tend to reify as exclusive categories.

Over the long term, it has been argued, north Indian elites became more directly involved in agriculture.[47] In the nineteenth century, of the usual routes to dominance, only military coercion was being inhibited; land control and economic power were on the whole encouraged. On the other hand, local environment and custom remained as guerilla bands, swimming among the

---

45 Bhaduri, *Backward Agriculture*, pp. 17–18.

46 Pouchepadass, *Caste et Classe*, p. 84: 'Those districts that are almost entirely the property of one or more very large zamindars, and where there are almost no peasant proprietors. Certainly, there will be numerous middle-ranking tenants. But how can one distinguish among these middling peasants, between those who enjoy some individual security, and others who are permanently subject to intimidation and to very varied, extra-economic constraints, arising from their semi-feudal situation.'

47 See Bayly, *Rulers, Merchants*.

people and thwarting the heavy armaments of capitalism. Hence 'commercial' production was dispersed; command over men and women remained the core. Workers were still captured through social and economic power for the profits from their semi-independent production. The prerequisite and the legacy were layers of intermediaries of distinct character and position. Their capital did not newly subject and dispossess agrarian labour; it reinforced subservience. Their role was both political (from land control, legal structures, and the exercise of physical power) and social (vested in status, value systems, and beliefs). They did not merely occupy a space left for local trade by a weak colonial power or by limited market encroachment; they maintained their position despite massive interventions by the state and by long-distance trade. Nor were they merely the local arm of the state or international capital; they sought, in Bihar, to isolate these external forces from actual cultivators. There is nothing immutable about the situations described, but they are not especially or necessarily transitional. Their origins, nature, and strength need proper description if we are to understand change. In this case, it should be no surprise that later, when population and property values rose and even petty holdings were seized, these mostly went to rural elites.

References

Ali, I., *The Punjab Under Imperialism 1885–1947*, Princeton, 1988.
Amin, S., *Sugarcane and Sugar in Gorakhpur: An Inquiry into Peasant Production for Capitalist Enterprise in Colonial India*, Delhi, 1984.
Bagchi, A.K., 'Colonialism and the Nature of "Capitalist" Enterprise in India', *Economic and Political Weekly*, (30 July 1988), pp. PE 38–50.
Baker, C.J., *An Indian Rural Economy: The Tamilnad Countryside*, Oxford, 1984.
Banerji, H., *Agrarian Society of the Punjab, 1849–1901*, Delhi, 1980.
Bayly, C.A., 'Indian Merchants in a "Traditional" Setting: Benares, 1780–1830', in C. Dewey and A.G. Hopkins (eds), *Imperial Impact: Studies in the Economic History of Africa and India*, London, 1978.
———, *Rulers, Townsmen and Bazaars: North Indian Society in the Age of British Expansion, 1770–1870*, Cambridge, 1983.
———, 'State and Economy in India over Seven Hundred Years', *Economic History Review*, 2nd ser., xxxviii (1985), pp. 583–96.
———, *Indian Society and the Making of the British Empire*, Cambridge, 1988.
Béteille, A., *Caste, Class and Power: Changing Patterns of Stratification in a Tanjore Village*, Berkeley, 1971.
Bhaduri, A., *The Economic Structure of Backward Agriculture*, London, 1983.
Bharadwaj, K., 'A View of Commercialisation in Indian Agriculture and the Development of Capitalism', *Journal of Peasant Studies*, vol. 12, 1985, pp. 7–25.
Bhattacharya, N., 'Agricultural Labour and Production: Central and South-east Punjab, 1870–1940', in K.N. Raj, N. Bhattacharya, S. Guha, and S. Padhi (eds), *Essays on the Commercialization of Indian Agriculture*, Delhi, 1985, pp. 105–62.
Bhattacharya, S. and R. Thapar (eds), *Situating Indian History*, Delhi, 1986.

Bose, S., *Agrarian Bengal: Economy, Social Structure and Politics, 1919–1947*, Cambridge, 1986.
Breman, J., *Patronage and Exploitation: Changing Agrarian Relations in South Gujerat, India*, Berkeley, 1974.
Buchanan, F., *An Account of the District of Shahabad in 1812–13*, Patna, 1934.
Byres, T.J., 'Modes of Production and Non-European Pre-colonial Societies: The Nature and Significance of the Debate', *Journal of Peasant Studies*, vol. 12, 1985, pp. 1–18.
Charlesworth, N., *British Rule and the Indian Economy 1800–1914*, London, 1982.
———, *Peasants and Imperial Rule: Agriculture and Agrarian Society in the Bombay Presidency, 1850–1935*, Cambridge, 1985.
Chaudhury, B.B. (Benoy Chowdhury), *The Growth of Commercial Agriculture in Bengal, 1757–1900*, Calcutta, 1964.
———, 'The Process of Depeasantization in Bengal and Bihar, 1885–1947', *Indian History Review*, pp. 105–65.
———, 'Agricultural Growth in Bengal and Bihar, 1770–1860: Growth of Cultivation since the Famine of 1770,' *Bengal Past and Present*, 1976, pp. 290–340.
———, 'Rural Power Structure and Agricultural Productivity in Eastern India, 1757–1947' in M. Desai, S.H. Rudolph, and A. Rudra (eds), *Agrarian Power and Agricultural Productivity in South Asia*, Berkeley, 1984, pp. 100–70.
Chaudhuri, K.N. and C.J. Dewey (eds), *Economy and Society: Essays in Indian Economic History*, Delhi, 1979.
Chayanov, A.V., 'Peasant Farm Organization' in D. Thorner, B. Kerblay, and R.E.F. Smith (eds), *A.V. Chayanov on the Theory of Peasant Economy*, Manchester, 1986.
Colebrooke, H., *The Husbandry of Bengal*, Calcutta, 1804; London, 1806.
Das, A.N., *Agrarian Unrest and Socio-economic Change in Bihar, 1900–1980*, New Delhi, 1983.
———, 'Changel: Three Centuries of an Indian Village', *Journal of Peasant Studies*, vol. 15, 1987, pp. 3–60.
Datta, R., 'Merchants and Peasants: A Study of the Structure of Local Trade in Late Eighteenth-century Bengal', *Indian Economic and Social History Review*, vol. 23, 1986, pp. 379–402.
———, 'Rural Bengal: Social Structure and Agrarian Economy in the Late Eighteenth Century', unpublished PhD Thesis, University of London, 1990.
Desai, M., S.H. Rudolph, and A. Rudra (eds), *Agrarian Power and Agricultural Productivity in South Asia*, Berkeley, 1984.
Dewey C., 'Some Consequences of Military Expenditure in British India: The Case of the Upper Sind Sagar Doab, 1849–1947', in C. Dewey (ed.), *Arrested Development in India: The Historical Dimension*, New Delhi, 1988, pp. 93–169.
Dewey, C. and A.G. Hopkins (eds), *The Imperial Impact: Studies in the Economic History of Africa and India*, London, 1978.
Dobb, M., *Studies in the Development of Capitalism*, London, 1963.
Epstein, S.J.M., *The Earthy Soil: Bombay Peasants and the Indian Nationalist Movement, 1919–1947*, Delhi, 1988.
Fisher, C.M., 'Planters and Peasants: The Ecological Context of Agrarian Unrest on the Indigo Plantations of North Bihar', in C. Dewey and A.G. Hopkins (eds), *The Imperial Impact: Studies in the Economic History of Africa and India*, London, 1978, pp. 114–31.

Friedman, H., 'World Market, State and Family Farm', *Comparative Studies in Society and History*, vol. 20, 1978, pp. 545–86.
Guha, S., *The Agrarian Economy of the Bombay Deccan 1818–1941*, Delhi. 1985.
Grierson, G.A., *Behar Peasant Life*, Calcutta, 1885.
———, *Notes on the District of Gaya*, Calcutta, 1893.
Harriss, J. (ed.), *Rural Development*, London, 1982.
Hill, P., *Dry Grain Farming Families*, Cambridge, London, 1982.
———, *Development Economics on Trial: The Anthropological Case for a Prosecution*, Cambridge, 1986.
Hunter, W.W., *A Statistical Account of Bengal*, Calcutta, 1876.
Islam, S., *Bengal Land Tenure: The Origin and Growth of Intermediate Interests in the 19th Century*, Rotterdam, 1985.
Kessinger, T.G., *Vilyatpur: 1848–1968*, Berkeley, 1974.
Khan, I.G., 'Revenue, Agriculture and Warfare in North India: Technical Knowledge and the Post-Mughal Elites, from the Mid-18th to the Early 19th Century', unpublished PhD Thesis, University of London, 1990.
Kling, B.B., *The Blue Mutiny: The Indigo Disturbances in Bengal 1859–1862*, Calcutta, 1977.
Krishnamurty, J., 'Deindustrialization in Gangetic Bihar during the Nineteenth Century: Another Look at the Evidence', *Indian Economic and Social History Review*, vol. 22, 1985, pp. 399–416.
Kumar, D., *Land and Caste in South India*, Cambridge, 1965.
——— (ed.), *The Cambridge Economic History of India*, II, Cambridge, 1983.
Ludden, D., 'Productive Power in Agriculture: A Survey of Work on the Local History of British India', in M. Desai, S.H. Rudolph, and A. Rudra, eds, *Agrarian Power and Agricultural Productivity in South Asia* (Berkeley, 1984), pp. 49–99.
———, *Peasant History in South India*, Princeton, 1985.
Mackeson, F. 'Journal of a Voyage from Lodiana to Mithankkot by the Satraj River', *Journal of the Asiatic Society of Bengal*, vol. 6, 1837.
Mandelbaum, D.G., *Society in India, vol. II. Change and Continuity*, Berkeley, 1970.
Marshall, P.J., *Bengal: The British Bridgehead, Eastern India 1740–1828*, Cambridge, 1987.
Marx, K., *Grundrisse*, Harmondsworth, 1973.
Mayer, A.C., *Caste and Kinship in Central India*, London, 1960.
McAlpin, M.B., *Subject to Famine: Food Crisis and Economic Change in Western India, 1860–1920*, Princeton, 1983.
Mishra, G., *Agrarian Problems of Permanent Settlement: A Case Study of Champaran*, New Delhi, 1978.
Perlin, F., 'Proto-industrialisation and Pre-colonial South Asia', *Past and Present*, vol. 98, 1983, pp. 30–95.
Pouchepadass, J. (ed.), *Caste et Classe en Asie du Sud*, Paris, 1982.
———, *Planteurs et Paysans Dans l'Inde Coloniale: L'indigo du Bihar et le Mouvement Gandhien du Champaran (1917–1918)*, Paris, 1986.
———, *Paysans de la Plaine du Gange: le district de Champaran, 1860–1950*, Paris, 1989.
Raj, K.N., N. Bhattacharya, S. Guha, and S. Padhi (eds), *Essays on the Commercialization of Indian Agriculture*, Delhi, 1985.
Ray, R., *Change in Bengal Agrarian Society, 1760–1850*, New Delhi, 1983.

Robb, Peter, 'Ideas in Agrarian History: Some Observations on the British and Nineteenth-century Bihar', *Journal of Royal Asiatic Society*, n.s., 1990, pp. 17–43.

———, *The Evolution of British Policy towards Indian Politics 1880–1920: Essays on Colonial Attitudes, Imperial Strategies and Bihar*, New Delhi, 1992.

Roseberry, J.R., *Imperial Rule in Punjab*, Riverdale, 1987.

Sengupta, N., 'The Indigenous Irrigation Organization in South Bihar', *Indian Economic and Social History Review*, vol. 17, 1980, pp. 157–89.

Sharma, G.D., 'Urban Credit and the Market Economy in Western India, c. 1750–1850' in Gareth Austin and Kaoru Sugihara (eds), *Local Supplies of Credit in the Third World, 1750–1960*, Basengstoke, 1993.

Singh, R.P., and A. Kumar, *Monograph of Bihar: A Geographical Study*, Patna, 1970.

Srinivas, M.N., *The Remembered Village*, Berkeley, 1976.

Stein, B., '"Arrested Development" In India—but When and Where?' in C. Dewey, (ed.), *Arrested Development in India: The Historical Dimension*, New Delhi, 1984, pp. 49–65.

Stokes, E., *The Peasant and the Raj*, Cambridge, 1978.

Subrahmanyam, Sanjay (ed.), *Merchants, Markets and the State in Early Modern India*. Delhi, 1960.

———, 'Commerce and State Power in Eighteenth-century India: Some Reflections', *South Asia Research*, 8, 1988, pp. 97–110.

Subramanian, L., 'Banias and the British: The Role of Indigenous Credit in the Process of Imperial Expansion in Western India in the Second Half of the Eighteenth Century', *Modern Asian Studies*, vol. 21, 1987, pp. 473–510.

Thorner, A., 'Semi-feudalism or Capitalism: The Contemporary Debate on Classes and Modes of Production in India', in J. Pouchepadass (ed.), *Caste et Classe en Asie du Sud*, Paris, 1982, pp. 19–72.

Torri, M., 'Surat during the Second Half of the Eighteenth Century: What Kind of Social Order?', *Modern Asian Studies*, vol. 21, 1987, pp. 679–710.

Ure, A., *The Philosophy of Manufactures*, London, 1835.

Washbrook, D.A., *The Emergence of Provincial Politics: The Madras Presidency, 1870–1920*, Cambridge, 1976.

Watt, G., *A Dictionary of the Economic Products of India*, vol. vi, London, 1890.

Whitcombe, E., *Agrarian Conditions in Northern India. I. The United Provinces under British Rule 1850–1900*, Berkeley, 1972.

Wright, H.R.S., *East-Indian Economic Problems in the Age of Cornwallis and Raffles*, London, 1961.

7. Hierarchy and Resources*
Peasant Stratification in Late Nineteenth-century Bihar

This essay considers changes in rural society attributable to British rule, but again stresses the difficulty of finding objective bases for classes even given colonial standardizations and zamindari oppression. The focus this time is on variability and the economic and political contingencies that affected status and well-being.

The rural history of modern India has been and is being written for the most part within the terms of that dictum of Louis Dumont—that 'a certain hierarchy of ideas, things and people, is indispensable to social life'.[1] Even a scholar who questioned the distributions of power between sections of the community in north India, arguing for interdependence of landlords, peasantry, and traders, still emphasized village controllers and 'momentum towards social differentiation' 'to produce groups of rich peasants, or rather to continue their existence'.[2] The identity of such rich peasants remains obscure or at least

---

* First published in *Modern Asian Studies*, 13(1), 1979, pp. 97–126.

1 Louis Dumont, *Homo Hierarchicus*, London, 1972, p. 54. In recent years, the 'rich peasant' has been most often studied, though I.J. Catanach, *Rural Credit in Western India 1857–1930*, Berkeley, 1970, prefers 'a solid middle peasantry' and David Washbrook, 'Economic Development and Social Stratification in Rural Madras: The Dry Region, 1878–1929' in Clive Dewey and A.G. Hopkins (eds), *The Imperial Impact*, London, 1977, finds magnates so dominant as to preclude a true peasantry of cultivators making their own economic decisions.

2 Peter Musgrave, 'An Indian Rural Society: Aspects of the Structure of Rural Society in the United Provinces, 1860–1920', PhD Thesis, Cambridge, 1976, Chapter 2. See also his 'Landlords and Lords of the Land: Estate Management and Social Control in Uttar Pradesh, 1860–1920', *Modern Asian Studies*, 6(3), 1972: he finds estates dispersed and intermixed, and management partly dependent on tenants for its power. The confusion that may arise is illustrated when C.A. Bayly writes of 'village-controlling peasants', contrasted apparently with non-occupancy tenants and 'area-zamindars' but identified either as 'often Kurmis, Kachchis and Ahirs' or as 'subdivided but literate Brahmin and Rajput small-holding communities' and moreover preceding in political awareness a 'thrifty but unprotected middle peasantry'; see *The Local Roots of Indian Politics*, Oxford, 1975, pp. 9, 51, and 220. See also note 22 below.

specific to the region being studied; but obviously it would be very useful to have similar generalizations about social stratification in the study of modern Bihar. Hitherto the foundation at least of political histories there has been caste or caste groups;[3] yet economic hierarchy, that related but more enigmatic pecking order, is surely equally important. In this paper, I seek a basis for making such generalizations. Grave difficulties stand in the way. My conclusion throws doubt on the applicability to Bihar of the idea of stable hierarchies and suggests an alternative approach.

It is quite possible to characterize different parts of the area in general terms, basing the social picture on the three roles of rent collection, cultivation, and labouring, which were more or less identifiable with ownership of land, surplus or at least subsistence tenancy, and landlessness either complete or partial. Thus Muzaffarpur and Patna become districts of small landlords; Champaran, Darbhanga, and Saran districts of a few large estates. But no two observers are likely to agree on what these situations imply. Were small landlords more oppressive than large because closer at hand, or less so because nearer in status to substantial cultivators? The categories, though mutually exclusive as roles in relation to a single plot of land, were not so in relation to any one person, and therefore in general none functioned uniformly as an indicator of wealth and social position—strictures that apply particularly to their use in the examination of change over time. Nor will analysis at this level of vagueness help with such questions as the impact of tenancy laws, the bases of Bihari poverty, or the development of politics. Above all, it does not help define the rich peasant.

More exact descriptions are needed. We may accept, however, one assumption of the hierarchy of landlord, tenant, and labourer, namely that rent collection (under which we may subsume moneylending by landlords) was generally more socially and financially rewarding than cultivation, and cultivation than labour. In the 1890s in Muzaffarpur, the range between these occupations was narrow (agricultural incomes of Rs 48, 18, and 10) and, on average, proprietary holdings were less than twice the size of occupancy holdings (1.64 acres). Holdings did not equate with individuals, but the proportion of 2:1 seems reasonable, seeing that an estimated five per cent

---

3 See, for example, Cletus James Bishop, 'Sachchidananda Sinha and the Making of Modern Bihar', PhD Thesis, University of Virginia, 1972; but also the criticism of Lucy Carroll, 'Caste, Social Change and the Social Scientist: A Note on the Ahistorical Approach to Indian Social History', *Journal of Asian Studies*, XXXV(1), 1975. Walter Hauser, 'The Bihar Provincial Kisan Sabha, 1929–1942', PhD Thesis, University of Chicago, 1961, stresses economic issues and political rivalry in the kisan movement, but still supports the general political importance of caste (pp. 13, 37–8, 75–8, and 82–4).

of the population (proprietors) had nine per cent of holdings and 15½ per cent of the land (ratios of 1:1.8 and 1:3 per cent) while 55 per cent of the population (occupancy ryots) had 82 per cent of the holdings and 74 per cent of the land (ratios of 1:1.5) and 1:1.34 per cent). The comparison suggests that even though the average cultivated area owned by each proprietor was only nine acres, most incomes that were much larger than others were likely to depend on rents, not on land directly held. The distribution was affected by competition for land—in populous and fertile areas zamindars cultivated more and probably in larger units, as true proprietary holdings tended to be about the same size as raiyati ones (1.68 acres) and other lands that proprietors cultivated directly were larger (4.34 acres). But it was apparently not altered by whether zamindars were petty or large, since in parts of Champaran 77 per cent of holdings similarly accounted for 82 per cent of the land.[4] The landholding pattern confirms what Bihari ideas of status imply, that labourers would be employed, or land let out, or rents farmed as soon as each was possible. It follows that the key to stratification must be in discrimination within the majority group of settled raiyats, and not between the three categories more easily identified. Moreover, if rent collection was the main source of income for landlords, then the ability to avoid or reduce rent payment was likely to be an important factor in differentiating between tenants.

In the bhaoli system, which prevailed over much of south Bihar, rent was theoretically a fixed share of the produce, usually nine-sixteenths, though payment might be made in cash if the raiyat undertook to market the landlord's share. Bhaoli tended to make actual rentals high, definite, and in step with any rise in agricultural prices, and moreover to prove relatively most disadvantageous to the raiyats on the best land and in the best seasons—unless of course, as quite often occurred, a raiyat held some land bhaoli and some on cash rents, with the proportion differing with each harvest.[5] Bhaoli had

4 Proceedings of the Government of India, Revenue and Agriculture Department, Revenue Branch, hereafter, R&A Revenue, B17–18, January 1897, National Archives of India, New Delhi; C.J. Stevenson-Moore, *Final Report on the Survey and Settlement Operations in the Muzaffarpur District 1892–1899*, Calcutta, 1901, pp. 285–363. I use the terms landlord, zamindar, proprietor, and malik (as also raiyat, tenant, and cultivator) more or less interchangeably to describe social and economic roles rather than, in most contexts, legal status. The important issues and distinctions have been much discussed (see Walter C. Neale, *Economic Change in Rural India*, New Haven, 1962, chapter 3); but provided there is full awareness of specific features in any explanation, it seems immaterial which of the admittedly approximate terms is used here.

5 On bhaoli, see R&A Revenue A16–46, July 1883, and A11–16, February 1890; Patna Collector to Patna Commissioner, 10 December 1880, Patna Commissioner's Records (hereafter PCR), *basta* 350, Bihar State Archives, Patna (formerly State Central Record Office); Patna Commissioner to Board of Revenue (Bengal), 25 August 1882,

various advantages, chiefly in ensuring the zamindar's performance of works called gilandazi, for example the maintenance of irrigation (which, as it usually involved the interests of more than one village or estate, was beyond the capacity of even a group of raiyats), and secondly in spreading the burden of scarcity in a region of uncertain climate so that, as one Koiri cultivator put it in 1880, 'under bhaoli I and my children can live, [whereas] paying naqdi [money rent] we live one year and starve the rest'.[6] (Money rents indeed were often associated with rent-farmers, or thikadars, who had bid competitively for short leases.) The disadvantage of bhaoli tenure, however, was (as officials were fond of insisting) that 'Nothing could be better adapted to pauperism and to destroy the growth of habits of foresight, economy and independence'[7]—or, expressing it less emotively, to discourage the emergence of substantial cultivators. The proviso to this was that the system operated in practice as it appeared in theory.

Officials and others anxious to argue a case have given a harsh picture of the zamindars of Bihar. Though overdrawn, it does enable us to identify some of the bases of landlord power. According to such accounts, the only check on a zamindar's exactions was his own self-interest.[8] On bhaoli estates, he would collect directly if possible or through a thikadar if necessary. Division of the harvest took place on the threshing floor, but the 'rokhing' (or seizure) of the crop in the field was common enough.[9] In law, the power of distraint supported zamindars of all kinds; in practice, intimidation and fraud sustained their hold over their tenants, and rent was everywhere augmented by additional, mostly illegal, dues or *abwabs*.[10] Rent suits were rare. Deliberate steps were taken, indeed, to prevent the incursion of the law into landlord–

PCR 336, 5/44. Hauser, 'Bihar Provincial Kisan Sabha', p. 26, notes that proportions taken by the zamindar varied each year and in practice were 'never' (often not?) more than a quarter.

6 Gaya Collector to Patna Commissioner, 20 January 1881, PCR 350.

7 Reynolds, 11 December 1880, R&A Revenue, A11–16, February 1890.

8 See Patna Commissioner to Board of Revenue (Bengal), 18 June 1890, PCR 345–6, 1887–8. It is important to note how much of the evidence is polemical, arguing for or against tenancy laws, in a situation in which the inadequacies of the statistics increase our reliance on subjective accounts. Hauser bases his views on anti-zamindari sources and favours their interpretation of landlord-tenant conflicts (see note 13 below); P.C. Roy employed some of the evidence used for this paper to argue for zamindari omnipotence in *The Rent Question in Bengal*, Calcutta, 1883, pp. 122–34 and 137–52.

9 Gaya Collector to Patna Commissioner, 19 May 1890, PCR 352, 12/4.

10 See Patna Collector to Patna Commissioner, 10 December 1880, PCR 350; Gaya Revenue administration report, PCR 347, 12/14, 1885–6; Muzaffarpur ditto, PCR 340, 12/4, 1884–5; Patna Collector to Patna Commissioner, 9 May 1892, PCR 357, 12/9; Saran Collector to Patna Commissioner, 30 April 1885, PCR 342.

tenant relations—zamindars seldom made written leases and hardly ever gave full receipts. They manipulated their records (and less frequently actual holdings) to prevent the growth of occupancy rights through continuous occupation, and also opposed other physical evidence of a raiyat's interest in the land (such as pucca houses) even though in custom the raiyat's interest might be freely admitted—for example, it seems that although before 1885 only about one per cent of raiyats were thought to be shown on landlords' jamabandi papers as having held the *same* land for over 12 years, 60 per cent had in practice held *some* land in the same village for that long.[11] But even where, say, an occupancy right did exist in effect in this way, obviously it was to the advantage of the stronger of two parties to keep the terms of their mutual transactions disputable in law.

Thus the twin props of zamindari power were prestige and force. The landlord needed prestige so that his demands would be met without question—if raiyats had legal rights (of occupancy or to transfer holdings), it would diminish the *izzat* of the landlord and weaken his position even if the rights were identical with those usually enjoyed in practice. Equally the zamindars needed to be able, in a sense, to choose their tenants—and thus objected to anything that reduced the power of eviction or allowed 'objectionable' strangers (such as indigo planters) to acquire tenancies without their consent. They used force in the sense of deploying armed retainers (sending men to guard the uncut crop, quartering *sowar*s on refractory villages, preventing a raiyat from having access to his fields or imprisoning him, and in extreme cases having resort to arson and murder); but they chiefly used force in the sense of keeping the raiyats as tenants-at-will if they could, regardless of the law. They would lend to their raiyats to keep them in debt or would claim, on paper at least, much higher rents than they expected to receive and enter the fictional balance as arrears, so that 'interest' was one of the most common of the additional cesses and eviction the constant implicit threat. Indeed in some senses, zamindars clearly liked to think of the raiyats as less than tenants-at-will—for though certain cesses were rationalized as charges for services (such as *dak* or *band behri*) or for the costs of rent collection, many were justified as contributions to any extra or unusual personal outlay of the zamindar himself (a new elephant, a marriage, the entertainment of a visiting official).[12]

[11] Gaya Revenue administration report, 1889–90, PCR 352, Shahabad Collector to Patna Commissioner, 8 November, and Saran Collector to Patna Commissioner, 15 December 1880, PCR 350; R&A Revenue A16–46, July 1883; J. Tweedie, Patna judge, PCR 356, 10/40, 1892–3.

[12] Patna Collector to Patna Commissioner, 10 December; Shahabad Collector to Patna Commissioner, 15 December; Saran Collector to Patna Commissioner, 15 December 1880; and Gaya Collector to Patna Commissioner, 20 January 1881, PCR 350. Also see Roy, *Rent Question in Bengal*, pp. 67–70.

According to the contemporary and now familiar indictment of the zamindar, therefore, the Western concept of private property—such as the British gave to the zamindar—penetrated but imperfectly to the level of the raiyat. The inevitable tendency of such oppression, it would seem, would be to depress almost all tenants to a uniform level of bare subsistence, the rare exceptions being those who were really zamindars in disguise—representatives and servants of absent, distant, or quarrelling landlords or members of zamindari families occupying raiyati holdings, perhaps at nominal rates to avoid government cesses. And yet, though it will not do for Bihar to exaggerate the difficulties faced by zamindars,[13] there is a sense in which even their oppression may be seen to be precarious once we understand its basis in prestige and force, commodities subject to shifts or erosion. If rural power was still in essence customary and informal, it might in turn be flexible in response to circumstances. Thus we may postulate the existence of well-to-do peasants to the extent that exploitation was not uniform.

The power of the landlord, then, was not absolute. Much might be concealed from him. No less an authority than W.B. Grierson, celebrated Collector of Gaya and opponent of the bhaoli system, admitted that 'even petty landlords who can call in the assistance of their relatives to check appraisement are cheated with respect to Bhaoli produce'.[14] The government itself could hardly avoid being deceived, and preferred cash rents largely for this reason.[15] The nature of individual holdings helped in the confusion—they were not compact units but 'small patches of land...interlaced with plots forming parts of other holdings, and marked off...by two paths a few inches in breadth and half a foot in height'.[16] Bihar zamindars seldom had a private servant in each village and depended on the patwari, in whose interest it often was to not report on changes. He could (for a consideration) allow influential raiyats to cultivate vacant, reserved, or waste land, or could falsify the record,

---

13 In the well-known descriptions by Bernard Cohn, for example in 'Political Systems, in Eighteenth Century India', *Journal of the American Oriental Society*, vol. 82 (July–September 1962), p. 316, all groups within a territory provided members of the dominant lineage with a share of the produce, cash dues, or goods and services as appropriate. Hauser, 'Bihar Provincial Kisan Sabha', accepts this and the implication that zamindars had 'overwhelming and uninhibited power' (p. 15), a description that Musgrave, 'An Indian Rural Society' and 'Landlords and Lords of the Land', seems to suggest would better fit rich peasants, village controllers. The truth for Bihar is probably between these two extremes. (Musgrave writes of UP—permanently settled areas favoured the zamindar by being less directly governed and paying much less revenue, only one third as much in Benares according to Neale, *Economic Change in Rural India*, p. 55).
14 Gaya Collector to Patna Commissioner, 2 March 1896, PCR 363, 15/24.
15 Gaya Collector to Patna Commissioner, 9 May 1881, PCR 336, 12/14.
16 Finucane, 7 July 1888, R&A Revenue A11–16, February 1890.

entering as *khas* (or 'in arrears') to former cultivators holdings that were in fact occupied by his associates among the villagers.[17]

In this way, thousands of bighas of *diara* belonging to the maharaja of Dumraon were cultivated each year as the flood waters receded, without payment of any rent in spite of the maharaja's efforts—a court order awarding him Rs 30,000 in damages proved unenforceable.[18] Raiyats, it was agreed, were not always helpless, but sometimes 'Brahmins, Babhans, Rajputs and Mahomadans who...are perfectly capable of maintaining their own interests...and...of combining powerfully against the zamindar'—they were by no means a small class.[19] In Patna in general it was thought that 'ryots in the north of the District have rather the upper hand than otherwise'. Maliks had to relinquish one estate to the government because the raiyats were 'well-to-do men, Gowallahs and Rajputs' who were 'extremely difficult to deal with, paying no rent until compelled to do so' (as the government also discovered to its discomfort). In Bhojpur pargana in Shahabad also, government tenants were 'a particularly hard and stiff-necked generation', while in Kharwan (Bhabua) the zamindar, Babu Ram Saran Singh, obtained decrees for rent arrears but 'was afraid to execute them'.[20] In Darbhanga, the tenants of the elder Madhubani Babus (Harukhdari and Tantradhari Singh) combined to resist the oppression of the Babus' agent, Meena Lal, and by 1890 'undoubtedly... [had] the whip hand'. The maliks were virtually bankrupt, having long mismanaged their property, calling on the tenants whenever they had need of funds but without keeping a proper rent roll and through agents who exacted as much as they could from the raiyats and passed as little as they could on to the zamindar. The estate had gradually dissolved into confusion and violence, resulting in a rash of civil and criminal prosecutions on both sides. The head constable at the local police post became 'an out and out partisan' of the raiyats. Eventually the maharaja of Darbhanga, one of the Babus' creditors, obtained a decree against them that he refrained from executing on condition that the Babus dismiss Meena Lal and come to terms with their tenants.[21]

What were the factors which decided that some would suffer and others avoid the landlord's oppression? An easy answer would be to discover stable

17 Muzaffarpur Collector to Patna Commissioner, 13 October 1892, with note by Bell, Manager, Darbhanga Raj, PCR 357, 17/9.
18 Darbhanga Collector to Patna Commissioner, 14 October 1880, PCR 350.
19 Patna Commissioner to Bengal Government, 20 April 1881, PCR 333, 17/3.
20 Patna Collector to Patna Commissioner, 10 May 1884, PCR 342, 12/4; Shahabad Collector to Patna Commissioner, 1 May 1894, PCR 361, 12/3.
21 Patna Commissioner to Board of Revenue (Bengal), 6 June 1895, PCR 363, 12/6; Patna Commissioner to Darbhanga Collector, 24 September and 22 November, and reply, 11 October; and Subdivisional Officer, Madhubani, to Darbhanga Collector, 6 October 1890, PCR 353, 17/4.

classes of cultivators whose position was stronger against the zamindar because they shared some consistent advantage, such as larger holdings, secure tenancy, high caste, freedom from debt, and so on. Most contemporary observers interpreted what they saw in these terms; more recent commentaries have associated social change with a growing ability to market as well as grow crops.[22] These explanations are the more plausible in that the chosen characteristics *were* self-evidently useful to cultivators in their social and economic relations. What is open to debate is whether they can take us much nearer to explaining the origins of rich peasants and whether they can safely be used in a structural analysis of society.

The type of tenure, for example, will not give conclusive answers in Bihar. The degree is not helpful as very few extended beyond the second and none below the third. There was no middle peasantry identifiable, as in Bengal proper, by its dominance over subtenants—a fact that led one observer to account for the wretchedness of Bihari raiyats by noting the lack of an example of opposition to the landlord.[23] Nor were non-occupancy and underraiyats invariably at a disadvantage in terms of rent, as Table 7.1 shows. The figures may have been distorted by indigo factories appearing as undertenants on kurtaoli leases, but we may presume from the non-occupancy rates at least that special circumstances, probably the availability of waste land (20 per cent in Champaran at the time), made for favourable terms for some tenants in Saran and Champaran.[24] The pattern is familiar from the eighteenth century,

22 Elizabeth Whitcombe, *Agrarian Conditions in North India*, vol. 1 (*The United Provinces under British Rule 1860–1900*), Berkeley, 1972, pp. 43–5, stresses 'blood or service relationship with the maliks'. Bayly, *Local Roots of Indian Politics*, p. 51, refers to 'village-based cultivators' who 'already controlled rural credit and sometimes dominated access to the market'. On marketing, see Colin M. Fisher, 'Planters and Peasants: The Ecological Context of Agrarian Unrest on the Indigo Plantations of North Bihar, 1820–1920', pp. 122–4, and also Neil Charlesworth, 'Rich Peasants and Poor Peasants in Late Nineteenth Century Maharashtra', in Dewey and Hopkins, *The Imperial Impact*. Charlesworth defines rich peasants by landholdings sufficiently large for growth and marketing of cash crops. Catanach, *Rural Credit in Western India*, pp. 16–17, claims for 1836–73 a 43 per cent increase in population, 10 per cent in bullocks, 25 per cent in cultivated area, 31 per cent in ploughs, 71 per cent in wells, and 220 per cent in carts—which suggests to me greater independence in marketing, but also retention of agricultural resources (except wells) in proportionately fewer hands.

23 PCR 362, 8/10, 1895–6; Rasik Lal Sen, Report on Land Acquisition Proceedings, Gaya, 1897–1900, R&A Revenue B26, April 1901.

24 R&A Revenue B3 and 4, May 1898; Stevenson-Moore, *Final Report on... Muzaffarpur*, p. 314. Interpretation is complicated because the figures are averages—in Nasriganj, Shahabad, 10 or 12 in each village held subtenancies at about 1½ times the occupancy rate; but some large jotedars sub-let 'at hardly any advance on the rental they themselves pay'—D.J. McPherson, 1883, PCR 356, 10/15, 1892–3. For kurtaoli, see note 60 below.

TABLE 7.1
Rent Rates on Surveyed Areas in 1898
(Rupees/Annas/Pice)

	Rents on total area			Rents on cultivated area		
Raiyats	Champaran	Saran	Muzaffarpur	Champaran	Saran	Muzaffarpur
Fixed rates	1/1/6	3/8/-	3/6/4	1/4/2	3/13/9	3/14/-
Settled and occupancy	2/0/3	3/14/6	3/15/9	2/3/5	4/1/-	4/5/5
Non-occupancy	1/15/5	3/10/7	4/13/9	2/3/11	3/13/2	5/1/6
Underraiyats	1/9/2	3/15/6	4/15/9	1/10/8	4/0/11	5/4/5

but still the consequences are far-reaching for our purposes. The implication is that an advantage (tenure) may be reversed by circumstances (waste land). If so, our search for factors producing a stable economic structure will not be straightforward.

Thus contemporaries have left us their conviction that the lot of the Bihari peasant would be greatly improved if only he could be effectively guaranteed the occupancy of his holding, and there are many indications that occupancy right was valuable, notably in the long campaigns zamindars fought against it and the reported eagerness of the raiyats by the late 1890s to pay for extracts from settlement rolls recording their rights and liabilities.[25] On the other hand, there is no pattern of advantage for occupancy tenants or any certainty that the prosperity of the peasantry increased consistently as their number grew—just as in Shahabad in 1889 thika holdings were more valuable than other forms of tenancy on average, but numerically the great majority of the richer holdings were held raiyati under inferior tenures.[26] In general it is likely that, as one official put it, 'The amount of rent payable seems to depend on the power of the proprietor to get it realized and the capacity of the ryots to pay it'[27]—rather than on the legal conditions of tenancy even where these could be enforced in practice. If so, and accepting for the moment that similar arguments could be applied to other advantages (caste, for example, is insufficient to explain variations of wealth among the dominant Rajputs and Babhans), then we are forced to look for varying combinations of factors behind stratification—which raises doubts, surely, about structural notions of hierarchy altogether.

Do we need, therefore, to look for the development of attributes not usually associated with peasants, to distinguish the more well-to-do by their profits

25 R&A Revenue B3 and 4, May 1898, and A40–2, May 1899; Roy, *Rent Question in Bihar*, pp. 192–200.
26 PCR 351, 21/44, 1889–90.
27 Rasik Lal Sen; see note 23 above.

from rent, trade, and loans? For a peasant, the basis of such activities must be the possession of a larger than average holding; and for any continuing polarization along these lines, there would have to be a market in tenancies. Indeed, the consensus among officials (in the nature of things, few reliable figures can exist) was that throughout Bihar occupancy holdings were freely mortgaged and sold in the 1880s, usually without the knowledge of the landlord.[28] The transfers would be concealed through collusion with the zamindar's servants or by the former raiyat's continuing to pay the rent on behalf of his successor, especially where only a part of a holding had changed hands. To a degree that one observer declared 'unknown' at the time in the North-West Provinces,[29] there was a market in and a known value for raiyat's land in Bihar. In this respect the positions of petty zamindar and substantial cultivator would have been similar.

There are some, though not unambiguous, indications that transfers were becoming more frequent in the last two decades of the nineteenth century. In the 10 years after 1881, registrations of the sale of fixed-rate occupancy holdings increased on average by over 100 per cent, and of occupancy holdings by nearly 490 per cent. Partial sales and mortgages may be assumed to have increased even more rapidly and the figures for raiyati holdings may be further swollen by the inclusion of most of the sales and mortgages under Rs 100, which increased by 173 and 297 per cent over the period. By contrast, sales and mortgages over Rs 100 increased by only 50 and 60 per cent.[30] There was of course much scope for increase merely in registration, as probably no more than 10 per cent of transfers were registered in the early 1880s. But the greater rate of increase in the smaller or raiyati holdings suggests qualitative change, however interpreted. To the extent that the increase was real, there was a growing market in such land, and to the extent that the increase was merely in the percentage of registration, there was a growing reliance upon the law and presumably less concern about the imposition of *salami* by the landlord, should the transfer come to his notice.

It is reasonable to speculate that at least a proportion of the transfers of land in the later nineteenth century involved the consolidation of holdings in fewer hands. If we again compare the five-yearly periods 1880–5 and 1887–92, we find that moneylenders' purchases increased from 1,137 to 7,019; other

---

28 Darbhanga Collector to Patna Commissioner, 14 October 1880, PCR 350; Board of Revenue (Bengal) to Bengal Government, 22 December 1883, PCR 342, 10/63; Muzaffarpur Collector to Patna Commissioner, 13 October 1892, PCR 357, 17/9.

29 T.M. Gibbon, Bettiah Manager, to Champaran Collector, 11 April 1892, R&A Revenue, A56–8, January 1895.

30 Patna Commissioner to Board of Revenue (Bengal), 31 January 1894, PCR 358, 12/9.

landlords' from 1,583 to 7,551; and other raiyats' from 3,780 to 27,987. We must allow for the ambiguity of the categories ('other landlord' might include ordinary moneylenders, and 'other raiyat' village mahajans), but here again the fact that the increase for other raiyats (740 per cent) is markedly greater than that for other landlords (480 per cent) suggests a significant change, perhaps that accumulation of land was taking place alongside moneylending as an investment for rural profits.

This is no more than we would expect to the degree firstly that agriculture was increasingly profitable for those able to sell a surplus and grow cash crops and secondly that the security of tenure for occupancy holdings matched in reality what was promised in law. Some indication that these conditions might be fulfilled may be seen in the high value of occupancy holdings— averages of Rs 80 per acre in Saran with rent at Rs 4/6/1, or Rs 50 in Darbhanga (rent Rs 4/5/5), or even Rs 17 in Champaran (rent Rs 2/4/7).[31] Certainly some officials in Bihar believed that increasing transfer implied some absorption of the holdings of the poor by their richer neighbours. Of course there were many instances where after foreclosure a raiyat ended up paying four times to the mahajan what he had previously paid to the zamindar. This was thought to be common in less prosperous areas; but in 'well-to-do' districts (Shahabad or Saran), the majority of purchasers at sales were believed to be genuine cultivators, and mortgages too were often explained as a form of conditional transfer to a fellow raiyat, so that such transfers were interpreted as a sign of selective prosperity and not of general indebtedness. It may even be that this difference between poor and prosperous areas existed more in terminology (masking different officials' attitudes) than in fact, in that the 'rapacious money-lenders' were agreed to be as local as the 'genuine cultivators' and both could have been acquiring land for either rent or cultivation.[32]

The usual picture of a rural moneylender, however, is that of the bania— 'the same man who buys the grain'[33]—or the zamindar lending to his more substantial tenants. The indebted raiyats were thus doubly bonded. True, it

31 R&A Revenue, B3 and 4, May 1898, and B26, April 1899; L. Hare, 'Keeping up the Record of Rights', PCR 357, 17/9, 1892–3; Patna Collector to Patna Commissioner, 10 December 1880, PCR 350.

32 R&A Revenue, B26, April 1899; L.H. Mylne, R&A Revenue, B52–3, June 1895; Darbhanga Collector to Patna Commissioner, 14 October 1880, PCR 350; Patna Commissioner to Board of Revenue (Bengal), 31 January 1894, PCR 358, 12/9. F. Tomasson Januzzi, *Agrarian Crisis in India: The Case of Bihar*, Austin and London, 1974, examining post-Independence conditions, found one village in which high-caste cultivators engaged in moneylending with net incomes of less than Rs 50.

33 Report on Cooperative Societies in Bengal 1904–5, R&A Revenue, B14, June 1906.

may be said[34] that neither the bania nor in many circumstances the zamindar was primarily interested in depriving the raiyat of his land—they looked for profit chiefly in their own callings. Widespread land transfers affecting raiyats' holdings might then seem to be safely attributed to acquisitive cultivators, and the bania with 'the sole aim...of obtaining the land of his client'[35] relegated to the imaginations of British officials. It would be mere chance or fashion which encouraged, for example, the heir to a two-anna share of Mauza Patihar in Saran to petition the government in 1900 for help against the mahajan who had possession of his land and refused to give it up even if the original loan and interest were repaid in full.[36]

A more reasonable assumption is that some who lent money were quite ready to foreclose for profit—for example, where a bania could obtain better security or a zamindar higher returns by employing the former cultivator as a labourer—and these cases need to be accounted for as well as those where a fellow cultivator could benefit by amalgamating several contiguous plots for irrigation, or to grow cash crops, or to employ excess family labour. Opportunities existed, therefore, for prosperous tenants to increase their holdings; at the same time, there is no conclusive evidence that very substantial proportions of the transfers were consolidations by rich peasants rather than alienation to banias or zamindars, or indeed purchases by raiyats that did not involve any increase in the disparities of income in the village.

We shall return below to the question of the size of the raiyats' holdings. First we need to examine some other advantages. Some found it possible, for example, to speak of a 'well-to-do patwari class'.[37] Patwaris in Bihar were notoriously dishonest and were often sued for embezzlement of rents. They

---

34 See P.J. Musgrave, 'Rural Credit and Rural Society in the United Provinces 1860–1920', in Dewey and Hopkins, *The Imperial Impact*; and Neil Charlesworth, 'The Myth of the Deccan Riots of 1875', *Modern Asian Studies*, 6(4), 1972. Exceptions would include times when the profits of agriculture were suddenly high without involving greater debts or, just possibly, where a bania wanted to avoid tax (his lending was liable for tax where a zamindar's was not). See Annual Licence Tax Report 1882–3, PCR 339, 37/7. On indebtedness, see note 67 below.

35 Ibbetson, 11 August 1884, R&A Revenue, A5–6, September 1894.

36 R&A Revenue, B12, March 1901.

37 Patna Commissioner to Board of Revenue (Bengal), 27 July 1894, PCR 361, 23/37. Clive Dewey, '*Patwari* and *Chaukidar*: Subordinate Officials and the Reliability of India's Agricultural Statistics', in Dewey and Hopkins, *The Imperial Impact*, describes the independent patwari, a picture which applies best to north Bihar and large, poorly supervised estates. But Musgrave, 'Landlords and Lords of the Land', stressing control of records rather than men, describes a variety of patwari types. See also Catanach, *Rural Credit in Western India*, pp. 21–2, on old *mirasdar* (village servant or artisans) groups who were usually not poor but also 'not necessarily' the wealthiest; or village servants, many but 'probably not all' poor.

also collected fees from the raiyats while ostensibly serving zamindar and government jointly. Their usual responsibilities—to keep accounts, collect rents, measure holdings, and (on bhaoli lands) estimate the value of crops—would obviously be potential sources of personal or factional power whenever some independence from the malik could be maintained. After the early 1880s, government registration of patwaris, for example, made it more difficult for the zamindars to dismiss them. And yet on the other hand maliks could often keep control by the threat of appointing another servant to perform those lucrative jobs (rent collection chiefly) that were not officially reserved to the patwari.[38] There was no certainty, then, that office would bring its rewards. Officials complained perennially that it was difficult to attract suitable candidates to be patwaris, not least among those for whom the calling was quasi-hereditary.

In general it seems that in Bihar government was less likely to be a direct ally of one villager against another than in some other parts of India. Virtually its only permanent representative in the villages was the *chaukidar*, who had little power or status and was anyway paid by the villagers. District boards were starved of funds and aroused little interest; no effective system of village organization was introduced. A few minor government servants might be able to help a few of their friends. In 1891 all but four of the security bonds taken in Patna Division covered landed property,[39] suggesting rural connections that might be put to advantage, as in *tauzi* frauds in which revenue was stolen and the arrears concealed by collusion between government and zamindari servants.[40] (Such opportunities increased in times of famine, when government loans were distributed on a larger than usual scale.) Or village factions might attack an enemy by laying information with the police—for example, that a cultivator was concealing opium, for it was well known that convictions could be obtained for possession of very small quantities retained by growers either by accident or for personal use.[41] But the only consistent large-scale government involvement was probably through the advances to opium cultivators—over Rs 29 lakhs were advanced between 1892 and 1894, and the significance of the crop to the economy may be seen in the very unfavourable balance of trade caused by imports of food grains, especially to

38 See Report by Patna Commissioner, PCR 333, 14/4, 1880–1; Muzaffarpur Collector to Patna Commissioner, 5 April 1881, ibid., 14/8; Darbhanga Collector to Patna Commissioner, 18 May 1881, PCR 336, 12/4; Champaran Collector to Patna Commissioner, 16 June 1881, PCR 334, 14/8.
39 Patna Commissioner to Board of Revenue (Bengal), 5 December 1891, PCR 354, 8/1.
40 See, for example, PCR 355, 14/6, 1891–2.
41 See Opium Agent to Patna Commissioner, 18 March 1883, PCR 338, 84/10.

Saran district.[42] Virtually all other government intervention was exceptional and unlikely to produce hierarchies in the villages. This was true of irrigation and public works—and even of that most obvious ally, the courts, for between raiyats litigation was of marginal significance if only for reasons of access. There were only 29 munsiffs in Patna Division, many fewer than in Bengali districts even though the judiciary was just as responsible for revenue and other rural cases in Bihar as in Bengal proper.[43]

We are left, then, with no secure and objective reasons why stable hierarchy should develop, and must return to questions of landlord-tenant relations. Here the impact of government may not be dismissed so readily. We find rather that by the later nineteenth century landlords seem to be subject to pressure from an accelerated rate of change prompted by British laws, zamindari partition, and rising prices. The effect of the first was felt through tenancy legislation and through survey and settlement proceedings—zamindars came increasingly to rely on legal sanctions to support their position and this initially altered the basis of and ultimately weakened their power. The effect of the second came both through the proliferation of petty zamindaris and through the long-drawn-out partition proceedings themselves. The third made increasingly necessary what the first two also encouraged—for zamindars to confront their tenants, in this case to raise rents or extend zerat at the expense of tenancies. These subjects are too large and complex to be dealt with here, but it is possible to outline the processes at work.

It is now a commonplace to say that the suprastructure of Western law and government that the British placed above rural India wrought remarkably little change at the lower levels of society. What is true about this (and to be fair, what is usually meant) is that the Western modes in which the law was couched and the administration devised were not reproduced in life—the British might pass a tenancy law to cover Bihar, but tenancy there did not change accordingly to the model of behaviour set out in the Act. But this does not warrant the suggestion that British government had little impact.

Thus, though the evidence is confusing and it is very difficult to pin down the precise effect of a specific measure, I am satisfied that the steady encroachment of the British in theory and in law into tenancy relations in Bihar after 1885 had the effect of increasingly defining those relations and thus (ultimately) of making the arbitrary exercise of power by landlords more difficult than before. (It should be noted that no such interference defined the relations between raiyats.) In short, we should not be deflected by the mass of

---

42 Patna Commissioner to Royal Commission on Opium, 11 April 1894, PCR 361, 29/9.

43 R&A Revenue, A54–5, September 1896.

evidence stressing, for example, the inability of the raiyat to pursue his interests in a court of law—a fact relevant to the failure of the British to instil their own system—from considering the equal weight of official (and zamindari) impressions by the 1890s that raiyats were slowly 'awakening to a knowledge of their rights', observations relevant to an understanding of change within existing institutions.[44]

As early as 1884, the manager of the Darbhanga Raj had argued that the raiyat in Bihar knew his own interests and would 'set his Landlord, however powerful he may be, at open defiance, if he deems his rights are being infringed', and though this is hardly evidence from a neutral source, it may serve to remind us of the importance of the raiyat's concept and awareness of his 'rights'.[45] Survey and settlement operation too were late and rare in the permanently settled areas, and at first resulted in less litigation than expected—even disputes over the record affected only three per cent of holdings, a fact the Secretary of State thought a tribute to the record's accuracy, but which was at least as likely to have reflected the degree to which it favoured the powerful.[46] And yet we have already seen tenants at the end of the century 'clamorous' to pay settlement dues to collect their copy of the record, and there is evidence that the new certainty about rights outlived the brief visits of the settlement officer. In the 1890s, there were repeated reports that abwabs were now levied only where raiyats acquiesced, and were gradually becoming less frequent. Revenue officers were more often called in to appraise crops. Leases were more common. Moves for commutation of produce rents were on the increase and would have been still more frequent, it was thought, if raiyats had been able to prove the average rentals of past years in cash terms and thus avoid too high a money assessment.[47]

The point is not that disputes were necessarily more frequent or that zamindars as a class were now weaker against tenants as a class, though this would be the case in the long term. The point is that a contract relationship was extending into areas formerly left to custom. Observations of this process do seem to have been the result of change and not merely of closer acquaintance with landlord-tenant relations as they had always been. The

44 Patna Commissioner, Revenue Administration Report 1882–3, PCR 338, 12.
45 Lt. Col. R.C. Money, PCR 341, 17/1, 1884–5.
46 R&A Revenue A15, February 1892. The lower levels of survey teams were not immune from partiality, and initially were recruited locally.
47 R&A Revenue, A40–2, May 1899; Shahabad Collector to Patna Commissioner, 12 May 1890, PCR 352, 12/4; Gaya Collector to Patna Commissioner, 12 May 1890, PCR 357, 12/9, 1892–3; Patna Commissioner to Board of Revenue (Bengal), 18 June 1890, PCR 345–6, 1887–8; Shahabad Collector to Patna Commissioner, 8 November 1880, PCR 350; Patna Commissioner, Revenue Administration Report 1894–5, PCR 363, 12/6.

British initially had helped the zamindar by assuming that all rights were definite when they were not and only the zamindar knew what rights he had in British eyes.[48] In the late nineteenth century, however, the government began deliberately to communicate its view of rights to tenants as well. Rights often remained indefinite in practice. But greater awareness of the British view of definite rights not only would benefit some zamindars in their dealings with tenants—as had already been the case over generations—but also might assist some tenants when they were resisting their landlords.

The testimony with regard to the effect of partition is also contradictory. On the one hand, the example of Muslim landholders may be cited to show in their 'present poverty and decay' the results of repeated partition, in this case by inheritance in the absence of testamentary rights.[49] To this school of thought, partition proceedings—a new phenomenon dreamt up by the British—would help the weak against the strong by allowing a small co-sharer to escape the oppression of his major partner and equally by making the tenants more nearly a match for the zamindar. It was indeed a devaluation of landholding status—one result clearly would be effectively to add to the ranks of the peasantry as owner-cultivators, former co-sharers whose holdings after partition were too small to allow them to be let. On the other hand, partition proceedings may also be seen as a weapon of the strong against the weak, especially to oust an unpopular partner, just as major co-sharers were known to withhold revenue in order to gain control of an entire estate (through the sale law) at the expense of their fellows. (It was thought that as much as nine-tenths of all revenue arrears were due to payments withheld by co-sharers.)[50] Similarly, petty maliks might seek partition to gain control of a specific piece of land, or as a cover for splitting up a raiyat's holding among several maliks or for enhancing rents (for example by using a shorter pole for the *batwara* measurement and then presenting the results as evidence in a rent suit). Here again British administration, by conferring definite rights that it assumed to be capable of judicial proof and setting up machinery to enforce those rights, may be seen to have benefited the strong against the weak to the degree that the rights remained in fact indefinite and incapable of judicial proof except on fabricated evidence.

On the whole, however, I incline to the view of partition as being debilitating in the long term. Partition proceedings were most common in areas of petty proprietors (to a degree not explained by the fact that more estates were

48 Gaya government pleader (a Babhan landowner), quoted in 'Memorandum on the Rent Question in Behar', R&A Revenue A16–46, July 1883.
49 Patna Commissioner to Board of Revenue (Bengal), 30 November 1882, PCR 337, 14/47.
50 Patna Collector to Patna Commissioner, 10 May 1890, PCR 352, 12/4.

potentially involved). The increase in the number of estates, for example in Darbhanga (50 per cent between 1880 and 1895), far outstripped the increase (in this case 21 per cent) in their estimated value; and of this rapidly growing number an overwhelming majority resulted in new estates in the lower revenue categories—in Muzaffarpur in the 10 years before 1894, only 54 of the 4,200 new estates paid more than Rs 100 per annum. And as this 54 fell far short of a compensatory increase even to maintain the percentage of bigger estates and as those affected by partition came to represent a large proportion of all estates, so an increasing polarization among landlords may be suggested. It may well have been paralleled by polarization among tenants, for whom there were obvious opportunities under very large or very small maliks. This would be true even if the number of maliks (as opposed to the number of estates) did not increase, because an estate shared between several co-proprietors tended to be run as one unit, especially when it came to coercing tenants, and the strength from such cooperation would be lost if the estate were divided.[51]

Certainly partition proceedings themselves as well as any rivalry between maliks could benefit tenants. Wherever there was a dispute, raiyats could agree to pay one of the parties at a favourable rate or more sagely (as they could be very badly off if their side lost) pay neither until the dispute was settled. In particular, the situation of flux introduced by partition, with perhaps a new malik, allowed raiyats to claim zerat land as theirs or to contest rents, especially given the tendency of rival proprietors to file contradictory jamabandis in order to reduce the revenue assessment on their own portions. In the case of the elder Madhubani Babus already described, the tenants supported one Ranju Singh, a claimant for much of the Babus' estates—some of the rioting concerned disputes about rents that had been paid to him instead of to the Babus' agents. That this was a tactic by the raiyats is illustrated by the fact that 'sixteen of the most turbulent spirits' were among those who deposited rents in Ranju Singh's favour and that Ranju himself was 'at best a pauper' whose legal expenses were being defrayed by the tenants.[52] The raiyats, then,

---

51 On partition, see R&A Revenue, A16–46, July 1883; A11–16, February 1890; and B49–71, January 1894 (*The Pioneer*, 7 January 1893). Also see Revenue Administration Reports—Muzaffarpur 1883–4, PCR 340, 12/4, and Patna 1889–90, PCR 352, 12/4. See as well Saran Collector to Patna Commissioner, 6 November 1893, Patna Collector to Patna Commissioner, 30 November 1893, Muzaffarpur Collector to Patna Commissioner, 3 February 1894, Champaran Collector to Patna Commissioner, 10 February 1894, and Gaya Collector to Patna Commissioner, 22–3 March 1894, PCR 359, 17/7; Patna Commissioner to Board of Revenue (Bengal), 6 June 1894, PCR 361, 17/2; Darbhanga report on cess valuation, 18 January 1896, PCR 362, 8/10.

52 PCR 353, 17/4, 1890–1.

knew the advantages of disputes over possession well enough to encourage or engineer them when opposing their landlord.

In Bihar, agricultural prices were rising significantly throughout our period, both in absolute terms and in terms of the substitution of cash for food crops. The response of zamindars was to increase rents—in the early 1880s, the most common cause for enhancement was the growth of such crops as poppy, cotton, or sugarcane, which would add one or two rupees per bigha. But in general, landlords sought to share in rising prices whenever these were the result of long-term trends rather than of immediate shortages (it was difficult to enhance rents in times of scarcity).[53] Rising prices were important for all landlords, though obviously most detrimental on lands leased out on fixed rentals. Elsewhere (as in most of north Bihar), a system of money rents would obviously benefit the raiyat to any extent that enhancements were outstripped by the rise in prices. In the case of high-caste tenants who did not cultivate their own land the benefit would also depend on labour costs and therefore on the relative local strength of the landless as well as the zamindars. There are good indications that wages did not keep pace with prices—better than for rents—but in particular areas, they must be set against a tradition of seasonal migration[54] and the availability of work on development projects or in towns.

The effect of price rises on bhaoli lands was to encourage some raiyats to seek commutation of their rents where the circumstances of irrigation, for example, allowed them to risk losing the landlord's gilandazi. Short-term fluctuation in prices might also be important. On some bhaoli lands where cash rents were paid, the value of the landlord's share of the crop was calculated while the crops were still in the field (the *danabandi* system); in others where the share was decided on the threshing floor (the *battaiya* system), the price for the landlord would be calculated at one seer per rupee less than the current price if the raiyat were to sell the crop.[55] Often of course a raiyat was so pressed for money that he would be forced to sell his crop immediately after or even before the harvest; but where this was not the case, any rise in price after the value of the landlord's share had been fixed would benefit the raiyat—and no doubt lead the zamindar to seek additional exactions in compensation.

As a result of zamindari pressure, average rents seem to have doubled in the 16 years before 1880 and for the most part the increases were 'tamely accepted'. The methods used were almost wholly derived from landlord prestige and force and not from law. As late as 1890, for example, there was very little interest in the government's price lists, which could be made the

53 Gaya Collector to Patna Commissioner, 20 January 1881, PCR 350; Muzaffarpur Collector to Patna Commissioner, 30 April 1884, PCR 340, 12/4.
54 See, for example, R&A Famine Branch, A6, January 1882.
55 D.J. McPherson to Shahabad Collector, 9 May 1884, PCR 341, 10/63–9.

basis of suits for enhancement. Nor did zamindars often sue for arrears (though these would appear in their books); if they did so, it was because they were on bad terms with their raiyats and not in order to raise rents. Instead, they would measure their estates with shorter poles to discover 'excess' area; they would levy additional cesses; they would seize crops to enforce payment of a higher demand; and only when not very strong would they take legal action for distraint in order to increase rents. The landlords, according to some reports, proved able in the great mass of cases to introduce the market into tenurial relations by offering or threatening to offer tenancies at higher rates. The result was, in part, acceptance of the increases by existing tenants, but also a 'very extensive...change of occupiers', with lands passing to 'lower labouring classes...trained and accustomed to field labour' and therefore able to increase productivity to match the higher rents.[56] Obviously the success of such zamindars was a measure not only of their powers of coercion but also of objective factors, such as the pressure of population on the soil, which limited the options available to the raiyat.

From the mid-1880s, the price rises began to accelerate—again in absolute terms and in terms of prices available to cultivators, in this case (I suspect) with the decline both in the incidence of *tut*, the system whereby zamindars bought their tenants' crops at less than the market rate, and in the differential (7½ to 11½ per cent in 1885 in Sassaram subdivision, Shahabad)[57] that poor communications and marketing had provided between prices at district markets and those at local haats. We may rescue from its prosaic context the description by an Indian Excise Deputy Collector in 1884 of the changes he had witnessed in Gaya. The railway had 'brought a remarkable increase in traffic, especially in seed, sugar, molasses, lac, and hardware; canals had 'improved...agricultural prospects' and given 'general impetus to...internal trade and commerce'; and the opening of roads had made the interior 'more easily accessible in all years'.[58] Moreover, the Bengal Tenancy Act began to or was expected (by zamindars) to make zamindari exactions more difficult. Landlord methods began to change too. The major signs of attempts to enhance zamindari profits were now the extension of zerat, the spread of kurtaoli leases, and the execution of *sharahnamah*s.

56 R&A Revenue, A11–16, February 1890; Patna Commissioner, Revenue Administration Report 1882–3, PCR 338; Patna ditto (fragment) 1893–4, PCR 361, 12/3; Patna Commissioner to Board of Revenue (Bengal), 18 June 1890, PCR 345–6 (1887–8); Darbhanga Collector to Patna Commissioner, May 1892, PCR 357, 12/9; Muzaffarpur Collector to Patna Commissioner, 13 October 1892, PCR 357, 17/9; Patna Collector to Patna Commissioner, 10 December 1880, PCR 350.
57 D.J. McPherson to Shahabad Collector, 15 April 1885, PCR 342, 10/13.
58 Prankumar Das, Sudder Excise Deputy Collector, Gaya, 30 January 1884, PCR 340, 7/69.

Attempts to extend zerat (I use this term to include all forms of zamindars' own land) may represent the recognition that the rise in prices was making cultivation relatively more profitable in relation to rent collection. This was certainly the case for small landlords in terms of economic advantage, although considerations of social prestige greatly restricted the change that might have occurred because of this. To some extent, this was also true in a great rash of disputes over waste land, grazing and forest rights, and so on, as landlords tried to reserve to themselves village resources because the rises in both prices and population were making them more valuable. But once the landlords had land, it would usually be let to individuals—by the mid-1880s, raiyats in Shahabad, for example, were complaining that large areas of waste land that had existed for their use 10 years before had now virtually disappeared into the hands of pahikasht raiyats—and the extension of zerat was much more generally an indirect attempt to enhance rents. In the first place, it might be a necessary step, ousting a settled raiyat, leading to a renewed lease at a higher rate. In the second place, in north Bihar zerat usually included land held by raiyats on bhaoli tenure and thus a zamindar who claimed that land had this status might well be seeking to replace a money rent that was declining in value with a share of the harvest. Equally, disputes might be started by raiyats on bhaoli land who wished to keep the increases to themselves. It was said that they refrained from applying for commutation in the north not so much because of the difficulty of proving past rents as because to do so would be to admit that bhaoli rents prevailed. Certainly there were many more disputes about zerat by the 1890s. In one case in Gaya, it was alleged that high-caste tenants had lived in peace with their landlord for 50 years until 'stirred up' on this issue by 'an old Babhan pleader'. The suggestion of course is that, whether the zamindars sought to extend bhaoli or the raiyats to limit it, by the 1890s there were reduced possibilities for additional cesses or arbitrary increases in money rents.[59]

The spread of kurtaoli leases and sharahnamahs reinforces this point. The former were not new but rapidly increasing after 1885. There were 3949 new ones recorded that year in Muzaffarpur. Under a kurtaoli lease, an occupancy raiyat agreed to sub-let his holding or part of it, usually to an indigo

---

59 Patna Collector to Patna Commissioner, 9 May 1892, PCR 337, 12/9; R&A Revenue, A16-46, July 1883; Muzaffarpur Revenue Administration Report 1883-4, PCR 340, 12/4; Board of Revenue (Bengal) to Bengal Government, 22 December 1883, PCR 342, 10/63; Gaya Collector to Patna Commissioner, 8 May 1894, PCR 361, 12/13. In the Nasriganj estate, demand for zerat was associated with numerous partitions as proprietors sank 'through improvidence into the position of cultivators', but it would be dangerous to assume that this was necessarily indicative of more than a continual flux that left constant the numbers of the wealthy—PCR 358, 10/12, 1893-4.

Hierarchy and Resources 171

planter, for long terms of 15–20 years; in practice, the leases were not as disadvantageous to the raiyat as they seemed because of a tacit understanding that the raiyat would stay in possession and that only part of the holding would in fact be taken up (to cultivate indigo). Raiyats entered into these agreements to borrow money or, by enlisting the help of the factory, to resist landlords who sought to increase rents.[60] Their prevalence over about a decade marked a period of stress in rural relations. Sharahnamahs were written statements by which raiyats agreed to pay for specified lands—in effect a general enhancement of rents. In the mid-1880s, the Darbhanga Raj, for example, began a systematic campaign to secure sharahnamahs; from Muzaffarpur, the effect on the raiyats was described thus:

> The malik has been bothering him for his arrear of rent, his crops have been poor and he has been only able to just pay his Mahajan; he can not pay off his arrear. Suddenly he is called up to the zamindari kutchery, where he finds himself one of a crowd of rayats, all in the same condition. The Putwaris, Goomashtas, jeth ryots &c., tell them, that if they execute a Sharanama, their arrears will be wiped off.[61]

Of course they agreed, and were then schooled by the village *amlah* to admit execution before the Registrar. They would go away with their rents raised 'but in a state of blissful ignorance until...next...called up to pay...'.[62]

It is clear that sharahnamahs became so prevalent because raiyats were objecting to rent increases by other means. Everywhere, it was said, they paid agreed rents but resisted those 'concocted' by the zamindar. Indeed in some cases, landlords were reported 'afraid' to claim the enhancements they had written into their rent roll.[63] In Darbhanga, 3000 raiyats of one zamindar deposited their rents with the civil court in 1887 (thus opposing an attempt at enhancement). By 1889, this same landlord had 'greatly and severely enhanced his rents' after obtaining kabuliyats from the raiyats.[64] In an estate in Patna at this time, tenants who had won a dispute in a civil court later entered into an agreement in which they conceded to their landlord almost all the points that they had won at law.[65] If these examples are typical, then the basis of the landlords' power was moving under the pressure of economic

---

60 Muzaffarpur Revenue Administration Report 1884–5, PCR 344, 12/4. See also Fisher, 'Planters and Peasants'.
61 Muzaffarpur Revenue Administration Report 1883–4, PCR 340, 12/4.
62 Ibid.
63 Shahabad Collector to Patna Commissioner, 8 November 1880, PCR 350; munsiff on Darbhanga rents, May 1892, PCR 357, 12/9.
64 Darbhanga Collector to Patna Commissioner, 20 February 1889, R&A Revenue, A11–16, February 1890. On the raiyats' reluctance to execute kabuliyats, see Roy, *Rent Question in Bihar*, p. 67.
65 The landlord was Raja of Maksudpur—Gaya Collector to Patna Commissioner, 8 May 1894, PCR 261, 12/3.

change. In the same way, formal leases, once rare, had become much more common as landlords sought use them in order to *restrict* rights tenants had in law by inserting clauses to waive such provisions.

Now we have already suggested that zamindari oppression might be felt to different degrees by different raiyats and that some raiyats were stronger than others. The stress put on landlord–tenant relations by these attempts to enhance rents can also be seen to impinge differently. My suspicion is that, from the second half of the nineteenth century at least, prices rose more rapidly than rents and that from about the 1890s landlords found it more difficult to make exactions other than agreed rents. In short, zamindari capacity to increase their incomes gradually declined at the same time as the rate of price inflation increased. (There were, of course, counter-indications in such factors as land hunger, population growth, and indebtedness.)

I do not dwell on this point here, firstly because its proof is fraught with difficulty but secondly because it is not central to my present argument. There is, after all, no doubt of the overwhelming power of major zamindars in most of Bihar throughout our period and beyond. There was room for a truly vast decline in their strength relative to that of their tenants before their supremacy was in any way threatened. My point is rather to demonstrate the possibility of relative decline or advance among the *peasantry*, and the probability that such polarization was on the increase. Whether or not zamindari incomes kept pace with inflation or tenants generally enjoyed improved conditions, the confrontations implicit in the economic change and the increasing incidence of formal rather than informal relationships in land argue for harder or wider differentiations between tenants. It is now time to draw out the conditions of that ranking, which have been implicit in the preceding discussion.

When we looked at a selection of possible advantages that might have generated hierarchies, we found that all of them were conditional and not absolute. We concluded that economic ranking among peasants in Bihar was actually or potentially in a state of flux. When we looked at landlord–tenant relations, we found that they too were conditional, liable to affect tenants differently; but we also found that from the late nineteenth century zamindars in general (though not invariably) were under some pressure. We concluded that any such pressure was likely consistently to exaggerate differentiation among tenants and that in general (though not invariably) there was some polarization among the peasants in this period.

The key question for our purposes was how this differentiation began. We saw firstly that if a peasant were to become richer than his fellows, then he must be able to avoid the exactions of his landlord. The main weapons of the raiyat were concealment and evasion. Contemporary observers agreed that in Bihar, unlike in Bengal, raiyats very seldom cooperated to oppose their malik. Individual avoidance therefore depended on individual or at least factional resources. There were such advantages as high caste in mixed villages and also in general (some cesses, for example, were not levied on high-caste raiyats), or a friendly patwari where the zamindar was strong but distant, or disputed possession and financial embarrassment where the zamindar was weak but at hand. A money rent was generally helpful. A shortage of land would not be, but conversely waste land might—thus we find 'well-to-do' pahikasht raiyats gaining control and sub-letting on Saran diaras, while rents were low but disputes frequent in relatively underpopulated Champaran.[66]

To these we may add—as they are suggested by the approach adopted here, though we have not discussed them—such variants as family size and composition by age or sex as well as ability to work. We shall see below, for example, in the case of Sahara village, quite different results for different cultivators from fluctuations in output and prices. Further, we have here also the key indicators of change, though now we may add to a raiyat's possible resources use of contract and the market, knowledge of legal 'rights', and appeals to the courts, officials, or other potential allies. Relative economic strength would vary over time according to the availability and effectiveness of such weapons as these for different raiyats. Thus the more the landlord needed to confront his tenants or the more relations came to be formalized in law (though still ambiguous in practice), the more effective the advantages of one tenant or group would be in preserving or extending a position relative to that of the less favoured. There would be, that is, many effects which benefited those who were already in the best position in regard to them; but—and this is the central point—no advantage or set of advantages would bring benefits in all circumstances. Thus a good harvest reduced the borrowing of grain for seed according to Licence Tax returns in the 1880s,[67] but even a succession of good seasons did not bring borrowing to an end. While some cultivators benefited because they started off relatively solvent, others stayed caught in the cycle of debt. On the other hand, the advantage of high caste, for example, was not essential in this case. The benefits might be enjoyed equally by those more energetic lower castes whom we have seen increasing productivity to match higher rents. Moreover, if one considers Bihar alone and examines output rather than price, the 1880s and 1890s were years of very mixed agricultural fortunes, and high-caste tenants, as employers of labour, were more vulnerable in poor seasons in that they needed to borrow not just for seed but also for workers.[68]

66 Shahabad Collector to Patna Commissioner, 8 May 1894, ibid.
67 See Muzaffarpur report in PCR 339, 37/7, 1883–4.
68 See Darbhanga Collector to Patna Commissioner, 3 May 1892, R&A Famine, A12, June 1892. Indebtedness does play a large part in contemporary and present-day explanations of nineteenth-century stratification. I have not examined it in detail. Partly

The point, as we have seen above, is not that a characteristic—say type of tenure—was never useful but that it was not uniformly so. Thus it is clear that tenants who had (or could claim to have) a fixed rental were at advantage if they could maintain their position at a time of rising prices. There were various such tenures known by various names (*sikmi, gujashta, maurasi*), amounting mostly to a kind of inherited occupancy tenure, usually dating back ostensibly to a money rent at the time of the Permanent Settlement. But such a resource as this was not a fixed indicator, I am arguing, because it was no better than the raiyat's ability to back it up. Thus sikmi raiyats generally paid increased cesses, maurasi rents were regularly enhanced at least before the 1890s, and small gujashta holdings were passing rapidly into the hands of local moneylenders or cultivators.

Variation shows up equally clearly in rent increases. The Muzaffarpur settlement of the 1890s allowed the comparison of rents in 100 villages that had been surveyed in 1885: 93 per cent proved unchanged, but no single factor conclusively explained the increases in the remainder. There was a 17.62 per cent rise where estates had been officially partitioned and 10.75 per cent where they had been divided privately, but only 2.65 per cent in undivided estates. A similar pattern was found where estates had been sold. Moreover, 92 per cent of illegal enhancements affected the lower castes, as did 88 per cent of the legal. Obviously, in these cases it did not do to be low-caste where there was an illegal enhancement during an official sale or partition; but low caste alone was not too damaging, given that only 7 per cent of rents were increased.[69] And even location might matter. Table 7.2 shows the changes in prevailing rents in Darbhanga between 1880 and 1895, a period when (as mentioned above) the value of property was estimated to have increased by over

---

it was less fashionable a problem in Bihar, partly it seems not to have been a primary worry (other disabilities being fundamental, and to some extent alternative credit being available through indigo planters and opium agents), and partly its effect is difficult to judge. For example, Whitcombe, *Agrarian Conditions in North India*, pp. 162–70, echoing her sources, considers freedom from debt essential for high economic status. But only Catanach's middle peasants (see note 1 above) were thus free, compared with the poor who borrowed to survive and the rich who borrowed to invest, and Charlesworth, 'The Myth of the Deccan Riots', finds the wealthiest often the most heavily in debt. Even Whitcombe remarks (p. 191) that 'cultivators considered it prestigious to keep a running account with the Bania for a sizeable sum'. The key question clearly was not debt itself but the relationship between payments owed and resources available, and it is in part with the origins and conditions of that ratio that this paper deals.

69 Shahabad Collector to Patna Commissioner, 8 November, Patna Collector to Patna Commissioner, 10 December, Saran Collector to Patna Commissioner, 15 December 1880, and Gaya Collector to Patna Commissioner, 20 January 1881, PCR 350; Shahabad Collector to Patna Commissioner, 1 May 1894, PCR 361, 12/3; Stevenson-Moore, *Final Report on Muzaffarpur*, pp. 412–17.

TABLE 7.2
Rent Increases in 53 Parganas of Darbhanga, 1880–2 to 1891–5

Nil	16	20–34%	11
1–5%	4	40–45%	2
6–10%	13	Not known	7

Note: Rents ranged between Rs 2/12 and Rs 5 in 1880–2 and between Rs 3/8 and Rs 5/8 in 1891–5. The dates represent the duration of valuation proceedings. The first and third columns indicate 'rate of increase' and the second and fourth columns indicate 'number of holdings affected'.

20 per cent.[70] In the figures from which this table has been calculated, there is no pattern such as of high rents being subject of high increases or low to low that would suggest the impact of, say, variations in the fertility of land. Yet we see that in more than two-thirds of all the parganas rents rose by less than half of much as property values; in nearly one third of the known cases rents did not rise at all; and on the other hand more than a quarter did rise by over 20 per cent. The chief explanation must be widely varying capacities to enhance rents—interestingly, in each of two of the parganas where increases were high, there operated a notoriously oppressive landlord, Raja Rameshwar Singh in Bachhaur and Babu Ganeshwar Singh in Padri.[71] Differences possible between one area and another should also be possible between raiyats on the one estate.

Finally, the value of any one resource could alter as circumstances changed. To take one example, an occupancy tenant on a Bettiah Raj village in Champaran was shown on the patwari's register in 1891 as holding over eight bighas at a low rent. At that time, however, the village was surveyed as it had been leased to an indigo factory, and the tenant proved to have a holding of over 15 bighas. The tenant thus became liable to pay rent for the excess at the prevailing occupancy rate. Even allowing a margin for initially rough measurement or the use of a different length of pole, the discrepancy suggests that the tenant's family had surreptitiously increased their holdings after the record was made. They had been thikadars when the village was first being brought into cultivation and had had the advantages of a superior tenure, favourable rents, and the existence of waste land. All of these, however, had been conditional upon loose supervision. No measurements had been carried out in the memory of the patwari, a man of 62. In 1891, however, external circumstances reduced the advantages and made the family, we may assume, somewhat nearer in status to their fellow tenants.[72]

70 Darbhanga report on cess revaluation, 18 January 1896, PCR 362, 8/10.
71 Darbhanga Collector to Patna Commissioner, 20 February 1889, R&A Revenue, A11–16, February 1890.
72 Finucane, 24 November 1891, PCR 355, 15/4.

We are talking, then, of resources rather than hierarchy, and I suggest that this is the only way in which the problem of stratification in Bihar can be approached. It may be said, however, that the difference is more apparent than real,[73] that the variations which are the essence of the conditional resources on which this approach is based were too slow in any one village to prevent advantages hardening into stable structures. Of course this hardening must have occurred; but we are looking, it will be remembered, for the basis of generalizations about hierarchy, and these will not be convincing unless we can show structures consistently over wider areas and times than seem to be possible for Bihar. Moreover, the degree of fluctuation even in a single village should not be underestimated. In the tables and figure that follow, we return as promised to those apparently most stable of conditions: the size and relative values of holdings. They show the problems that would be met in an attempt to impose any sort of static stratification on the basis of total land cultivated and total rental paid by the more substantial villagers on a government estate.[74]

The village, held *bhaoli*, was apparently homogeneous in caste (most of the cultivators named Singh or Jha) and contained one relatively large landholder, probably the former zamindar or thikadar. His rental varied from nearly triple to one-and-three-quarters the amount of that of his nearest rival. His area of cultivation was greater than that of anyone else to similarly fluctuating (though smaller) degrees. In addition, about 20 holdings were never larger than five bighas, which was at the time the average area below which

[73] Note, for example, Charlesworth's distinction between quantitative resources such as land, which might fluctuate to produce 'floating' elites, and qualitative differences such as freedom to manoeuvre, which tended to perpetuate advantage (see 'Rich Peasants and Poor Peasants', pp. 98–9). This distinction is difficult in Bihar because of the variability of circumstances. See Januzzi, *Agrarian Crisis in India*, for one low-caste village with 61 landed and 12 landless households and an absentee zamindar controlling five-sixths of the land; another village with 28 Bhumihar (Babhan) and 2 Koiri ex-zamindars or tenure-holders, and 42 landless; a third with low castes dominated by a patwari; and a fourth with 209 landed Rajputs and 158 landless Yaddavas, and 30 absentee zamindars. Endless variations of this kind could be presented as a smaller number of types. There are some consistent factors—landed households, for examples, were significantly larger on average than landless ones—but the problems of such analysis are that not only characteristics but also the effects of each characteristic varied, and that generalizations would need to be made at one point in time—a snapshot in the same way as survey proceedings were.

[74] The charts are calculated from and the discussion based on enclosures to Stevenson-Moore, Settlement Officer, Muzaffarpur, to Director, Bengal Government, Revenue and Agriculture Department, 12 June 1896, PCR 366, 15/11. The village had 61 holdings, for 44 of which figures are available in full. (Three more are included because each was amalgamated with one of the 44; the remaining 14 have been omitted, except that the village totals in Table 4 are for all of the 61 holdings for which a return was made in each year.) The figures do not take account of income from external or non-agricultural sources, but concentrate on the primary question of surplus to sell.

a raiyat would have been very unlikely to have had an effective surplus for sale. Most of these families must have supplemented their incomes by service or labour. Outline stratification is straightforward: into 'landlord', 'raiyats' (income from surplus), and 'labourers' (income partly or largely from labour). These divisions, it should be noted, are not reflected in rates of rent, except very broadly in a tendency for more of the higher rates to be paid by holdings above the presumed subsistence level in cultivated area.

The real difficulties begin, however, when we examine the 'raiyat' group more closely. Among this group, one is clearly the most substantial on average, but he is not the biggest rent-payer in all years. All the other rankings are gradual and the range very large (from Rs 22 to Rs 77), so that if we were to identify the 'rich peasants', say from two to ten in the average rankings, many in that 'group' would have had more or at least equal affinity with others outside it.

If we turn to the annual statistics, this impression becomes even stronger. Table 7.3 shows the average rankings of the top twenty rent-payers in each

TABLE 7.3
Average Ranking of Top 20 Rent-payers, Mauza Sahara

Rank	1891/2	1892/3	1893/4	1894/5	1895/6
1.	1	1	1	1	1
2.	6	2	2	2	2
3.	2	4	3	3	10
4.	4	5	4	4	3
5.	3	3	5	14	11
6.	8	7	7	10	14
7.	5	9	8	12	12
8.	9	6	6	6	4
9.	7	15	9	7	6
10.	11	8	11	11	8
11.	13	10	10	9	9
12.	12	16	14	8	5
13.	17	19	12	17	19
14.	16	23	13	20	13
15.	15	13	18	19	7
16.	18	20	15	16	16
17.	10	11	16	13	18
18.	22	12	20	15	17
19.	19	17	23	21	20
20.	21	22	17	18	21

Note: This table shows the ranking (1 to 20) in each different years (columns 2 to 5), according to the amount of rent paid, in comparison with the average ranking over the same period (column 1).

178 Peasants, Political Economy, and Law

year and Figure 7.1 illustrates the variations in ranking from one year to the next. In no two years would our groups be the same, whatever the size or method of division, except for the outline we started with of landowners, raiyats, and labourers. It *is* interesting to note the lack of interchange across the middle of the Figure, identical with the line already drawn between surplus and

(a) By value of annual rent   (b) By cultivated area

Year

Note: Each line represents the change in ranking for one holding, from first at the top to forty fourth at the bottom. The years were (1) 1891/2, (2) 1892/3, (3) 1893/4, (4) 1894/5, and (5) 1895/6.

FIGURE 7.1: Graph of Annual Changes in Ranking, Mauza Sahara

subsistence holdings; but there is nothing similar to help us distinguish within the surplus group. Yet a holding ranked seventh on average may be sixth or fifteenth annually, ranging from relative affluence to near-subsistence—variation that virtually rules out stratification as a basis for analysis.

The problem is not just the occasional mavericks whose fortunes fluctuate wildly. (Family circumstances must come in here—a personal disaster apparently struck in about 1894 at the holding ranked number 5 on average, and about the same time numbers 14 and 34 were able to extend their cultivation.) A more important problem is the general variety of responses to economic and climatic conditions. Table 7.4 demonstrates that different holdings were affected to widely different degrees by the forces that made for fluctuations in the output and profitability of the estate as a whole. Our

TABLE 7.4
Percentage Variations from Average in Annual Value of Output, Mauza Sahara

Holding	1891/2	1892/3	1893/4	1894/5	1895/6
Village	+18	−4	+36	−29	−52
2.	+2	+8	+41	−7	−48
3.	+25	−10	+65	−22	−60
4.	+37	+9	+54	−26	−68
5.	+3	+15	+70	−90	−67
6.	+93	−8	+6	−31	−63
7.	+4	+9	+12	−7	−17
8.	+52	−11	+50	−33	−57
9.	+60	+13	+13	−29	−56
10.	−17	−2	+12	−7	−5
11.	+45	−36	+26	−11	−29
12.	−35	−38	+19	+16	−35
13.	+66	−27	+30	−39	−48
14.	−53	−40	+47	+63	−2
15.	+21	+51	+32	−32	−68
16.	+32	+28	+14	−28	−46
17.	+50	−12	+12	+7	−54
18.	+37	−25	+75	−49	−49
19.	−4	−21	+4	+17	−25
20.	−18	+9	+36	+27	−50

Note: The 'village' line is the average for the whole mauza. The other entries show the percentage variation each year from average output, for each holding, identified by the numbers (the average ranking) used in Table 7.3. The calculations are from bhaoli rents. The assumption is that the variations in the government's share are equivalent to variations in the value of output, as any ability to falsify rents was likely to be reasonably constant.

conclusion must be—especially if we imagine these variations extended over a much longer timespan—that peasants differed from one another in Bihar through a complexity of different advantages and disadvantages. Thus one could impose arbitrary divisions on the above figures and no doubt with ingenuity relate these to other factors of social and economic dominance; but though interesting, such analysis would not show us the essence of the difference in relative standing from one peasant to another.

To emphasize resources, not hierarchy, therefore is to assert that explanations for the variability of ranking from year to year must relate to different individual circumstances dictating decisions about how much land to cultivate and so on. Therefore generalizations should be couched in terms of these circumstances, and not in terms of a kind of fictional statistical summary that blurs the kind of fluctuation we see in Sahara. The feature of fixed hierarchy we have already examined—a high correlation between rank on the one hand and ability to resist or benefit from external conditions on the other—is notably absent from Table 7.4, in which such ability appears to be distributed quite at random. Thus within the global categories such as subsistence or surplus peasantry the abstractions cannot be in terms of definite groups of people such as 'rich peasants', but must be expressed as resources in relation to conditions, as social and economic forces that are implicitly in a state of flux. Only in these terms may the polarization of which I have spoken be more fully examined.

8. Labour in India, 1860–1920[*]
Typologies, Change, and Regulation

This essay, in addition to reiterating the points in Chapter 2 about indigo raiyats, broadens the discussion of the state's measures of intervention and of class-formation to include bonded, plantation, and industrial labour.

In recent years, several important books have discussed aspects of labour in India. Some have been significant in their fields more generally, and the subject as a whole can be seen to be changing. This essay reflects on four works, a three-volume collection of documents published by the Indian Council for Historical Research, and Gyan Prakash's monograph on Bihar, which together might be taken as representing the transition in Indian labour studies.[1]

We begin with the collections of documents. Their avowed purpose is to demonstrate that a 'labour movement' appeared in India earlier than used to be supposed. The definition of labour is basically Marxian: workers created

---

[*] First published in *Journal of the Royal Asiatic Society*, series 3, 4(1), 1994.

1 S.D. Punekar and R. Varickayil (eds), *Labour Movement in India. Documents: 1850–1890*, vol. I: *Mines and Plantations*, New Delhi, 1989; vol. II: *Factories*, New Delhi, 1990; and A.R. Desai, *Labour Movement in India. Documents: 1891–1917*, vol. III, New Delhi, 1988. There are 18 volumes projected in all for the *Documents* series; those under discussion are cited hereafter as *LMI*, vols i–iii. See also Gyan Prakash, *Bonded Histories: Genealogies of Labor Servitude in Colonial India*, Cambridge, 1990. Other important recent works not directly discussed here include Dipesh Chakrabarty, *Rethinking Working-Class History: Bengal 1890–1914*, Delhi, 1989; Jan Breman, *Of Peasants, Migrants and Paupers: Rural Labour Circulation and Capitalist Production in West India*, Delhi, 1985; and V.K. Ramachandran, *Wage Labour and Unfreedom in Agriculture: An Indian Case Study*, Oxford, 1990. Since this essay was written, a collection of readings with an introduction by Gyan Prakash has also appeared in the *Themes in Indian History* series, namely *The World of the Rural Labourer in Colonial India*, Delhi, 1992. See also Mark Hölmstrom (ed.), *Work for Wages in South Asia*, New Delhi, 1990, and Peter Robb (ed.), *Dalit Movements and the Meanings of Labour in India*, Delhi, 1993. The present essay continues the discussion begun in my introduction to the last volume.

by and subordinated to capitalism. In particular, these books assume that this workforce was formed from peasants (not artisans or labourers) either because the peasantry was the original social formation, destined eventually to become a proletariat, or because a process of 'peasantization' occurred after traditional crafts had been destroyed. Moreover, the editor of volume III of the series tells us—though this must have rung hollow even at publication—that by 1914:

The bourgeoisie which strode as a triumphant ruling class...throughout the nineteenth century, had exhausted its creative potentiality...Mankind entered a phase described by Lenin...[,] crying for setting up a new social order based on the end of the last exploitative system founded on private ownership of means of production.[2]

In other words, the point of these volumes is the 'life and struggle of [the] Proletariat in India'.[3] In this framework, the inevitable antagonism of labour and capital is the key. The subject is the consequential suffering of the 'workers'. Labour as such, in the production process, is a secondary concern so are the perceptions of workers themselves.[4]

This chronology and rationale are unsatisfactory in several ways. One is that we need to understand much more about labour in India and will not do so while diverted by a teleological concentration on the emergence of a proletariat and a working-class movement. A restricted definition of 'labour' prevents a complete assessment of the particular forms and position of labour in India. Indeed, a more interesting narrative is suggested by the documents presented here than is recognized by the editors. Another problem is that the concern with exploitation diverts attention from potentially more interesting stories of change. We need to ask if exploitation did take particular extreme forms under colonialism and capitalism, but also if it did so under the influence of South Asian conditions. In the record, moreover, colonial rule is not only complicit or acquiescent in the oppression of workers; it is also the agent of a gradual encroachment by law and other political forces into the lives of producers. The point in basing a more extended discussion on these volumes

2 *LMI*, vol. iii, p. ix.

3 *LMI*, vol. iii, p. xiv. Compare: 'The Indian labourer was turned into an industrial worker as a result of a revolution', *LMI*, vol. i, p. ix, and vol. ii, p. xi; also 'the conditions...expose the myth that capitalists whether British or Indian were acting as trustees of the workers', *LMI*, vol. i, p. vi, and vol. ii, p. viii.

4 For a discussion of the problems and possibilities of a study of culture from below, see Carlo Ginzburg, *The Cheese and the Worms: The Cosmos of a Sixteenth-Century Miller*, translated by John and Anne Tedeschi, London, 1980, especially pp. xiii–xxvi. Some attempts have been made at similar studies for South Asia, notably by Shahid Amin, Sekhar Bandyopadhyay, B.S. Cohn, Dipesh Chakrabarty, Ranajit Guha, David Hardiman, and Majid Siddiqi.

is not the merit of their points of view,[5] but rather the possibility they provide for exploring some of these issues.

II

Volume I of that series is arranged to show how indigo was produced in nineteenth-century Bengal under a repressive agrarian system controlled by European planters. There is a hint of 'labour movement' in the combination of raiyats in Nadia district refusing to sow indigo in 1860. The well-known affair was apparently local in inspiration (the Indigo Commission of 1860 could find no evidence of 'trouble-makers' from outside), but it was hardly a workers' revolt.[6] Otherwise there is little here to justify the place of indigo in an account of developing capitalist labour relations. Its inclusion implies merely that raiyats became workers because Europeans managed the plantations. On the contrary, the indigo system repeated and distorted features of an earlier and continuing politico-economic regime. It was based on advances and debt and also extra-economic power. It involved an alliance between rentier, trading, and administrative powers and also between village-level and external elites.

---

[5] It has to be said that the first two fall below the minimum of competence in their presentation. None of them provides much in the way of scholarly apparatus: identifying individuals, providing background, and so on. Presumably because the work was sadly interrupted by the death of Professor Punekar, volumes i and ii present documents out of order, often out of context, sometimes misleadingly identified and sometimes not identified, and almost wholly without dates. Even the titles of the works are inappropriate: the first (*1850–1890*) contains material from 1860 to 1906 and in the second (*1891–1917*) the earliest document dates from 1875. No newcomer to the subject could safely be encouraged to use these books. The third volume, edited more professionally by A.R. Desai, provides a useful and usable collection, though it too has some oddities. One is that it claims to draw *inter alia* on archives, legislative debates, records of the International Labour Organisation, and papers from many associations. In fact there is no direct use of official records and the collection comprises, almost without exception, extracts from the Bombay-based *Times of India* and the *Bombay Chronicle*. These are important materials, but a collection drawn from them alone (even when reporting events as far afield as Lahore, Calcutta, Jamshedpur, and Madras) is obviously a different matter from one based on all possible sources. The volume also is a transparent attempt at slanting the reader's interpretation. It includes an extract from V.V. Balabushevich and A.M. Dijakov (eds), *A Contemporary History of India*, New Delhi, 1964, which presents labour unrest as part of a 'nation-wide... anti-imperialist struggle'; this is undermined by most of the documents and by a further extract from a secondary work. To the summary provided by the latter—V.B. Karnik, *Strikes in India*, Bombay, 1967—parts of this collection add little more than detail. Nonetheless, overall the volume is more balanced than its declared motivation makes one fear. The historian got the better of the polemicist.

[6] Report of the Indigo Commission (hereafter IC), 1860, paragraphs 120–31, *Selections from the Records of the Government of Bengal*, 1861; see paragraphs 120–31, *LMI*, vol. i, p. 39–41.

Hereditary obligations played an important part in securing indigo production, as did local and personal rather than general or public law.

I have written elsewhere on indigo and the subject has been well covered by others.[7] Can one justify the implication in the volume under discussion that the system whereby it was produced in Bengal represented an example of, or at least a step towards, a capitalist exploitation of labour? Two main systems of cultivation existed—*nijjote* and raiyati. The first was carried out by planters on owned or rented lands, using hired labour. The second depended on the use of advance payments and extra-economic sanctions to ensure that 'independent' cultivators devoted certain lands to indigo. This second, raiyati form, by far the more prevalent, is chiefly discussed in these materials (and the literature) and not easily described as a new form of labour relations.

If the indigo raiyats are to be presumed to be a proto-proletariat, then they must have been involved in common in relations of production radically different from those they had previously experienced. But, first, they were differentiated amongst themselves. Included even among those introduced in these pages as suffering the oppression of the planters were village office-holders, former factory agents, the owners of brick houses, and people owed large debts.[8] Indigo cultivation was often resented, but some of the more effective resistance to it came from small rivals of the planters. A key to the indigo systems, as to social control, was the existence of intermediaries, each claiming a percentage and seeking to oppress those below them (not altogether unlike the

---

[7] See essay 4 and 'Bihar, the Colonial State and Agricultural Development in India, 1880–1920', *Indian Economic and Social History Review*, XXV(2), 1988; Jacques Pouchepadass, *Planteurs and Paysans dans l'Inde Coloniale: L'indigo du Bihar et le Mouvement Gandhien du Champaran (1917–1918)*, Paris, 1986, and also *Paysans de la Plaine du Gange: Croissance Agricole et Société dans le District de Champaran (Bihar) 1860–1950*, Paris, 1989; B.B. Chaudhuri, *The Growth of Commercial Agriculture in Bengal (1757–1900)*, Calcutta, 1964; C. Fisher, 'Planters and Peasants: The Ecological Context of Agrarian Unrest and the Indigo Plantations of North Bihar, 1820–1920' in C. Dewey and A.G. Hopkins (eds), *The Imperial Impact: Studies in the Economic History of Africa and India*, London, 1978; B.B. Kling, *The Blue Mutiny: The Indigo Disturbances in Bengal, 1859–1862*, Philadelphia, 1966; G. Mishra, *Agrarian Problems of Permanent Settlement: A Case Study of Champaran*, New Delhi, 1978; and H.R.C. Wright, *East Indian Economic Problems of the Age of Cornwallis and Raffles*, London, 1961. See also the entries in G. Watt, *A Dictionary of the Economic Products of India*, London, 1890.

[8] After the disturbances at Nadia, indigo raiyats judged liable to damages had the resources or access to credit to be able to pay out Rs 31,225 within days of being fined; in Jessore, 157 just as quickly paid Rs 6,226. Given that the annual advance to cultivators, a cash outlay to cover the costs of cultivation, was 'invariably Rs 2 per bigha' (two fifths of an acre), such payers were apparently, as the Indigo Commission claimed, 'men of substance'—see IC paragraph 175 (see *LMI*, vol. i, p. 43). See also paragraphs 94–9, pp. 32–3 and *Selections*, 1861 (*LMI*, vol. i. pp. 2–10).

patrons, placemen, and deputies of the English eighteenth century). As the Indigo Commission explained, the taking of '*dustoori*, or perquisites' was characteristic of the indigo factory servants—the hierarchy of '*dewan gomashta, amin*, and *takidgir*'—but also was 'done unfortunately in all establishments, public or private, official or unofficial, whenever cash passes through the hands of native subordinates'.[9] It was no doubt because of these layers of agents and brokers that coercion by the planters was not directed only at poor peasants but also or even particularly at 'respectable' persons and office-holders.

Secondly, as the Commission of 1860 clearly recognized, the practices of the planters conformed in large part with 'local custom', whereby the means used to enforce production of particular crops or to extract general agricultural surplus included rent, debt, 'moral compulsion', and the fear or experience of physical force.[10] These weapons persisted throughout the countryside and over time, perpetuating equally the dominance of the high castes and the economic exploitation indicated by abwabs (illegal cesses). They resulted typically from collusion between powerful families and institutions, an alliance which that between planters, zamindars, and the local magistracy merely echoed.[11] Even of kidnapping—that is, 'confining recusant or obstructive parties'—the Commission noted that 'it may be urged, unfortunately with truth, that the practice was not invented by the planters, but was previously practised, and is still practised, by others'.[12]

Hence the raiyati system was not introduced at the whim of the Europeans, but was necessitated by local expectations and by conditions of dense population and complex land rights. Planters mostly found it impossible to acquire large units of land for direct cultivation. A common reason was the *strength* of land rights at village level even in this area where, by some accounts, they had been destroyed by British property laws after 1793. Moreover, one explanation of the general recourse to advances and lenders by agriculturists was that it was sustained from income and convenient in spreading costs, that:

the sale of hides, and the raising of jute and ordinary rice crops, are profitable to the parties who supply these articles; and as to the ordinary Mahajani [moneylenders'] dealings, it suits the ryots to borrow money or grain to eat at a season of the year when the market is tight, and to repay the loan after the gathering in of the harvest.[13]

9 IC, paragraph 107 (*LMI*, vol. i, p. 34).
10 IC, paragraph 48 (*LMI*, vol. i, p. 20).
11 The Indigo Commission reported that planters and zamindars generally cooperated and that local European officials tended to give support too, at least before the 1850s (magistrates had 'not been sufficiently alive to the position of the ryots, and...not accorded to them a due share of protection and support'—IC, paragraphs 40–55 and 112–19 (*LMI*, vol. i, pp. 18–22 and 37–9).
12 IC, paragraphs 94–102 (*LMI*, vol. i, pp. 32–4).
13 IC, paragraph 176 (*LMI*, vol. i, p. 44).

Less favourably for the raiyats, it was also often thought that they were forced to seek seed and food for want of resources and to seek credit in order to meet rent and other demands made in money and out of step with the harvests.

Certainly it is likely that the advent of the planters represented some degree of change in agrarian relations. Apart from the obvious long-term impact of an increased reliance upon distant markets and capital, the arguments for change include enforced modifications in land use and decision-making, both in the move to indigo (though cash-cropping was hardly new) and in the lands secured by the planters for direct cultivation. Such lands included *chur* (riverine) tracts and other areas formerly used in common or for occasional cropping. The thrust of such interventions could be seen to be an attempt to reduce the possible range of decisions taken locally and the flexibility available to the agriculturists. Secondly, the intrusions by indigo planters may have been more disruptive in practice than other controls whose form they took. There were many systems of advances; perhaps the indigo planters' were more onerous and more rigorously enforced.[14] There were repeated pleas and reports that indigo cultivation was not remunerative; its persistence thus indicated coercion which, though certainly not unique, may have been extreme. In Bengal, though not elsewhere to the same extent, the planters attempted a close supervision of cultivation, which was loudly denounced by the raiyats.[15]

Nonetheless, the tale to be told of indigo is not an uncomplicated one of workers' subordination to capital, their impoverishment, and emergence as a 'class'. Though we might identify some reduction in the skills required and in the variety and choice available to labour, there is only a very loose and insignificant approximation between the working conditions of raiyati indigo cultivation and those of, say, a late nineteenth-century agricultural gang in England (let alone a production line set up by Henry Ford), and no certainty of a trend towards such 'industrial' patterns. Questions are raised as a result about our economic stereotypes. In particular, the consistency in the terms of indigo advances of different kinds argues for the importance not of external economic 'systems' ('feudal' or 'capitalist') but of immediate context and custom. The Indigo Commission explained:

The contracts, which all the ryots enter into, are either for one year, or vary from three to five or ten years. The advances made in October and November, are invariably at the rate of two rupees a beegah [bigha], and for this sum, the ryot usually agrees to give land suited for indigo, which lands would be marked off by the servants of the factory, to prepare them, to sow the indigo, weed it, and deliver the plant at the factory. The plant, when grown and delivered, is measured, and credit is given to the ryot at a rate which now ranges from four to six or eight bundles for the rupee. The bundles

---

14 IC, paragraphs 31–5 (*LMI*, vol. i, pp. 16–18).
15 Ibid.; and IC, paragraph 59 (*LMI*, vol. i, p. 23).

are measured by a six-foot chain passed round the centre of the plant.... The same process is repeated year after year.... With some local distinctions...the above are the main features of *ryotti* cultivation....[16]

The importance of custom is suggested in hereditary obligations and in standard terms of agreement and rates of payment perpetuated over years. There were so-called 'free advances', whereby the raiyat was not charged for seed or cutting and carting, and 'also a third system under which he takes no advances, but gets seed for which he pays, not at a fixed rate of four annas a beegah [as was usual], but at the market rate'. But both these variations were discovered only 'to a very limited extent'. More marked differences in rates and terms could be found between rather than within regions (say between Bengal proper and north Bihar); but even then, certain features of the system— the advances, the involvement of parts of many holdings, the indirect control— were still very general.[17] As said, they arose out of tenurial, ecological, and social conditions. There was little direct cultivation because unencumbered land was not available. But why was there hardly any purchasing of crops from independent raiyats? Only in Rangpur district did the Commission find much of a market whereby the cultivators were able to sell their indigo freely despite having taken advances. One suspects even this may be a case of mistaken identity. During the nineteenth century, parts of Rangpur were being developed by medium- to large-scale entrepreneurs, giving rise to a distinctive system of largish village-level controllers (*jotedars*), poor sharecroppers (*bargadars*), and semi-tribal harvest-time labour (*adhiars*). The jotedars were often major creditors and grain dealers, providing seed at high rates of interest to the sharecroppers.[18]

Something similar seems to have prevailed in northern India in Aligarh, Mathura, and Farrukhabad districts, where an extensive cultivation of indigo pre-dated British rule. The crop 'used to be brought to the factory, and there sold by natives'. The factory made advances to 'contractors, zamindars and cultivators, who grew the plant with less supervision than is usual in Bengal'.

16 IC, paragraph 31 (*LMI*, vol. i, pp. 16–17). Obviously there is a superficial resemblance between this indigo system (and other labour and management strategies to be discussed in this paper) and the 'putting-out' arrangements found in Britain and Japan (and indeed most places) before, during, and after industrial revolutions. Generally, too, they are regarded as liable to abuse and subjected to legislation: there are repeated instances in nineteenth-century England, prompted by indignation at conditions in such 'sweated' industries. The Indian examples perhaps differ in the range of the extra-economic controls and in their ubiquity, completeness, complexity, and resilience.

17 See above, note 14.

18 See Sugata Bose, *Agrarian Bengal: Economy, Social Structure and Politics, 1919–1947*, Cambridge, 1986, pp. 12–15 and 254–6.

Indeed, 'in the case of contractors, men of substance, the planter never inquired where or how the plant was grown'. With such a system, as presumably also under the jotedars of Rangpur, it was uncertain (thought the Indigo Commission) that 'the poorer class of cultivators derived much profit'.[19] In other words, they were likely to have been subjected by intermediaries to controls very similar to those which elsewhere were exercised more directly by the planters or their agents.

The Indigo Commission was concerned with two elements of 'improvement'. The first was economic expansion through trade; the second prevention of abuses by law. The Commission is pilloried by the editors of these volumes for believing that 'the Planter has a ground to justify his squeezing the ryots as he (Planter) has to maintain himself'. In fact, it argued in partial exculpation of the planters that they themselves worked on capital borrowed at high rates of interest and that at least they extended cultivation and provided much employment. It remains a very pertinent issue in development and environmental studies whether and in what circumstances general well-being can be assured by means of economic growth, that is, by 'efficiencies' and expansions of production. We will return to this question. The second instrument of improvement according to the Commission, and the dominant one in these pages, was intervention designed to identify and regulate conditions of work in accordance with specific Western theories. This we will now consider in some more detail.

The chief defects of the indigo system identified by the British officials were the 'compulsion of the cultivation' and the legal 'imperfections' which permitted it. The analysis of the problem was neo-classical—want of freedom and want of certain and effective law—and so was the remedy: it was to be 'the earliest and most vigorous reform', not of labour law, but of contract and property law, on the argument that as the indigo raiyats supplied their own bullocks and land they were not labourers according to the 'first principles of political economy as to what represents capital'.[20]

The indigo system flourished not with the aid of colonial power so much as outside it, in a world of personal, local, and social control rather than of abstract or general rules and rights. The Bengal government is criticized here for its failure to respond to petitions about abuses; but it was really advocating a new system of individual protection. In its replies to petitions, it referred petitioners to regular tribunals or declined to comment on matters that were *sub judice*. It showed none of the later (and earlier) British hesitations about

19 IC, paragraph 35 (*LMI*, vol. i, pp. 17–18).
20 IC, paragraphs 69, 175, and also 162 (*LMI*, vol. i, pp. 27, 43, and 52). (The order of sections of documents is sometimes rather arbitrarily shuffled in these volumes).

the appropriateness of such approaches in Indian conditions; it was quite certain, to paraphrase a Resolution of 30 January 1860, that any oppression or injustice was subject to the jurisdiction of the courts, whose job it was to redress wrongs and punish offenders with the support of the local authorities.

By the same token, the raiyats themselves were bound to fulfil any legal contracts into which they had entered. The law was 'equally fair to all parties', to quote another resolution of 28 February. The government was thus not—in theoretical terms—in dereliction of its duty to protect the weak (as the editors of these volumes claim). Rather, it was trying to carry out that duty by means of an extension of 'objective' legal principles and processes.[21]

The Indigo Commission was appointed to consider *legislation*. It looked in turn to the European planters not only to protect European rule in the countryside but for 'a sort of guarantee that violent abuse shall not long remain undetected'; they could represent a new 'public opinion' that would begin to redress the habitual inequities of Indian life. This was to some degree a triumph of hope over experience. The Commission recognized 'the delay and difficulties of the law, the corruption of the police, the venality of the native clerks of courts, and the opposition, direct or indirect, which the European may encounter', though it did not accept that the excesses planters were known to have committed could thus be excused.[22] On the same basis, the Commission supported missionaries and others who had been blamed for fomenting the troubles in Nadia. It was appropriate that they should publicize the 'rights' of cultivators to decline indigo contracts. The Commission's minority report also wanted to improve the police and outlaw *lathial*s (the cudgel-bearing strongmen employed by local elites, including planters); it wanted an indigo inspectorate; it called for indigo contracts to be registered and regularized and then to be enforceable under the criminal law. Hence the story contained in this volume is less one of Indian labour (only small proportions of which are represented) as of the evolution of state and legal responsibility for the world of work.

21 *Selection*, 1861 (*LMI*, vol. i, pp. 10–13). Possible consequences of this attitude are discussed in the conclusion, below. Note also the comments in IC, paragraphs 117–18 (*LMI*, vol. i, p. 38), on the order by the future Lieutenant-Governor of Bengal, Ashley Eden, while magistrate of Bariset, to the effect that 'the ryots can sow on their lands whatever crop they like' and that police would be 'sent to the ryots' land to prevent any disturbances that are likely to ensue from any compulsory cultivation of their lands'. This ruling was upheld by the government at the time and was, thought the Indigo Commission, 'strictly in accordance with the law'. However, it was partly because of the outcry at this decision, as well as the explanation by the erstwhile Commissioner that it was not intended to afford police protection to indigo raiyats who were defaulting on their contracts, that the Commission concluded that normally a greater partiality had been shown to the planters.

22 IC, paragraph 101 (*LMI*, vol. i, p. 33).

The rights thus to be protected were regarded as both standardized in law and inherent. In just this way, Bengal property laws—from the Permanent Settlement of 1793 to the Tenancy Acts of 1859 and 1885—were supposed equally to define future rights, which thus owed their existence to the legislation, and to reflect 'historic' rights that could be explained according to theories of social evolution.[23] By depending on law for enforcing rights of whatever origin the British assumed the achievement in reality in India of a Hobbesian 'sovereignty' though the reach of the colonial state remained limited. Indeed, in many aspects of British involvement in India one finds that theoretical imperatives were able to override a more pragmatic recognition that the rulers could not determine the execution of policy nor control its impact.

In addressing the problem of indigo, the Commission elaborated on why Europeans as foreigners must behave very much better towards the raiyats than Indian planters and zamindars. In the raiyati system, *as in other aspects of rural life*, the raiyat appeared to the Commission to be 'deprived of his free will'. He was 'bound to continue a cultivation, which does not give him fair or adequate profit, which in its worst aspect he absolutely dislikes, and in its most favourable aspect he is only induced to tolerate'.[24]

This argument is worth examining further. First, it contained a nationalist element, typical in its essentializing and appeal to the past: 'Experience teaches us, in every department, phase, and period of Indian history, that the lower orders will endure patiently at the hands of one of their own colour or creed 10 times the oppression which they would at the hands of a foreigner.'[25] The assumption was that Indian raiyats recognized Indian zamindars and planters as fellow nationals, and for that reason would resent their demands less than they would those of 'aliens'. Secondly, this argument embodied the belief on the part of the Commission that European ways were superior to others (as, by the same token, were high culture and ideals to popular understanding and practices). This was not a simple racism. The Commission observed that Europeans were involved in abuses and it expected Indians to be amendable to 'improvement'. What it was expressing mainly was confidence in 'progress', defined in terms of improved output, wealth, and public morality, and in

---

23 See Robb, 'Law and Agrarian Society in India: The Case of Bihar and the Nineteenth-century Tenancy Debate', *Modern Asian Studies*, XXII(2), 1988, and 'Ideas in Agrarian History: Some Observations on the British and Nineteenth-century Bihar', *Journal of the Royal Asiatic Society*, vol. 1, 1900; and Asok Sen, Partha Chatterjee, and Saugata Mukherji, *Perspectives in Social Sciences*, 2. *Three Studies on the Agrarian Structure in Bengal, 1850–1947*, Calcutta, 1982.
24 IC, paragraph 70 (*LMI*, vol. i, p. 27).
25 IC, paragraph 67 (*LMI*, vol. i, p. 26).

absolute remedies, marked by the refusal to be deterred by obstacles thrown up by custom or social barriers.

In these respects it offered a specific view, to be encountered equally in public commissions reporting on England. It showed awareness of the role of capital, asserted the value of enterprise, and espoused an 'organic society' and civic gospel': views which were distilled not only from Adam Smith and Jeremy Bentham, but also from Thomas Carlyle, John Stuart Mill, Matthew Arnold, and John Ruskin. The Commission had a Utilitarian faith in the influence of law and in increased production and commerce for the general good. But also, for example by arguing that the planters' and the rulers' self-interest demanded a greater benevolence towards the raiyats, it was foreshadowing *Unto this Last* (1862). Other public commissions too had said as much, as had Coleridge: 'Your *heart* must believe, that the good of the whole is the greatest possible good of each individual: that *therefore* it is your *duty* to be just, because it is your *interest*.'[26] Wordsworth too pointed out the implications for the state in his postscript to the *Lyrical Ballads*: 'Is it not indisputable that the claim of the state to the allegiance, involves the protection, of the subject?' By linking improvement in material conditions to social responsibility, and indeed by adding to the recognition of very rapid 'mechanical' change a reassertion of the old humanist concerns with nature, spirit, and happiness, these writers and thinkers added new dimensions and expectations even to the dutiful inquiries of a growing officialdom in India. Though they did not prevent the oppressions of planters or the opportunism of colonial government, these ideas and policies should not be judged by standards of other times nor dismissed as being without influence.

---

26 *The Watchman* (1796), no. iii, in Stephen Potter (ed.), *Coleridge: Complete Verse and Select Prose*, London, 1962, p. 146. Obviously parts of this view—and particularly its appeal to the past—owed much also to Locke's views on property, which will be mentioned below. But matters were being taken further. Compare the attack on 'Liberty as the Law of Human Life' in Matthew Arnold, *Culture and Anarchy*, edited by J. Dover Wilson, Cambridge, 1963, for example, pp. 184–98: '...in the policy of our Liberal friends free-trade...is specially valued as a stimulant to the production of wealth.... Therefore, the untaxing of the poor man's bread has...been used not so much to make the existing poor man's bread cheaper..., but rather to create more poor men to eat it.... And...our free-trade policy begets such an admirable movement, creating fresh centres of industry and fresh poor men...that we are quite dazzled and carried away.... If...we persist in thinking that our social progress would be happier if there were not so many of us so very poor..., then our Liberal friends...take us up very sharply.' Their 'error...is, perhaps, that they apply axioms of this sort as if they were self-acting laws which will put themselves into operation without trouble or planning on our part'—in short, pursuit of them 'has been too mechanical' because it ignored the facts that 'about one in nineteen of our population is a pauper' and 'that the relations between capital and labour' are not understood.

III

If the indigo system provides a paradigm of labour and change well outside the expected track of Marxism and most economic theory, are those approved models to be found instead in more 'industrial' modes of production? Two discussed in this volume concern coal and tea, both distinguished by depending, unlike indigo, largely upon impermanent migrants and wage labour. But these systems too do not unequivocally represent new working regimes. First, against the old stereotype of settled village 'republics' and despite serious, long-term, and mainly socio-political constraints, it is now recognized that some labour had long been mobile in India.[27] Arguably the same areas and peoples were often the most subject to labour recruitment in the colonial period. Notable instances include Ratnagiri district south of Bombay or the Gangetic districts of eastern Awadh and western Bihar, all of which sent out large numbers (from different social levels) as military recruits, as harvest labourers, and later into cities, factories, and plantations within India and abroad.[28] There were also 'tribals' such as the Santhals of southern Bihar and northern Orissa, for whom migration may be regarded as an extension of historic processes of incorporation into (though then also of marginality within) the mainstream of South Asian economies and societies.[29]

Secondly, in terms of the methods of labour recruitment and management, coal mines and tea plantations bear a family resemblance to indigo cultivation rather than to 'modern' factories. In Punekar and Varickayal, *Mines and Plantations*, the case of coal is represented by information on labour shortage

[27] See Jan Breman, *Labour Migration and Rural Transformation in Colonial Asia*, Amsterdam, 1990.

[28] On Ratnagiri's links with Bombay city (as also with Mauritius), see Gill Yamin, 'The Character and Origins of Labour Migration from Ratnagiri District, 1840–1920', *South Asia Research*, 9(1), May 1989. On Bihar, see especially D.H.A. Kolfe, *Naukar, Rajput, and Sepoy: The Ethnohistory of the Military Labour Market of Hindustan, 1450–1850*, Cambridge, 1990; Seema Alavi, 'North Indian Military Culture in Transition: 1770–1830', PhD Thesis, University of Cambridge, 1991; Anand Yang, *The Limited Raj: Agrarian Relations in Colonial India, Saran District, 1793–1920*, Berkeley, 1989; and Jacques Pouchepadass, 'The Market for Agricultural Labour in Colonial North Bihar, 1860–1920' in Hölmstrom, *Work for Wages*. The Continuation of independent and unassisted emigration (mostly seasonal) from Bihar and the North-West Provinces was recognized by B. Foley's Report on Labour in Bengal, Calcutta, 1906 (which is reproduced but not identified in *LMI*, vol. i; see pp. 125–6). These included seasonal, mainly cold-weather, movements to East Bengal and Assam for harvesting, roadmaking, and railway work and, on a different rhythm, to Calcutta for domestic and mill labour. See also Arjan de Haan 'Migrant Labour in Calcutta Jute Mills: Class, Instability and Control', in Robb, *Dalit Movements*.

[29] See the articles by Corbridge, Bourz, and Engels in Robb, *Dalit Movements*; and also Ranajit Guha, *Elementary Aspects of Peasant Insurgency in Colonial India*, Delhi, 1983.

and a sorry collection of mostly fatal accidents. We learn little of the recruitment and management of the workforce, but just enough to raise doubts that the key opposition was between capital and labour.[30] Rather the line is once again blurred by the use of intermediaries. There were instances too of mine owners acquiring villages in order to use zamindari influence to secure workers.[31]

Similarly with regard to tea the 'existence of the middleman between the planter and the emigrant was regarded as a necessary evil, for which in the then existing circumstances...no remedy could be devised'.[32] And once again, advances played an important part. Garden *sardars* were recruiters employed by the tea gardens and drawn from experienced coolies returning to their own villages. They received Rs 10 initially from the planters' local agents and then Rs 10 per recruit; the actual payment after the workers arrived on the plantations (Rs 5 to Rs 40 per coolie) was regarded as a bonus.[33] In some contrast with the generalizing optimism of the Indigo Commission, the Assam Labour Committee of 1906 favoured the *sardari* system because it approximated to what was thought of as Indian norms. 'The best way of working with natives of the coolie class', it advised, 'is...through headmen

30 See also Colin Simmons, 'Recruiting and Organising an Industrial Labour Force in Colonial India: The Case of the Coal Mining Industry, 1880–1939', *Indian Economic and Social History Review*, XII(4), 1976.

31 Dietmar Rothermund and D.C. Wadhwa (eds), *Zamindars, Mines and Peasants: Studies in the History of an Indian Coalfield and its Rural Hinterland*, New Delhi, 1978, for example p. 8. See also Detlef Schwerin, 'The Control of Land and Labour in Chota Nagpur, 1858–1908', in ibid.; and for a later period, Gunther Dienemann, 'Labour Force and Wage Policy: An Analysis of their Structural Characteristics and Patterns of Development' in Rothermund, E. Kropp, and Dienemann (eds), *Urban Growth and Rural Stagnation*, New Delhi, 1980.

32 Report of the Assam Labour Enquiry Committee 1906 (hereafter ALC), paragraph 77 (*LMI*, vol. i, p. 168). On the recruitment systems generally, see paragraphs 25 (pp. 189–90), 48–61 (pp. 176–85), 67–98 (pp. 163–76), and 222–31 (pp. 185–9).

33 ALC, paragraph 92 (*LMI*, vol. i, p. 173); also see paragraphs 20 and 90–7 (pp. 139 and 172–5). Garden sardars were legalized by Bengal Act II of 1870 and by Act VII of 1873. Local agents were recognized in Act I of 1882. An oft-recognized result of the systems used was to link plantations with particular districts and villages, though patterns changed over time. In eastern U.P. and western Bihar, for example, Ghazipur was the leading district sending workers to Assam because, it was thought, of its convenience. Though only 341 registered migrants were recorded in 1890, far larger numbers participated in 'free' emigration. However, in 1915/16, 94,911 emigrants went to Assam from the provinces of Bihar and Orissa, an increase attributed almost entirely to bad harvests and more extensive use of garden sardars (following the abolition of contractors) in Orissa. In the previous periods (1913/14 and 1914/15), no emigrants at all were recorded as having come from the districts of Patna, Saran, and Muzaffarpur in Bihar. See Government of India, Revenue and Agriculture Proceedings, Emigration Branch, A series, nos 1–4, January 1890, and no. 25, April 1890; and compare Commerce and Industry Proceedings, Emigration, B27, January 1916, and B72–3, December 1916, National Archives of India, New Delhi.

who understand their likes and dislikes in a way which no European can do.'[34] The Committee advocated again and again that conditions of work and housing needed to accord with the expectations of the workers and that by this means, the coercive aspects of recruitment and employment could be avoided. It also had a 'village community' view of the kind of society that should be created in Assam on moral and economic grounds. It thought that garden sardars should be encouraged at the expense of independent contractors because they brought in families with a high proportion of women and children rather than single men, the 'easily duped' single women, and 'waifs and strays'.[35]

The perceived accommodation between West and East, market and custom, capital and labour, was characteristic of the mood of British administration towards the end of the nineteenth century. The evidence shows that keen competition between planters at first encouraged long contacts and legal measures to punish absconding; but later produced higher and higher prices for labour, not as wages for the employees but as profit for increasing layers of intermediaries who supplied it: *daffadar*s (freelance recruiters), sardars, *arkati*s (village-level recruiters), and so on. With regard to working conditions too, the planters in the tea gardens of the Assam valley had once attempted, according to the Committee of 1906,

> to do for the coolie what the Englishman thought best for him, and to exact in return the service which the Englishman thought could be fairly demanded. It, however, did not follow that these terms... were congenial to the coolie. The coolie was expected to work six days in the week although he preferred to work five; to turn out at the hours his master chose and not at the hours he himself preferred; to live in the house which his master thought best for him and not in the house he himself thought best; to stay on the garden where he was fairly well-off instead of returning to his home or taking to cultivation.[36]

This approach failed. In some places the planters even had to allow liberal leave in order to adapt to what was regarded as their workers' preference for leisure over pay. Working regimes and pay levels generally had to adjust to different local conditions, including ecology; and it proved the case that the 'more easy it is for a coolie to abscond from the garden, the more necessary it is to make it worth his while to stay'.[37] In some places where suitable land was available, a strategy was developed to retain labour by granting smallholdings to coolies formerly housed in 'lines'. The change was marked by growing numbers residing in the bastis (squatter settlements), by increases in rice growing and ownership of animals, and by a decline in the tasks required

---

34 ALC, paragraph 97 (*LMI*, vol. i, p, 175).
35 ALC, paragraph 74 (*LMI*, vol. i, p, 167). See also paragraph 192 (p. 158).
36 ALC, paragraph 151 (*LMI*, vol. i, p, 148).
37 Ibid., paragraph 152.

on the plantation and in the percentage of the total labour force at work at any one time. The resultant bi-employment in intensive private cultivation supplemented incomes and thereby at the same time increased 'loyalty' and reduced the pressure to raise wages. Similar devices had long been used to entice and exploit agricultural labour in the migrants' home regions and of course were implicit in the various indigo systems. One occasion of these changes in Assam was a reduction in the region's isolation (resulting in part from the extension of the railway). It is an irony that this opening-up reduced the trend towards central management and money wage-payments in the tea gardens.[38]

Once again however, for both coal and tea, there was consistent state interference. It is usually regarded as having been in aid of capital, but may also be interpreted as intended to place bureaucratic and legal limits on the exploitation of labour. The tea gardens and the recruiters were subject to regulation almost from the first and, when it was found that much had escaped the law and that the industry was 'disfigured by many evils',[39] the proposed remedy was almost always further legislation. Controls were introduced in 1863 by means of an extension of Act XIII of 1859, which had penalized breaches of contract by workers in the Presidency towns; from the 1890s, this provision again gained greater acceptance than its successor, Act I of 1882. The alternative—'free' emigration sponsored by daffadars and the 'scum of the earth', arkatis—was blamed for most of the ills and unpopularity of migration to the tea plantations.[40] Typical was the attitude of Sir Charles Rivaz, introducing a regulatory bill in 1901. He described these contractors, as if it were condemnation enough, as a 'horde of unlicensed and uncontrolled labour purveyors'. From such 'illicit' agents (it was argued), 'ignorant men and women, chiefly from the most backward districts', should be protected by government.[41]

In 1906, it was still thought that ideally 'all contractors' should be 'licensed'.[42] Assam was largely to retain its special laws, unlicensed recruiting was to be banned, and the two classes of sardar were to be 'assimilated' to

38 ALC, paragraphs 141–62 and 193–200 (*LMI*, vol. i, pp. 144–56). Between 1899 and 1906, the percentage of labour working daily dropped from 87 to 73 per cent and the task was reduced by 25 per cent at the Empire of India and Ceylon Tea Company in Tezpur, 'probably the most conservative district... in labour matters' (paragraph 152, p. 148).

39 ALC, paragraph 151 (*LMI*, vol. i, p. 148). On the early history of regulation, see paragraphs 15–24 (*LMI*, vol. i, pp. 134–5 and 137–40).

40 ALC, paragraph 97 (*LMI*, vol. i, p. 176). See also paragraphs 2–8, 16–24, 48–53, 59–61, 222–8, and 232–91 (pp. 140–3, 137–40, 176–8, 183–4, 185–8, and 194–213). (See note 20, above)

41 ALC, paragraph 48 (*LMI*, vol. i, p. 176).

42 ALC, paragraph 76 (*LMI*, vol. i, p. 167).

those provided by one of the laws.[43] Such recommendations were made, despite a new preference for many of the controls to be phased out, though one standard 'system' was no longer the goal and when thinking generally had come to favour a greater 'freedom' for labour. The idea—at once neo-classical and relativist—was that planters should compete for workers by offering appropriate and favourable terms, for example a relaxation of penal sanctions, reduced contract periods, and higher wages.[44] General law could then replace specific regulation. All along, an alternative bastion had been bureaucratic: the appointment of official superintendents to inspect the conditions of emigration and employment, a device favoured also by the minority on the Indigo Committee and for regulating conditions in coal mines, as well as of course by a host of inquiries into factories, health, and other aspects of public life in England.

Evidence that officials did not see or justify these efforts merely as a means of easing the way for the capitalists is once again readily to be found. According to the Committee of 1906, the 'main idea' throughout had been 'a contract binding the emigrant to serve on a tea estate for a certain number of years, and in return for his being thus bound, the law provided that he should be "protected"'.[45] Though aspects of the resulting law were 'totally indefensible in principle', they had to be judged by their actual operation. The Government of India had explained this in a despatch to the Secretary of State, on 5 October 1891, to the effect that however 'objectionable in principle' it appeared, Act XIII of 1859 was 'a more lenient and popular penal contract law, from the labourer's point of view, than the Act of 1882. As such it is serving a useful purpose as a transitional stage between strict penal contracts and a system of civil contract under the ordinary law.'[46] There is a certain Alice-in-Wonderland quality about this and we can read it of course as a late-nineteenth century gloss on a mid-century pragmatism. A law happily convenient for colonial trade and European capital, and presumably formulated to be so, was being justified in the fashion of the 1880s and 1890s by its appropriateness to India's 'backwardness' and for bringing India nearer to the enjoyment of laws that were analytically 'correct'.

When priorities were being identified, the well-being of the workers inevitably competed with the importance attributed to tea as a valuable export,

43 ALC, paragraph 98 (*LMI*, vol. i, p. 176).
44 The point is made repeatedly in ALC. See paragraphs 57–61 (*LMI*, vol. i, pp. 180–5), 156 (p. 150), 201 (p. 190), 237 (p. 195), and 240–73 (pp. 196–208).
45 ALC, paragraph 25 (*LMI*, vol. i, p. 189). This paragraph also (p. 190) suggests that planters should adopt 'more elastic' labour relations.
46 This assessment was made in a special report compiled between 1886 and 1889; ALC, paragraphs 224–5 (*LMI*, vol. i, pp. 186–7).

especially given the worries about the perennial labour shortage in Assam—the Inquiry Committee of 1906 estimated a shortfall of some 18 per cent, which it attributed partly to the unpopularity of work in Assam.[47] Yet the 'protectionist' clauses and rationale also appear consistently, as do harsh criticisms of tea planters' conduct. Official interference was prompted partly by the high mortality among workers en route to Assam and because the conditions encountered after arrival were notoriously just as bad. The officials recorded and tried to respond to the local riots, to instances of planters' violence and racial abuse, and to low birth- and high death-rate statistics suggestive of poor health among the tea coolies. At one level, this can be regarded as mere paternalism, illustrated by what might nowadays be called the 'infantalizing' of the 'ignorant' and 'backward', and it may be argued that that process was extended to Indian society as a whole because, even though 'wily' Indians were among the exploiters, controls were supposedly remedying failures of indigenous civilization. Government interventions were often rationalized on the basis of particular inadequacies, a 'backwardness', or failure to develop in Indian institutions and practices. On the other hand, the 'special case' argument was rhetorically useful in a climate of laissez-faire and it was applied to English as well as Indian situations. Again an element here was the extending of the responsibilities of the state, attributable to general and not colonial tendencies. Certainly the Committee repeatedly advanced the argument that 'self-interest' as well as 'altruism' demanded reform.[48]

IV

This intervention is also the effective subject of the second volume edited by Punekar and Varickayil, which focuses on employment in factories, especially the Bombay cotton mills. One point becomes increasingly evident: that pressure for regulation was augmented by new professions and their expertise. Doctors and civil engineers fed a professional interest in working conditions into the

---

47 ALC, paragraphs 26–9 (*LMI*, vol. i, pp. 135–6). This percentage has been calculated from estimates in para. 28. In crowded districts Malthusian fears also encouraged the opposite reaction from officials, leading some of them to welcome emigration. A scheme in Bihar is discussed below (see note 88). But official ambivalence is illustrated in the attitude recorded in the Report of Labour Immigration into Assam for 1888, which noted the increase in 'free' emigration as something that in itself, as 'Government has observed', was 'not to be regretted', though it did regret, however, 'the practice of... inducing persons by deception to leave their homes'; Government of India, Revenue and Agriculture Proceedings, Emigration Branch, A series, nos 1–4, January 1890.

48 One planter too thought it 'to our interest to see' that the workers were contented and comfortable—ALC paragraph 155 (*LMI*, vol. i, p. 201). See also various similar and some contrary opinions in paragraph 58 (pp. 181–3).

official enquiries on factory legislation, the Commissions of 1875, 1884, and 1890. As a result, by the early twentieth century, views and reports had been largely standardized. They provided a set of norms and laws against which the conditions of labour were judged. Among the new rules, for example, was the axiom that men worked at their best for only eight or nine hours a day, that long periods spent standing would induce flat feet in children, or that certain amounts of light and ventilation were necessary to health and efficient production. Specific diseases were traced to occupations, such as lead poisoning in brass foundries, dye works, and so on. A checklist was established for factories: on temperature, ventilation, humidity, dust, general cleanliness, protection of machinery, and means of escape.

Over time, rules and inspection spread from larger to smaller establishments. Normative concepts set the agenda for inquiries, recommendations, and ultimately law. So workers were assiduously canvassed as to their preference between higher pay and shorter hours of work; children and women were now 'known' to be weaker and more vulnerable than men, and their work and conditions were particularly monitored. Professionalization was marked also by the collection of statistics, for example of accidents. These records were designed to provide comparisons and to measure progress. All of these changes in 'knowledge' gradually provided weapons in the hands of inspectors. The 'scientific' rules were then employed by increasingly vocal publicists and lobbyists to influence what was provided by law. The *Times of India*'s celebrated article on 'Bombay's Slaves', published under Lovatt Fraser in 1905, registered not only a general humanitarian concern, but also specific charges framed in terms of science and of law—on hours of work, factory conditions, child labour, and so on.[49]

International labour conventions were increasingly important and much pressure came, for example, from the International Congress of Hygiene and Demography, 1891, or later the International Labour Organization. But in India, the basis of the norms, the yardstick of success, was British experiment and experience. Investigation in India was secondary. For example the Haldane Committee of 1902, a British departmental enquiry into ventilation in factories and workshops, provided a standard measure of ventilation according to the

---

49 *Times of India*, 13 May 1905 (*LMI*, vol. ii, pp. 68–81; also see pp. 66–7 and 81–7). For other points in this paragraph, see *LMI*, vol. ii, *passim*. No attempt is made here to discuss the extensive literature on Indian factory labour; see for example M.D. Morris, *The Emergence of an Industrial Labor Force in India: A Study of the Bombay Cotton Mills 1854–1947*, Berkeley, 1965; R.K. Newman, *Workers and Unions in Bombay 1918–1929: A Study of Organisation in the Cotton Mills*, Canberra, 1981; and Dick Kooiman, *Bombay Textile Labour: Managers, Trade Unions and Officials 1918–1939*, New Delhi, 1989.

proportion of carbon dioxide in the air and thus superseded measurements of workroom capacity. The new calculations were devised by chemists. Humidity and whether clean water was being used could also be checked according to a test laid down in Home Office regulations of 1906.[50]

Against these imported standards, 'Indian' norms were also proposed, sometimes as a reason for different expectations or policies. There were appeals to supposed social or cultural peculiarities, as when T.M. Nair, author of a remarkable minute of dissent to the Report of the Indian Factory Commission of 1908, proposed that '[a] small percentage of low caste women... may accept work in all the departments of a mill and work alongside men of all castes. But the large majority never will.'[51] Most commonly, however, the arguments were ones to which the employers were particularly attached: that more Indian than British workers had to be employed to achieve the same level of output and that the standard of comfort and contentment of Indian mill workers was higher than that of other Indian workers.

This was an excuse for applying lower standards in India than in Britain. In support of it were relatively objective points about the organization of production in India. For example the Berlin International Conference in 1890 provided a maximum of 11 hours' work for women, but accepted an exception proposed for India on the ground that in Ahmedabad cotton mills, where one woman and a boy looked after a machine, the work was not too arduous and breaks were possible during the shift.[52]

There were also, more often, arguments drawing on the character and poverty of Indian labour, some of them making a point still heard today about the social advantages of overmanning. Thus Indian factory work was supposed to suffer inevitably from disabilities when judged against the norms that were being established. When faced with criticisms, especially regular press campaigns on hours of work and employment of children, the Bombay mill owners argued (in the words of Tata and Sons) that 'Labour in India is not cheap. It is inefficient.'[53] Indian factory workers were scarce, unskilled, and

50 The 'Pettenkofer' system was used to measure carbon dioxide. Humidity was important in cotton manufacture. The test stated that any water was injurious 'which absorbs from acid solution of potassium permanganate in 4 hours at 60°F more than 0.5 grain of oxygen per gallon'—Indian Factory Labour Commission 1908 (hereafter FLC), *LMI*, vol. ii, p. 195.

51 T.M. Nair, minute of dissent, FLC, quoted from *Indian Textile Journal* (hereafter *ITJ*), XIX(218), 1909 (pp. 57–8 *LMI*, vol. ii, p. 59). Extracts from this minute appear at several points in *LMI*, vol. ii, misleadingly attributed to the Labour Commission of 1875. Its importance has been noticed before, but is worth reiterating.

52 Indian Factory Commission 1890 (*LMI*, vol. ii, pp. 280–1). Sorabji Bengallee dissented from this exception (p. 281).

53 Letter from Swadeshi Mills Ltd. Bombay, to the Secretary to the Mill-owners' Association, 16 March 1897 (*LMI*, vol. ii, pp. 89–91).

agricultural in background. They lacked training, they were also peripatetic; and they were recruited, managed, and paid indirectly.

This brings us again to the second of our major questions: India's 'peculiar' features. Indigo, tea, and coal production were not creating a proletariat, but nor was one to be found in factories. It is well known and amply illustrated in this collection that factories too were very slow to adopt systems of direct recruitment and management. The lynchpin of this indirect system was vividly captured by a writer in the *Indian Textile Journal* in 1890:

> The jobber is an important personage in an Indian mill. A big red turban, a black coat reaching to his knees, a sheet of white calico thrown across the chest distinguishes the jobber from the ordinary workman. He invariably carries a stick while a silver or brass chain hangs from a watch of the same metal in his coat pocket. He has worked his way up from the lowest beginning and...gets enough himself to keep him and his family comfortably besides enabling him to save up and buy land in his native village...[54]

His job was to maintain the machinery and to recruit and manage the staff. He was paid on piece rates and by exactions from the workers. The dangers were plain: 'An intimate knowledge of the native hand's character is absolutely necessary on the part of the manager or overlooker. Otherwise the jobber and his workmen gain the upper hand.'[55] A possible example of tension between factory and jobber was a strike in 1894 occasioned by an argument over the quality of yarns between Framji Billimoria, manager of the New Great Eastern Mills in Bombay, and his head jobber Dhakoo.[56]

Sometimes management was blamed for Indian conditions. It did not consider, say, that a labourer recruited by a jobber and paid by him a month in arrears would inevitably remain in thrall to the jobber or other creditors;[57] it did not understand that such a worker, 'finding himself compelled to work a long number of hours', would be bound to reduce 'the intensity of labour as a safeguard to his own physical well-being'.[58] Additionally, given the conditions of factory work, the jobber would continue in employment only for a few months or years at a time. T.M. Nair, a doctor by profession, argued that 18 months was the average period of employment for mill workers—not from choice (they were poorly paid and indebted) but because of the strain

---

54 *ITJ*, I(6), 1890, pp. 91–2 (*LMI*, vol. ii, p. 97).
55 Ibid.
56 Reported in *ITJ*; see *LMI*, vol. ii, pp. 306–7. This was also a time of wage disputes, as mentioned below.
57 Report on the shortage of labour in industries by an officer on special duty, 1906 (*LMI*, vol. ii, p. 260).
58 Nair's minute of dissent, *ITJ*, XVIII(216), 1908, pp. 395–6 (*LMI*, vol. ii, p. 43). This same passage is also attributed to the *ITJ* of October 1893, p. 5 (*LMI*, vol. ii, p. 227). On working hours, see also *LMI*, vol. ii, pp. 50–60 (Nair again) and 209–50.

of the work upon health. Most of the workers, he suggested, returned to the countryside to become agricultural labourers, not having access to land. The decline in their health was often missed by medical witnesses either because occupational diseases went unrecognized or because, by definition, only those who were for the moment fit and at work presented themselves for inspection at the mills.[59]

But mainly it was alleged that India explained all. The jobbers were supposed to be peculiarly Indian intermediaries paralleling others, including those discussed above. Factory absenteeism was said to be explicable in epidemics or the social and agricultural calendar. It was India too that made it hard to regulate child labour or to raise the age at which persons were deemed to be adult. Indian conditions meant that age was difficult to judge (various measures were used, including development of the teeth), and when the 1890 Commission proposed raising the age for adult work from 12 to 14 but no further, it adduced arguments that reflected its view of Indian customs and expectations. At the higher point, it explained, age might be more easily determined, which was clearly desirable given the different capacity of 'adults' and 'children'. But on the other hand in India 14 was an age at which marriage often took place. Moreover, in joint families children were often important earners; indeed 'a tropical climate and the diseases common to it often age the parents so rapidly, and throw them out of work, [so] that a son or daughter, aged 15 to 16, is frequently found to be the mainstay of the family'.[60]

A tension was implied between Eastern 'culture' and Western 'efficiency'. The contrast is nowadays acceptable only in disguise as an indictment of capitalist values and practices and otherwise is condemned as 'Orientalist'. Yet real issues here should not be lightly dismissed. In some senses, labour is a universal condition; but in many other ways, it is plainly various. Its situation in India depended on indigenous characteristics as well as colonial *force majeur*. The 'Orientalist' critique is relativist to the extent of admitting civilization to be 'separate but equal'. These Indian cases argue that societies differ in 'efficiency' and 'morality'. The assertion will be explored further in the next two sections.

V

The two factors implicit in the documents, the Indian legacy and the external categorization, have been explored by Gyan Prakash. His important study of the Bhuinya *kamia*s, bonded labourers in Bihar, is focused both on indigenous forms, including the consciousness of the workers themselves, and the concepts

[59] Nair's minute, *LMI*, vol. ii, pp. 25–51.
[60] Indian Factory Commission 1890, pp. 4–6 (*LMI*, vol. ii, p. 283).

and regulation of labour advanced by British law and government.[61] This two-pronged attack on the problem greatly widens the definition of labour and the scope of Indian labour studies. In breaking out from narrow, Eurocentric categories of analysis and by attending equally seriously to the popular and the official voice, this book exemplifies the methods needed to understand the social and economic interplay of work and status in India. Of course as a pioneering study it leaves questions still to be considered. Some of these will now be discussed, as an illustration of the intricacies of the path advocated in this essay. There are three parts in Prakash's story. The first is that of law or categorization: bondage represented a legal construct. The second is that of context or contingency: bondage resulted from the power of money, but only where social inferiors were indebted to superiors, and this differed from subjection to a lord or as a slave. The third is that of kamia self-perceptions and the extent to which they contested or acquiesced in inferiority of status and opportunity.

For the first two aspects, the key question is the impact of colonial interventions. Prakash argues that bondage was imposed upon marginal people in south Bihar as a new system—which made them kamias and was a creation of British and capitalist legal concepts. Such 'bondage, far from being a relic of pre-modern times, was constructed by the colonial discourse of freedom', namely a post-Enlightenment emphasis upon equality in 'nature', and the extension of money as a basis of social relations.[62] These suggestions raise serious and difficult issues, among which those about labour occupy one small corner. They relate to the basis and impact of European ideas and perceptions, to the nature of cultures and of cross-cultural contact, to the possibility of translation and conversion, to the character and consequences of colonialism, and so on. With the paradox presented by Prakash—that measures intended to empower individuals in practice enslaved some of them—we are dealing with an incompatibility of understanding between Europe and India (as in

[61] See note 1 above. The discussion that follows is supplementary to my comments on this work in *Dalit Movements*, pp. 13–21. Categories of unfree labour shade into one another; here the concern is with bondage in productive agrarian labour (excluding forced employment on one hand, or ceremonial and domestic servitude that treated the worker as a commodity on the other). For a useful, balanced summary of these possibilities and the ubiquity of coercive labour relations in colonial India, see the essay by Tanika Sarkar in Utsa Patnaik and Manjari Dingwaney (eds), *Chains of Servitude: Bondage and Slavery in India*, New Delhi, 1985.

[62] Prakash, *Bonded Histories*, p. 220. See also pp. 143ff. for a valuable discussion of early British consultations about slavery, showing the plurality of their initial approach, respecting Indian religion and custom as well as asserting moral certainties, so that judges in Bihar 'recognised generally the rights of masters over their slaves, to the extent of enforcing any engagements voluntarily entered into by parties, according to the customs of these parts, and provided they be not repugnant to the feelings of a British judge'—Report of the Indian Law Commissioners, 1841.

the terminology and approaches to labour already discussed). The British made false diagnoses and introduced remedies that, being inappropriate to India, created new problems. They were related to another paradox at the heart of European thinking as it related to India in the nineteenth century: an emphasis upon individuality, but also upon a search for types. The kamias, though entitled to objective and equal legal rights as individuals, suffered from being categorized as a bonded community.

As we have seen, this is a far from uncontroversial view. Most problematic may be its implication that Western concepts of the person and hence Western categorizations differed in essence from those of Indians. One difficulty is that this reifies and freezes or at least cordons off what is probably varied, fluid, and negotiable. It is important to be clear therefore about the features of Western thought that are distorting the perception of Indian labour according to this essay and which according to Prakash worsened the standing of Bihari kamias. In some part, it is that same ambiguity between the self and the category.

At one level in European thinking, these are successive emphases in the evolution from Enlightenment universalism, through the individualism of the Utilitarians, to the sociological relativism of historicists and Idealists. Thus re-interpretations of Indian village communities may be linked to European reactions to industrialization and with a re-assessment of the European middle ages—embracing Henry Maine and Maitland, Ruskin and Rossetti, Tolstoy and Gandhi.[63] But at other levels the individual and the type are mutually dependent, for example when Adam Smith, focusing his study on human personality, emphasized both primary selfishness and 'natural' sympathy for others. The first impulse was directed to the survival of the individual and the second enabled the existence of groups or society.[64] Together, they implied general human characteristics within each individual, in moral and intellectual terms as in physical.[65]

63 See particularly Clive Dewey, 'Images of the Indian Village Community', *Modern Asian Studies*, VI(3), 1972.

64 Smith, *Theory of Moral Sentiments*, 1790. Of course this differs markedly from Bentham's argument that the greatest happiness could be achieved by the exercise of egotistical interest, but it is plain from labour legislation and much besides that such unbridled Utilitarianism was not consistently applied in India. There is a mix in all of these viewpoints with regard to India. Thus Macaulay's Eurocentric universalism was ignorant of India but expected Indian 'improvement', while the influence of Henry Maine's comparison with medieval Europe shaded off into racism, essentialism, and social Darwinism, as relativist anthropologists of the late nineteenth century understood much more of India, reinstated the value of community, but were more pessimistic about 'improvement'.

65 This is a reason perhaps for the dogged search in ensuing centuries for a material demonstration of moral worth, be it in physiognomy, in art, in manner, or in self-made, self-improving wealth.

This does seem to be a post-Renaissance European contribution. Where rulers, systems, and deities are expressions of personal will, it may be easier for individuals to be subsumed in groups or hierarchies. The expectation is of duty and the tendency towards monism. But where there are impersonal forces, the individual seems to escape to the centre of the stage. The expectation is of rights and the trend towards dualism or plurality. Then there arises a further need to categorize, starting with the Self and the Other and going on to define separate spheres, such as for man or things secular. Whereas monism invites exegesis of a single truth, individuality presupposes difference, which calls in turn for classification. The categories themselves are then conceptualized as individuals, as in corporative legal entities, and that process may make for essentialism. The outcome is a reformulated order, which seeks still to privilege the individual. It does so, if not unequivocally,[66] then certainly in the long musing of British philosophers upon the origin and limits of political power from Bacon, Moore, and Hobbes, through Locke, Blackstone, and Bentham, on to the present day—an evolution that increasingly stressed the separation of public and private and the state's contract with the individual. In this Indian case, the kamia was a type because of concepts of individual rights derived from a range of sources, including Locke's concept that property (ownership or authority) originated in acts of creation, as by God of man and by parents of children, and was thereby inherent in the individual and expressed in labour.[67] It was this property of which the bonded worker was deprived.

All this supports the case for contrasting pre-colonial with colonial forms in India. Yet though Locke linked his idea to that of liberty, we may wonder whether these complex antecedents can be reduced to the issues of freedom and money chosen by Prakash. And still more serious questions are whether the dichotomy of free and unfree (much illustrated in the present essay) was really novel in Europe, characteristic of colonial interventions in India, and

---

[66] Being ill equipped to discuss this point, I merely assume from ignorance that the individual is still the focus even when perceiving ultimate principles by reason (according to Kant) or the absolute as expressed in phenomena (after Hegel). To speculate on whether reality exists independently of the 'idea' at least centres attention upon the perceiver-individual. It seems rather different in this respect from the idealism of Indian philosophy, which may begin in knowledge of self, but which leads to an ultimate unity that transcends reality and perception, a unit that is unknowable. The self too is moderated through *dharma*, *artha*, and *kama*, generalizing drives, aims, and roles. It is subsumed in transmigration (kama being a bondage to be escaped rather than an opportunity for improvement) and as the highest goal, it seeks to escape itself, in literal self-less-ness.

[67] For the most famous passage on mixing labour with, for example, land, see John Locke, *Two Treatises of Government*, edited by P. Laslett, Cambridge, 1960, pp. 328–9.

in some way influential, as Prakash seems to claim, in determining the conditions of labour in nineteenth-century Bihar.

Clearly ideas of freedom and the market are to be contrasted with hierarchical doctrines of nature, monarchy, and mercantilism (whether in seventeenth-century England, or during the nineteenth century, or indeed in the present day). But the opposition of freedom and tyranny is hardly new, being evident for example in Cicero's 'Complete Orator' or Plutarch's life of Caesar,[68] and the political context has remained important. Nor was it new to conceive a comparable, even related freedom in relations of employment. Tennyson, having just been raised to the peerage, regarded the freedom of his own day as greater than that of the ancients, when, he wrote, 'Freedom' was 'pained/To mark in many a freeman's home/The slave, the scourge, the chain'.[69] Tennyson had earlier written poems celebrating the moderation of the steps towards political 'freedom' in the Reform Bill of 1832, so that one may imagine that the Corn Law controversies and the Chartists firmly established in the public mind the supposed connection between free trade, labour freedom, and political liberty. And yet at least a parallel to this had been obvious to the Romans in their concepts of slaves, of freedom, and of citizens. We see in *Utopia* too (especially in the absence of property and money) a link between political and occupational conditions, even an implicit attack on monarchy, which have often been regarded as a humanist response to felt changes—the enclosures and commercial agriculture in particular.[70] Even Hobbes, in his exposition of sovereignty as power and order, as a kind of bondage, traced its origin to implicit and competitive acts of will on the part of men, so that the limits placed upon such acts derived from a kind of agreement.[71]

Thus in explaining the fate of Bihari kamias, Prakash is perhaps doing too little in terms of the complexity of influences, but also too much by way of accommodating the kamias' status to a European evolution. The chief fallacy, it may now be thought, of the philosophical school of history and all its followers—in which one may include Hume, Smith, Hegel, and Marx—is that (alongside the development of the novel, interestingly enough) they treat history

---

68 See Georges Barnes (tr.), *Cicero on the Complete Orator*, London, 1757, p. 228: 'the yoke of tyranny', or Sir Thomas North (tr.), *Plutarch's Life of Julius Caesar* in T.J.B. Spencer (ed.), *Shakespeare's Plutarch... in the translation of Sir Thomas North*, Harmondsworth, 1964, p. 77: 'they chose him perpetual Dictator. This was a plain tyranny.'

69 'Freedom', written in 1884—*Poems of Alfred, Lord Tennyson*, selected by Charles Tennyson, London, 1954.

70 Utopia means of course 'nowhere'. The work was surely intended as an ethical ideal rather than a social blueprint. Sir Thomas More, *Utopia*, translated by P.K. Marshall, New York, 1965.

71 Thomas Hobbes, *Leviathan*, Harmondsworth, 1981.

as a single or serial narrative in which human societies not only are bound to change but also tend to evolve from more primitive to more developed stages. In a limited way, Prakash shares this assumption, while at the same time arguing (as did many Europeans of their own case) that the change is not beneficial in all respects or for all people. Moreover, in order to make this point, Prakash needs to subscribe (as those Europeans did also) to a contrary narrative, the decline from a better past. When he explains that the formal abolition of slavery and later the introduction of labour laws paradoxically made possible the kamias' bondage, it is difficult not to conclude that we are supposed to regard earlier instances of forced labour as aspects of a moral rather than a material economy. Prakash even hints at the isolated village community being 'penetrated from outside' during British rule, though the countryside had had a long involvement with the military, with merchants, and so on. Indeed in the colonial period there was much that appears to be bondage in Gangetic Bihar as well as on the southern fringes; but its beneficiaries, Prakash's local chiefs, the maliks, are presented rather as village patrons distributing surplus. If this is not entirely convincing, it may be because Western discourse has here become not just a subject of analysis but an explanatory principle. On offer is a substantivist critique of the formalism of colonial attitudes, positing a disjunction between altruistic man (the Indian past) and economic man (the nineteenth-century Western ideal). My view is that one should look not for necessary evolution, times at which either a social or an economic logic must prevail, but for varied mixtures and fluctuations of these different rationales.[72]

72 See Prakash, *Bonded Histories*, chapter 3, especially p. 97. The speculative discussion of land rights and cultivation patterns in this chapter is one of the less convincing parts of the book. Issue is being taken here with Prakash's view of colonial discourse and of the impact of concepts on the basis of Western thought and Indian conditions. In support of the latter doubts are numerous other accounts that have made plain that bondage was far from new in colonial India: at least one essay (by Dingwaney in Patnaik and Dingwaney, *Chains of Bondage*) that has traced the inability of law to prevent it, from Manu to 1843 (with regard to slavery); from 1837 to mainly 1854 (with respect to indentured emigration); and between 1920 and 1976 (against debt bondage). For early examples and types of slavery, including debt bondage, see also Uma Chakravarti's and Salim Kidwai's essays in the same collection. They refer in turn to Irfan Habib's recognition (in 'Potentialities for Capitalist Development in the Economy of Mughal India', *Enquiry*, winter 1971) that a 'landless' servile class can exist in conditions of apparent land surplus because of social and political power, and to the fact that the character and incidence of servitude depend on a variety of conditions, as shown in Benedicte Hjejle, 'Slavery and Agricultural Bondage in South India in the 19th Century', *Scandinavian Economic History Review*, XV(1&2), 1961. On the variety of bondage, important to this debate, see also note 60 above and Ramachandran, *Wage Labour*. Moreover, though there is clear evidence of a rising proportion of agricultural 'labourers' over recent centuries, much of the increase would be explicable in the worsening man : land ratio even without changes affecting the distribution of economic and social power, and hence access to land and control over people.

The third issue, of workers' self-perception, could be an obvious corrective. It refers (in the most interesting and original part of Prakash's book) to continuities of oral myths among Bhuinyas, especially the notion of a caste hero (*bir*), and explanations of their low status in terms of some early loss. Again, we are invited to see this as an illustration of that better or at least different past that the European concepts displaced. But such materials are difficult to interpret. It is possible to regard them as a subversive alternative in that they treated the existing hierarchy not as natural but as historical and accidental,[73] an interesting parallel to the shift of emphasis in Western thought when it also valued the 'real' over the supposed and the 'original' over the present. But the Bhuinya myths did not contest that present. The deduced self-respect was hidden; and actual resistance, for example by avoidance or combination, was not couched in mythic terms. Instead, the portrait of the warrior ancestor Tulsi Bir was 'drawn from the relations of domination'; the feared ghost of Gaya, Raghuni Dak, though combining male and female and crossing caste, re-affirmed those same categories;[74] the ambivalent village deities, the *malik devata*, also endorsed the existing hierarchies—their protection was 'bought' and controlled by landlords, extending maliks' 'property' rights over the kamia's person and possessions. The myths can be seen as extending and thus reinforcing 'hegemonic' notions of status and pollution and what Prakash admits to be 'traditions' of subordination as well as long-term, caste-based divisions between people of similar economic and social standing.[75]

Prakash refers to Bourdieu's warning of the danger of either demonstrating incoherence or imposing coherence. But (in common with all writing and analysis, to varying degrees) Prakash is imposing coherence by yoking mythic and actual practices, by linking the world of spirits and the world of work. This is no bad thing. Though ritual (and any) practices are constituted of 'discontinuous' and 'dynamic events' whose function is 'cultural inconsistency', yet they do play a part in constructing culture; there are 'grand cultural plans' (continuous events) as well as negotiations or circumstances.[76] Here there are spirit-cult practices that can regenerate the malik's dominance. Prakash is reluctant or defensive about this because in the end he wants to assert the motive primacy of capitalism and colonialism. In his examples, however, there is an unmistakable mutuality between dominance by money and state and that by religion and custom.

73 Ibid., chapter 5, and also chapter 2.
74 Ibid., especially pp. 77–9, 197, and (for Raghuni Dak) 204.
75 Ibid., pp. 77–9 and 207–16. The malik devata would also punish any undetected theft from the landlord unless first propitiated; then theft would be disguised as a gift, the exact opposite of Proudhon's famous dictum on property.
76 See ibid., pp. 206ff., quoting from Pierre Bourdieu's *Outline of a Theory of Practice*.

Prakash regards the malik's power and the subjection of the kamia as being 'reified' and 'commoditized'. There was an 'objectification', revealing (as in the abolition of slavery or in debt bondage) the 'power of things'.[77] But the book clearly shows, too, patronage extending beyond the money bond,[78] and makes it plain that dominant roles could not be simply bought. The successful possession of property and power either depended on social standing or brought social status with it (the money-purchaser gaining social resources, like a commoner marrying into royalty). As a result, in social terms at least, bondage was not uniform, as Prakash himself tells us (while drawing the opposite conclusion):

With agrarian relations objectified in land, kamia-malik relations juridically represented in money and grain advances, bondage was unleashed in the agrarian landscape. With hierarchy no longer in control, now even the low-caste rich peasants began to hire kamias, new groups were subjected to debt bondage, fresh areas for the expansion of the kamia labour system were discovered.[79]

Unless the intention is to write caste differences out of Bihari history (an unlikely project) and to replace them with a caste-blind category of 'rich peasant' (as opposed to the relatively rich low-caste peasant), this must mean varieties, even layers of coercive control.

What, one wonders, could have been the mechanisms for any hardening of labour subordination? It is a familiar argument that something like that happened gradually with regard to land rights; but the argument rests upon the observable impact of records, measurement, surveys, partition, settlement proceedings, legal enactments, court decisions, and taxes. By contrast, the kamias, despite their theoretical transformation, suffered in practice from a marked lack of such intervention—their situation fitted nowhere in the colonial state's schema but fell unseen (until very late in the day) somewhere between the abolition of slavery, the preservation of landed estates, the promotion of commercial agriculture, the investigation of plantation conditions, the tenderness for occupancy-tenant rights, the regulation of factories and workshops, and the monitoring of migration and emigration.

Thus it seems that the key ideological or terminological difficulty was not the conception of labour freedom (which anyway is relative), but the compartmentalizing of work within the dualist pattern of European definitions—that is, work as opposed to leisure, to home, to hobby; work at once individual (a contract and payment for each worker) and generalized (by standardized terms, hours, places, and tasks); work that has been discussed

77 Prakash, *Bonded Histories*, pp. 151–2.
78 See ibid., p. 175ff.
79 Ibid., p. 162.

here for differing in meanings in the Indian context. Prakash reveals much of the context, but wants to relegate some of it to a pre-colonial past. There are too many continuities of economic and indeed of social behaviour to make this convincing. In particular, considering the evidence, it cannot be that the bondage described in pre-colonial or pre-capitalist India was just an imaginary Other of the capitalist West.[80] There must be circumstances reflected in the admittedly distorted mirror held up by the British. If there was injustice in the past and economic as well as social forces of control, then the kamias of colonial Bihar prove to be doubly bonded, by custom as well as capital. That alone would make it entirely plausible that their position worsened during the nineteenth century.

By 1900, bondage remained a strategy for low-level survival. The seasonality of employment was still high, as was the contribution of non-agricultural jobs. But terms and options must have been affected by the increasing value and exclusive possession of land and by the rising population, while countervailing influences remained few. Kamias could seldom appeal to the courts; concerted resistance remained a desperate throw; protest, as in the past, was best expressed by fleeing or by taking on additional work, sometimes in secret.[81] None of these held much hope of radical improvement.

VI

Such may have been the consequences for some sections of Indian labour. The outcome is obscure in Prakash's account because in the final analysis it is unclear whether the subjection of labour derives from legal categories and their imperfections, from history and culture, or from economic and demographic happenstance. This uncertainty is an argument for multiple explanations rooted in historical, ideological, and material factors. On that basis, among many possible conclusions about labour in colonial India before the institutionalizing of mass politics, before the demographic upsurge, before the Great Depression of the 1930s, there are two which may be singled out.

First, it was partly because of the circumstances of Indian labour, in particular the power of intermediaries, that a 'class' solidarity was hardly to be expected. The third volume of documents under discussion here details the growth of organized labour as of wider political awareness, but in the end it too demonstrates how long both remained partial and incomplete—as they

---

80 Ibid., p. 142.
81 There is a valuable account of income and work cycles in ibid., p. 169ff. On evasion strategies, see p. 175ff.

do to this day.[82] Of course there were many instances of concerted action in the mills as among rural labourers, and we must be wary of denying workers' consciousness of their position merely on the negative ground that they left few records. However, the point here is rather the positive evidence available of other forms of organization and mentality. A petition from Bombay's mill workers was presented in 1889, for example,[83] but such moves were insignificant in their effect on labour relations in comparison with the jobbers and of course the various complaints from mill owners and managers about the shortage and unreliability of labour. There were eventually economic, legal, and administrative pressures, then inputs from 'modern' organs of opinion, chiefly the newspapers and local professionals, and later still from political parties and organized labour. There were strikes in Bombay under the leadership of jobbers, for example in 1893–4 against employers' attempts to reduce wages by 10 or 15 per cent.[84] By the early 1900s, indeed, there were clear beginnings of organization. But there was hardly yet a 'proletariat'. It was a Maratha Aikya Itchu Sabha (that is, a body for Marathas) that sent a millhands' petition to Lord Curzon in September 1905.[85]

A few years later, the *Indian Textile Journal* expounded a theory to explain the delay in labour organization and the lack of trade unions in India. In Bombay, a union had been formed in 1908 by a 'retired weaving master... and a committee of pleaders' after strikes in reaction to the arrest and conviction of the politician and journalist B.G. Tilak on charges of sedition. (This was the Kamgar Hitwardhak Sabha or Association for Promoting the Interests of Workpeople, which then had 100 members, Hindu and Muslim; but apparently no subscriptions or funds were collected, other than Rs 1,500 from a meeting at the mill where its president had formerly worked. Its declared aims were charitable.) In England, by contrast, said the *Journal*, the unions had grown out of provident societies rather than anti-employer agitations. Such associations were neither feasible nor necessary in India, where workers

---

82 Space does not permit a full discussion (see above note 1), though there are many points at which it could be adduced in support of arguments in this paper. The first short section deals with the formation of unions in a wide variety of industries. The second, longer section describes strikes in Ahmedabad, Bombay, Lahore, Karachi, Sholapur, Calcutta, Jamshedpur, Madras, and elsewhere. The third section more briefly outlines the formation of the All-India Trade Union Congress (reprinting an AITUC publication edited by S.A. Dange, with a *Times of India* report). The final section deals with the International Labour Organisation's Conferences in 1919 and 1920. The appendices include some extracts from the Annual Reports of the Bombay Millowners' Association. See also notes 5 and 49 above.

83 Bombay mill-workers' petition 1889, see *LMI*, vol. ii, pp. 303–6.

84 *ITJ*, IV(42), pp. 149–50. (*LMI*, vol. ii, pp. 306–7); see also *ITJ*, various extracts, 1890–1900 (*LMI*, vol. ii, pp. 308–9 and 317–19).

85 *Times of India*, 25 September 1905 (*LMI*, vol. ii, pp. 325–8).

would not pay dues, were not permanent, and (because of caste, temple, and private charity) did not starve when out of work.[86] The argument is that, as the impulse for regulation was largely external and labour management remained indirect, the experience of factory work did not necessarily create solidarities; it is that even the idea and procedures of trades unions had to be imported. They would be grafted onto other solidarities (also then being extended and generalized) of linguistic group and religion. These are points that have had to be incorporated into theories of change for Indian labour.[87]

One lesson of Prakash's work, and of other studies with a similar range, is that the development of labour organization (as of 'class' awareness) must rest on a complex of *desiderata*. The nineteenth century saw many of the necessary changes. Both the individual and work were increasingly defined (becoming interdependent as concepts). Moreover, these definitions proceeded on a basis of experiment (one might compare the test of the Famine Codes, which sought to ensure that relief work was 'needed'), and thus of 'objective' criteria (that is, fixed measures and rules), and thereby of value (of people, work, even foods). As 'value' may be assessed either by analogy with price (as in a market) or according to moral worth, one may contrast its different meanings as belonging to separate families of understanding. In the case of food, for example, one has at one extreme calorific measures, or the established minima applied in colonial prisons and famine relief, and at the other extreme Indian ritual and social hierarchies of foods, and more-or-less subjective assessments of dietary 'healthiness' (including the popular equation of eating meat with strength). If such kinds of assessment stand together with mutual repercussions, then the measure of work, the test of need, and the standard of food all relate to ways in which the body and its actions are perceived through particular and not necessary or universal judgements. These mutualities delimit the possible in varying spheres, including the celebrated spectrum between caste and class, custom and contract.

There was a change away from one set of criteria towards another in nineteenth-century India. Yet on the other hand conceptions do not move evenly across a broad front. Just as 'objectivity' and 'materialism' were not peculiar to the nineteenth century, nor could they effect a thorough revolution at that time. That too is a conclusion to be drawn from the relativist definitions

---

86 *ITJ*, XXI (246), pp. 190–1 (*LMI*, vol. ii, pp. 336–41; and see replies, pp. 339–41). There was also a Sahaykari Mandli, a workers' defence association. A secretary of the Kamgar Hitwardhak Sabha visited Europe and North America, studying labour relations, between 1901 and 1911. For the disturbances following Tilak's conviction in July 1908, see *LMI*, vol. ii, pp. 329–36.

87 For a recent discussion of union-formation and identity among workers, see Chakrabarty, *Rethinking Working-Class History*.

applied in India—as in those Labour Commission debates that constituted an adult at work according to sociological rather than biological criteria, and by many other aspects in our foregoing discussion of the conditions and imperfections of India's so-called labour market. And so it is (as has often been observed but not always explained) that, say, factories need not produce proletariats.

Similarly, the kamias, according to investigations in the 1930s, continued to suffer in south Bihar in ways quite unchecked by legislation and despite improvements in communications and job opportunities. A sample inquiry of 392 cases showed that most worked for 9½ to 10½ months a year, that many of the workers had some land, and that most of the bonds were informal and oral. Typically, they were based on debts of Rs 10 to Rs 36, incurred in some 85 per cent of cases for marriage expenses and often by parents on behalf of children who were then bonded. Of those investigated, more than 150 (40 per cent) had been recruited within the previous 10 years; only 31 had escaped their bonds over the same period and one of those who had paid off a bond was reported as wanting to enter into another one in order to obtain homestead land. What produced this effect? Blame was placed on the kamia's 'inertia'. 'I despair,' wrote one official, 'of overcoming this by legislation, orders, or reports.'[88] The inertia was attributable partly to the attraction for the very poor, in the first place, of work however poorly it was paid (wages in kind could be sold for cash to buy salt, liquor, tobacco, and cloth, while the workers ate only one meal a day) and, in the second place, of small plots of land—many kamias held plots for houses and kitchen gardens and had access to ploughs and bullocks (and sometimes seed) for their own use. (They paid for these not only by being bonded, but by working unpaid for about two months in the year.) The kamia system might thus be presented as a device for securing or regulating access to resources made scarce by population pressure or legal and social controls. But this argument—applied to those who created and exploited the scarcity or to the motives of those who acquiesced—already contains an appeal to cultural norms. These are shown most poignantly in the bonding of children by parents for marriage costs and in the frequent inheritance of bonds from one generation to another. Such practices evoke a particular view of human individuality, of life, and of responsibilities.

88 Note by J.D. Sifton, 24 January 1936 Bihar and Orissa Revenue File No. 2 of 1936, 1–48, Bihar State Archives. This discussion is based on that file. The government had eventually, in 1920, got round to trying to regulate the employment of kamias. The law sought to limit the conditions and terms of the bonds, but little effort was devoted to the enforcement or reporting thereafter and the legislation was later thought to have failed. The question was shelved until the mid-1930s. The increase (if such it was) in bondage in that period was then attributed to a growing amount of *bakasht*, that is, *sir* or directly managed zamindari land.

In short, the stereotype is more than a mere creation of imported juridical and political concepts. Moreover in Bihar 'kamia' was applied not only to bonded workers but sometimes to 'ordinary' day labourers; conversely others not known by that name were indebted and unable to withdraw their labour or were bound to provide labour, plough, and bullocks free to the landlords and thus were bonded in effect, at least to some degree. This apparent confusion of terminology marks another of the limits to the conceptual standardizations imposed by colonial rule, but it also persisted because the circumstances of these deprived groups did in reality approximate to each other. The poor workers and the kamia were of low ritual status, unable to avoid its consequences without extraordinary effort; their customs, aptitudes, and opportunities were supposedly but also in practice engendered by caste. We can observe this equally in truisms and in evidence of caste propensities. For example in the late nineteenth century, when an official scheme sought to promote Bihari immigration to Burma, the promoters showed a marked preference for recruiting Koiris as an industrious cultivating caste. Family units too were preferred for the severely practical purposes of shackling cultivators to the land through their dependants and of providing a pool of cheap additional labour during harvest and other peaks of demand. Accordingly, most of the settlers were Koiris and very few were of castes that supposedly had a tradition of wage labour (such as Dusadhs, Kahars, and Nonias) and therefore might be expected to take up better-paid heavy labour in preference to cultivation. But experience also endorsed these predictions. High proportions of all castes deserted from the scheme, with the notable exception of Kurmis (and also Chamars). Moreover, invoking another set of customary expectations and practices (unwelcomed though to some extent shared by the officials), disproportionately many of the quite large numbers who died on the scheme were women and children.[89] It is to make the same

---

[89] See Government of India, Revenue and Agriculture Proceedings, Land Revenue Branch, B series, nos 52–3, June 1895, and ibid., nos 3–4, January 1898, National Archives of India, New Delhi. The emigrants were provided with bullocks and seed and were paid wages at local rates while they cleared land and became acclimatized. Then gradually they were moved on to crop-sharing arrangements with a view to effecting their gradual 'transition from...coolies to...independent cultivators'. The transfer of whole families so they would 'take root and develop into healthy communities' was supposed to include the 'decrepit and aged as well as the infants in arms'. A better known and far more important instance of such paternalism was the Punjab canal colonies. The moral may be as recently drawn on another issue by Clive Dewey: 'Again and again one finds Indian imperatives—Indian values, Indian stereotypes—overwhelming official prejudices', see 'Racism and Realism': The Theory of the Martial Caste', paper presented to the seminar on the Concept of Race in South Asia, SOAS, 4 December 1992).

point that we note that kamias were often forbidden to leave their village and that the ban was enforced by violence of course, but also by social deference. The limited emergence of a 'proletariat' resulted, in short, from Indian social and cultural conditions—just as perhaps organized labour reflected the weakening of alternative forms of solidarity and connection.

A second conclusion concerns the means whereby labour conditions might be improved. These stories of Indian labour imply a qualified pessimism. Plainly there is no such thing as 'modern' agriculture and industry, meaning a single form or set of characteristics. Practices contain different elements and their impact will depend on circumstances. There is a superficial similarity but a wide difference in impact between, for example, the sarkar or jobber and his dependent workers on the one hand and, on the other, an independent section manager and a team of generalists such as are nowadays popularly considered a Japanese improvement on the production line. Moreover in each environment there will be more or less competitive methods. Therefore the dilemma of social concern is, as said, how to curb excesses without preventing profitability. The comparisons implicit in the colonial laws did invite improvements in India to the minimum acceptable in more prosperous places. The British government in India oscillated between lower national and higher international comparisons, but generally and increasingly favoured the latter, egged on by 'experts' and their predominantly universalist laws. The advantage of this for workers was spelled out by T.M. Nair: 'The assistance of the law may be needed...because...only law can afford to every individual guarantee that his competitors will pursue the same course...without which he cannot safely adopt it himself.'[90]

The purpose of labour legislation is to establish minimum standards; international conventions are designed to extend them internationally. By means of this framework, the bargaining power of workers is increased without penalizing any one employer in a competitive market (or benefiting those more rapacious than others). Given this argument, it is curious that the application of legal standards in India has been presented as a colonialist intervention on behalf of British industrial interests. The assertion is represented in these volumes by a note on the discrepancies between English and Indian factory law that was sent to the India Office by Henry Harrison, president of the Blackburn and District Chamber of Commerce. It contains detailed expressions of concern for Indian workers, but also special pleading—the suggestion that by watering down the 'enlightened English Factory Acts' in its Bill of 1890, the Indian government had allowed its judgement to be 'warped by the clamour raised by the Indian mill-owners, who desire an unfair field for competition

---

90 *ITJ*, XIX(218), pp. 55-7 (*LMI*, vol. ii, p. 57).

with England'.[91] Indian legislation may have had the effect or indeed motivation of restricting that (largely imaginary) competition, and the needs of labour provision rather than protection were paramount in initially prompting enquiries and legislation over factories as for plantations and mines. Yet in the longer term, as Nair suggested, legal standardization was designed to benefit workers—it should ultimately have advantaged those Indians who were in work.

To expand on these points is to address the impact of British attempts at regulating labour in India. The conclusions of this paper contain an ambiguity. The claim is that state regulation of labour marked a major initiative during the late nineteenth century, but also that many features of Indian relations of production persisted. Indeed, attempts to balance the two contradictory criteria—the universal principle on the one hand and the Indian special case on the other—were consistently made in the official literature.

One way of resolving the paradox lies in the general failure of state regulation to transform conditions in any of the production regimes we have discussed. The argument here has been neither that Western laws perpetuated nor that they ameliorated the conditions of India labour. Of course in the longer term, the extension of abstract 'rights' could be a better insurance for the weak than the exercise of arbitrary power, however benevolent. And perhaps despite the feebleness and ambiguity of British legal interventions, they brought some benefits. The 1906 Committee in Assam noticed changing attitudes, a 'general advance in prosperity', and improvements in the systems and in conditions of life for the tea coolies;[92] it may not have been wholly mistaken.

Yet the key improvement often recommended by official inquiries (as in Assam or for cotton mills) was the use of improved conditions and wage levels rather than extra-economic means to attract and retain labour. Throughout the period, despite legislation, this advocacy seems to have had very little effect. There were wage increases—in 1904, Kanpur carpenters were reportedly paid more than double what they had received in 1858, with about 25 per cent of the increase occurring after 1900—and there is some evidence of a employers' response to supply factors, as when rates were increased at times of 'special pressure', for example plague epidemics. But such responses could be observed also in daily harvest rates for agricultural workers and did not necessarily disturb

---

91 Harrison to Secretary of State for India, 5 April 1890 (*LMI*, vol. ii, pp. 350–3). The Bill in question became the Indian Factory Act, XI of 1891. See also Clive Dewey, 'The End of the Imperialism of Free Trade' in Dewey and Hopkins (eds), *Imperial Impact*, London, 1977, on the limits of the influence of English commercial and industrial interests on British polity in India.

92 See ALC *passim*, but especially *LMI*, vol. i, pp. 147–53, 154–5, 192, and 198–208.

the norm. Wages seem rather to have been characterized first by the persistence of certain customary rates in cash terms. This was implied when early in the twentieth century a monthly rate for coolies in Kanpur of Rs 7 or 8 coexisted with daily rates of 4 annas (Rs 0.25). Naturally it proved hard to retain monthly workers in such conditions. Hence—and presumably for parallel reasons in other circumstances—wage regimes were characterized secondly by the persistence of non-money wages (on the model of tiny land-holdings for agricultural workers), of middlemen, and of other means of coercion or enticement, including credit. It is hardly remarkable then that the labour laws often missed their target. They were designed to regulate wages, hours, and conditions in accordance with British ideas of work, management, and payment.[93]

Considering the regulation of labour from the employers' side, we find that just as the indigo system thrived in the absence of law, so too the laws were relatively little used in Assam, except perhaps as a threat. Thus it is easy to exaggerate the assistance provided by the colonial authorities to the planters. For example, penal liabilities were placed upon workers in Assam. There were perhaps 2,50,000 immigrants in the tea gardens at the turn of the twentieth century. Quite large numbers were indentured under Act XIII of 1859 or Act VI of 1882. But fewer than 600 criminal cases were brought against labourers each year, only a minority were successful, and below one tenth led to custodial sentences.[94]

Equally from the point of view of the workers, the measures taken—statute, enquiry, inspection—had grave limitations. In the short term particularly, the application of general principles, for example to indigo cultivation, surely caused grievous harm to some individuals and sections of the people. And then, though mid-century universalism and pro-market strategies were soon eroded by stronger enunciations of particularity and of state responsibility, and hence by legislation to 'indigenize' the Indian law, yet it was still very easy for the tea planters' recruiters to avoid regulation. Rules were then extended, even though it was officially recognized that fear and ignorance of the existing law had assisted sardars and others to coerce the migrants.[95] In

---

93 *LMI*, vol. ii, p. 259. The question of wages is a difficult one; but the deduction here is supported from other sources and has been suggested before. See my article in Clive Dewey (ed.), *Arrested Development in India: The Historical Dimension*, New Delhi, 1988. In this example from Kanpur, note also on the special rates that 'when the pressure is relaxed the old rate returns'. It seems plain that rates were not always identical with payments, especially where there were payments in kind and the intervention of jobbers or of debt, and that they were entangled with non-economic expectations and influences.

94 ALC, paragraph 226 (*LMI*, vol. i, p. 178).

95 On the limitation of statute and inspection and other forces promoting improvements, see *LMI*, vol. i, pp. 192–3.

Indian mills too, regulation was often ineffective and certainly tended to be evaded if possible. Conditions were probably often worse than reported. It would happen, for example, once hours of work were stipulated for children, that a visit after these hours by an inspector or a European would be heralded (according to the *Times of India*'s account) by a 'perfect chorus of whistles', 'invariably followed by a regular stampede of half-naked children' and jobbers 'driving the children before them with cuffs and blows'.[96] Enforcement was difficult because, like regulation, it nearly always had to be managed from outside. Though there were instances when workers went to court in disputes over the non-payment of wages, they were unlikely to attempt to thwart their bosses over rates or conditions. The reason was put by Balloo Atmajee, a Maratha aged 35 and the ninth witness before the Factory Commission sitting in Bombay on 8 October 1890: 'The operatives are really afraid to go to Court, because the mill-owners employ vakeels [lawyers], and oppose them with great persistence.'[97] The law did little to change the ways labour was managed, nor affected the prevalence of strategies that combined low wages with enticement and coercion.

Once we emphasize the special importance of Indian conditions, we must also be concerned that the regulation was so externally inspired. We have noted the modifications wrought upon government policy (comparing tea with indigo) by the *fin de siècle* crisis of confidence, the relativist, 'anthropological', or if we like 'infantilizing' arguments about India's special character. Perhaps that is what Prakash was driving at. In the colonial period, the impulse for change in India and the idea and manner of state intervention—though not the concept that a ruler had a duty of care for his subjects—was imported from the liberal tradition in Britain. The fact that any amelioration had not gone very far is revealed by the descriptions of conditions in European-managed and -owned mills. But Nair remarked:

> speaking generally, the labourers fared worse under Indian employers than under the European. Even some of the most enlightened and educated Indian gentleman...had not a single word of sympathy with the labourers to express. They were all anxious to make up for lost time and to push on their industrial ventures and to accumulate wealth. But as for the workers, they were part of the machinery of production, and nothing more.[98]

If this comparison is fair, it reveals the greater exposure of European employers to specific intellectual and social pressure and appeals to self-interest. (Nair, a graduate of Edinburgh, was himself avowedly a follower of Cobden and an

---

96 *LMI*, vol. ii, p. 76.
97 Indian Factory (Lethbridge) Commission 1890 (*LMI*, vol. ii, p. 101).
98 *ITJ*, XIX(218), pp. 55–7 (*LMI*, vol. ii, pp. 59–60).

admirer of J.S. Mill. His mechanical and hence quasi-scientific metaphor was a commonplace, in this context and others, as we have seen.)

There was no guarantee anywhere that 'enlightened' treatment of workers would prevail, not even when time was no longer lost, industrial ventures were secure, and wealth had been amassed. But at least in Britain and among Europeans such ideas resulted in part from their being affordable, as Nair acutely observed. One danger was that they were not affordable in India. Regulation to international standards would not necessarily help all the people or the Indian economy should a low-paid labour force be needed to compensate for a lack of competitiveness in other aspects of production. This is why it is crucial not to pretend that all circumstances of production are potentially the same. Some of the suffering attributed to colonial rule can be traced to the British assumption that conditions were universal or that one could create a 'level playing-field' by legislation. Because some things can be changed and some cannot, given capacities, will, and awareness at any one time, there is always a real—and everywhere a different—balance to be struck between social justice and profitability.

Should imported standards reduce the competitiveness of Indian production they would preclude the general improvements in wealth needed for a widening prosperity. This dilemma remains. Having been at the heart of the controls formerly placed upon the Indian economy, they are now being raised most vehemently by critics from the Left in response to the present liberalization. These do not seem problems that can be solved. During British rule and presumably partly because of the fears of disorder and alienation specially felt by a colonial government, the preferred response to a very imperfect labour market was extra regulation. The policy interventions interposed market restrictions and considerations of equity; possibly they encouraged local resilience. The cost for labour was a failure to apply market solutions. Just as the indigo system could have been replaced, in theory, if cultivators had been offered adequate remuneration and fair conditions, so we can imagine terms on which labour could have been procured more competitively in Bihar or would have flocked to the tea gardens. Whether tea (or indigo, or other marketable crops) could then have been produced is of course another question. The educated middle-class politicians who have ruled India since Independence have applied somewhat analogous measures from a somewhat similar political and intellectual position. They too have had very limited success in improving living conditions for the majority. Market-led strategies are now being applied in India, having been eschewed by and large for more than 100 years. Once again the outcome will depend not only on economic 'laws' but on the impact and resilience of local conditions and expectations.

Index

agrarian, change 122–3; policy, 5–15, 18, 27–8, 51–4, 74–5, 77, 79–80, 90–2, 96–7, 115–18, 130, 143, 211; conditions in Bihar and Bengal 61–2
agricultural, department(s) 14–15; production *see* land use.
Akbar, Mughal emperor 8
anti-salt tax protests 3
Asiaticus (Philip Stanhope) 4
Assam Labour Committee, 1906 193, 196–7, 215; and labour shortage 197

Baker, Christopher 4
Banerjea, Surendranath 63
Bayly, C.A. on property and agricultural classes 23, 113; on 'village-controlling peasants' 151n
Bengal 77–9; landed property in 14–15, 42, 73, 77, 79, 82–3, 87; networks in 82
Bengal Tenancy Act 1885 5, 12–13, 62, 80, 93n, 97–9, 109, 112, 115, 169
bhadralok 43, 48; *see also* caste
Bihar(i), agricultural decision-making in 124–5; economic catastrophes in 81; labourers in 54; pre-colonial 109–10
Bombay (Mumbai) 5, 43, 115, 183n, 192, 217; cotton mills 197–200; labour 198, 210–11
bondage *see* debt

Bose, Sugata 4
British Indian Association of Awadh 42
Buchanan-Hamilton, Francis 24, 34–5, 131, 140
Buck, Edward C. 14, 94

Calcutta (Kolkata) 9, 42–3, 192n, 210n
Campbell, George 14
capitalism 86, 87–8, 139
caste(s) 24–5, 34–5, 38–42, 44–6, 48, 102–3, 112, 114, 145, 152, 159, 173–4, 207–8, 213
categorization viii, 46–50, 58–63, 99–100, 114, 125–6, 152, 203–4
Chaudhury, Binay 84–5
class(es) 7, 10, 13, 20, 22–3, 25, 33–4, 42–3, 46–8, 50, 64, 87–8, 116–18, 121–2, 131, 146, 157, 209–11
coal production 192–3, 195–6
colonial economy 122–3; C.A. Bayly on 23; crisis in 58; *and see* commercialization
colonialism in India vii, 2–4, 41, 46, 56, 64, 202, 207; and liberalism 217
commercialization, of agriculture 9, 18, 25–6, 29–30, 32–3, 70–1, 81–3, 86–7, 104–8, 111, 120, 128–30, 132–142, 145; of land 17, 75–6, 90–2 , 138–42
Cornwallis, Lord 9, 91
Cotton, Henry 4
Court of Wards, 11–12, 86
cultivator *see* peasant

Das, A.N. 143
debt, indebtedness 9, 11–12, 17, 24, 31, 39–40, 69, 73, 82, 107–8, 120, 125, 128–9, 137, 155, 161–2, 208, 212n; bondage 39, 202, 204–6, 209
depression, of 1930s 209
Dutt, Palme 39
Dutta, Rajat on land rights 73–4; on rice trade 129

East India Company, British 7–10, 24n, 57, 75, 77–82, 113, 129n, 140
ecology 40–50, 83, 104, 139
economic development 69–72, 86–8, 109–11, 121–5, 139–41, 217–18
Eden, Ashley 14; on Bengal government 93
elections and rural voters 3
Elliott, Charles 94–5
European(s) 4, 32, 42, 48–50, 59–62, 78, 80–2, 88, 132–40, 185, 189–190, 194, 202–7, 217–18

factory, Commissions 198–9, 217; legislation viii, 197–201, 214–17; workers 199–200
Famine Commission 14, 94; report, 1880–1 51–2
famine, 10, 14, 50–8, 96, 130, 163; and endemic poverty 56; and epidemic diseases 51; explanations of 51–2, 54–6, 101; nature of 53–5; politicization of 56–7; Ramesh Chandra Datta on 51; Michael Finucane on 54; W.W. Hunter on 50, 52; Eric Stokes on 53; John Strachey's report on Moradabad 51; Richard Temple on Bihar (1874) 53
Field, C.D. on Rent Law Commission report 94
Fisher, Colin 135–6
Francis, Philip 63

Gandhi, M.K. 3, 33–4, 37, 43, 63
Garth, Richard 95
Gaya Revenue Administration Report 155n
Grierson, W.B. 156–7
Guha, Sumit 4; on labouring dependants 23
Gupta, P.N. 37

Habermas, Jürgen 47–8
Harrison, Henry 214
Hastings, Warren 8–9
history, uses, influence of 59–63, 94–5, 205–6
Hudson, W.B. as head of Planters' Association 29

Ibbetson, Denzil 97
identity(-ies) 5–6, 50, 64–5; *and see* caste, class, peasants
India(n), civil society 47–8; class identities 88–9; commercialization 69–70; economic development of 69; economic history and evolution of capitalism 81; foreign trade and 8; indigenous knowledge in 64; lower-class 47; market for 8; modernization 62, 69; as notion of universality 88; pre-colonial 100; as source of raw materials 7–8; trade and state interference 111; Western categorization 64–5
Indian National Congress 87
Indigo Commission 185–8, 193–6; and legislation 189–90; minority report and troubles in Nadia 189
indigo cultivation 25–37, 42, 107, 135, 183–90, 186
industrialization 7, 145
intermediaries 47, 71; landholding 10, 16, 26, 73–4, 76, 99, 84, 87, 103, 121, 130, 133–4, 143, 146, 158n, 187–8; commercial 86–7, 103, 105–8, 120, 122, 124, 126,

135–6, 146, 185; *and see* jobbers, peasants
international labour conventions 198–9

Japan(ese) 69–71, 214
'jobbers' 199–201, 210
Jones, Richard 95

kamias 212–14; 201–3, 205, 212–14; Bhuinya 201–2; Bihari 203, 205, 209; bondage of 206; hiring of 208; *and see* labour, debt
Kawai, Akinobu 85
kisan see peasants; *sabha*, formation of 42
Koiris 34–5, 103, 213 cultivator 154
Krsi-paràsara 22–4, 63–4

labour viii, 5, 17, 20, 22–4, 38–40, 71, 81, 86, 112, 116, 118, 121, 126–7, 131–2, 137–8, 143, 152, 181–218; bonded 202–9, 212–14
land, -lord(s) 8–10, 12–13, 16–18, 22–5, 31, 40–2, 57, 71–6, 83–6, 96–9, 101, 105, 116–18, 127, 131–3, 152–8, 154–6, 164, 168–72; land law 16–17, 74–8, 98–9, 113, 115, 118, 121, 168–9; land-transfer, market 76, 160–2; landlord-tenant relations 27, 83–4, 96, 101, 107–8, 121, 133, 154–8, 164–6, 170
Landholders' Association of 1838 41–2
land use/agricultural production 18–19, 22–5, 73, 77–9, 102–3, 118–20, 122, 125, 131, 137–8, 140–5, 153
Laissez faire 58, 79–80, 97
Law, legal system 4, 10, 13–14; tenancy 92–102; *see also* Bengal Tenancy Act, land
Linlithgow, Lord 39
Ludden, David 4, 113

MacDonnell, Antony P. 52–5, 94–5, 101
MacKenzie, Alexander 93–5

Madras (Chennai) Presidency 10, 32, 43
Maine, Henry 50–1, 95
malik *see* landlord
Mann, Harold 39
Maratha(s) 47, 63, 77
Maratha Aikya Itchu Sabha 210
Market, and agricultural production 128, and ideas of freedom 205; system 111; *and see* land use
Marx, Karl (Marxist, -ian) 23, 26, 38–40, 59, 62, 70n, 73n, 87, 95, 140–1, 144–5, 182, 192, 205
Mayo, Lord 14
Menon, Dilip 4
Mill, James 10; on British dominion 59–61
moneylenders 160–2; and control 107; as social inferiors 129; *and see* debt
Mughals 47
Munro, Thomas 10

Nair, T.M. 199, 214–15, 217
Nakazato, Nariaki 85
Nandy, Ashis on 'masculinity' 44
Nation(alism) 20, 56, 62–3, 87, 190

O'Kinealy, J. 94
opium cultivation 132–46, cultivators 163–4; Datta on 129; East India Company's monopoly 7; lower castes as growers of 108; growers and *lambardars* 105; land given to indigo 29; and zamindar's hostility 133
Orissa, emigrants to Assam 193n; famine 1870 14; Santhals of 192

Panda, Chitta 84
partition of estates 164, 166–8
patwari 162–3
peasants/raiyats/tenants 3, 23, 34–53, 60–1, 84–5, 125, 151–2; associations 3, 37–42; identity, character 23, 34–6, 38, 44, 46,

60, 70, 72, 86, 98–9, 112, 117, 121–3, 125, 126–7, 142, 151–2, 155–7, 160–1, 171–8, 182; and intermediaries 99, 104–5, 114–15, 126, 128, 130–3, 135–6, 142–6; mobilization, organization 3, 25, 26, 33–4, 37–8, 45, 87–8, 172–3; occupancy or settled 12, 13, 16, 27, 31, 46, 97–8, 112, 114–15, 119, 146, 152–3, 155, 158–9, 160–1, 170, 174–5, 208; poor, poverty of 29, 54, 86–8, 101, 118–21, 146, 159, 172, 185; production 25–7, 33, 35–8, 42, 44, 46, 50, 95–6, 98, 142,155, 159, 183; pro-peasant school 11, 13, 18, 43, 61, 80, 93–102, 107, 115; proprietors 10–11, 13, 20, 29, 43, 53, 61, 80, 97, 99–100, 113, 114–16, 119–21, 153; 'resident' (*khudkasht*) and/or 'non-resident' (*pahikasht*) 17, 72, 83, 94, 116–17, 170, 173; rich 13, 39, 83–5, 88, 121, 125, 133, 136, 151–2, 156–7, 160, 166, 168; rights, protest 11, 13, 18, 25–7, 33, 35–8, 42–4, 46, 50, 61, 95–6, 98, 107
permanent settlement 9–10, 91, 190; *and see* land law
Pinch, William 44–6
planters 26–7, 29–30, 32–3, 132–8, 143, 183, 189; *and see* indigo
poverty, impoverishment 20, 53–4, 57, 81, 86–96, 101, 113–14, 118, 145; *and see* peasants
Prakash, Gyan 181, 201–9, 211, 217
pre-colonial stratification 117
'pre-capitalist' economy 70–1
production *see* land-use
Punjab 11, 13, 18; Alienation of Land Act, 1900 12; *and see* peasant

raiyat see peasant
Rajputs 157

rebellion of 1857–8 11, 115
Reid, D.N. 28–9; and raiyats 31
Rent 11–14, 17–18, 24–5, 28, 30–1, 35–7, 41, 51, 53, 70, 75, 82–5, 88, 92, 95–6, 98–102, 105–7, 111, 114, 117–21, 125, 128, 130–3, 136–7, 139, 142–3, 146, 152–79, 185–6; *see also* tenancy law
Rent Law Commission of 1880 93–4
resistance 3, 10, 33–47, 39, 42, 84, 143n, 156–8, 184n, 209; *and see* peasant
revenue settlement(s) 8–12, 42–3, 61, 74–5, 77–8, 91–2; *and see* land-law
Ricardo, David 11
rights vii–viii, 13, 16–17, 27, 35, 37–8, 41–2, 45, 47–8; in land 15–17, 72–3, 165
riots, Deccan in 1875 12
Ripon, Lord 15, 27–8
Rivaz, Charles 195

Sahajanand Saraswati, Swami 38–41, 49, 62
Sasmal, B.S. 87
Sen, Amartya 51–2, 81
Shore, John 9
Smith, Adam 29n, 59, 87, 191, 203, 205
state, roles of 14–15, 20, 47–8, 58–9, 78, 95–6; and economic change 78–80
Stevenson-Moore on agrarian interests 35; indigo disputes 35
sugar production 33, 135, 139
Sultan, Tipu 47
survey (revenue) 11, 13, 35–7, 49
Sweeney, J.A., report on Champaran 36

taxation 19–20
tea 192–7
tenants/tenancy *see* peasants; law, legislation 9, 12–14, 62, 80, 92–102, 109, 112–13, 115–17, 152, 164–6, 190

Thompson, Rivers 14–15
Tilak, B.G. 210
trades unions 3–4, 48, 210
trade 7–8, 21, 32, 80–3, 105–6; and government 121; local 128–9; and society 102–13
Utilitarian(s) 10, 75, 191, 203

van Schlendel, Willem 81

village(s)/countryside 3–15, 21, 70, 103–4, 117–18; character of 4–5, 104–7, 126–8, 141–2, 144–7; *see also* government and countryside

Washbrook, David 4, 151n; on law and society 90–2

zamindar(s) *see* landlord